The World Economy

GLOBAL TRADE POLICY 1995

Edited by

SVEN ARNDT *and* CHRIS MILNER

Blackwell Publishers

ISBN 0-631-194118

First published 1995

Blackwell Publishers Ltd
108 Cowley Road, Oxford OX4 1JF, UK
and
238 Main Street,
Cambridge, MA 02142, USA

British Library Cataloguing in Publication Data
applied for

Library of Congress Cataloging in Publication Data
applied for

This book is printed on acid free paper
Printed in Great Britain by Redwood Books, Trowbridge

The World Economy

GLOBAL TRADE POLICY 1995

Global Trade Policy

Editorial Introduction

Sven Arndt and Chris Milner

MANY significant changes have taken place in the world trading system in recent years. At national, regional and global levels trade policies and trade regimes have been fundamentally transformed in a number of ways. Indeed, John Jackson writes in his paper in this issue: 'The combination of events and institutional developments of the last few years, with the NAFTA in North America, the EC evolution towards deepening and broadening integration, the extraordinarily elaborate Uruguay Round results, as well as developments in China and East Europe, probably amount to the most profound change in international economic relations, institutions and structures since the origin of the Bretton Woods structure itself in the immediate post-war period'.

At the multilateral level, the Uruguay Round was finally completed in late 1993. It was the longest and most complicated of all the rounds; it looked more than once during its tortured history that it would expire; yet it produced far-reaching changes and significant improvements in the international trade regime. It brought services and agricultural trade under the purview and discipline of the GATT, established procedures for the protection of intellectual property rights, and set up for the first time in the post-war era a proper legal and institutional framework for trade relations among nations.

These changes came none too soon, for many countries — not the least of them the United States — had begun to doubt the ability of the multilateral system to deal with the problems facing a modern and highly complex community of trading nations. American critics of the GATT accused it of being too slow and cumbersome and to lack the teeth to prevent free riding and abuse. The United States, for its part, had decided to raise the profile of unilateral and preferential approaches in trade policy. Aggressive unilateralism was elevated to parity with multilateralism. The US created NAFTA, jointly with Canada and Mexico, took a leading role in APEC, engaged Japan in increasingly acrimonious bilateral disputes, and pursued China over intellectual property rights and other grievances.

SVEN ARNDT is from the Lowe Institute, Claremont McKenna College. CHRIS MILNER is from CREDIT, University of Nottingham.

It may very well be, as some have argued, that these extra-GATT activities on the part of the US helped spur other nations to complete the Uruguay Round. But completion now raises questions about the continued use of extra-GATT approaches.

There is at present little prospect that the momentum of regional collaboration will be slowed by completion of the Uruguay Round. But the proliferation of preferential arrangements throughout the world raises questions about the long-run compatibility of preferential and multilateral approaches. The question as to whether preferential arrangements represent building blocks or stumbling blocks for an open global trading system has not been answered.

Meanwhile, NAFTA has been completed and a decision made to consider its expansion throughout the western hemisphere. The European Union has just been enlarged by the entry of Austria, Finland and Sweden, and now looks eastward toward further expansion in the years to come. The APEC group of nations has agreed to search for ways of implementing its vision of regionalism, namely 'open regionalism'. For the United States, Canada and Mexico, implementation of an APEC programme would bring membership in overlapping preference areas. Whether such dual membership can be made to work and how is not known.

One of the reasons interest in trade blocs has grown in recent years, at least in the western hemisphere, is that developing countries, having abandoned their anti-trade-biased, import-substituting, inward-looking growth policies, need access to large markets in order to pursue export-led or pro-trade-biased policies. Many feel that preferential relationships with large, industrialised partners are particularly well suited for that purpose by guaranteeing access.

Although economists have long argued that unilateral trade liberalisation is typically the first-best trade policy, and although many developing countries have accepted that argument and unilaterally reduced their trade barriers, unilateral liberalisation does not guarantee access to large markets and such access is important if countries with small domestic markets are to take advantage of scale economies. Unilateral openness is still welfare-creating in the main, but reciprocal openness — when provided by large efficient trading partners — is better.

ORGANISATION OF THE REVIEW

The special annual issue of *The World Economy* will examine these and other topics in depth. Each annual supplement will feature sections on global and regional developments. It will examine trade policy developments at the country level by reviewing a handful of the latest Trade Policy Reviews (TPRs) of the World Trade Organisation (WTO). And it will feature articles on special topics related to trade and trade policy.

In the current issue, Robert Baldwin considers the accomplishments of the

Uruguay Round and John Jackson evaluates the World Trade Organisation. In the area of regional developments, Paul Wonnacott and Mohamed Ariff examine aspects of economic integration in the Pacific region. Reviews and evaluations of the TPRM exercises are provided by Kym Anderson on Australia, V.N. Balasubramanyam on India, Merle Holden on South Africa, Tim Kehoe on Mexico, Anne Krueger on the United States, and Sübidey Togan on Turkey.

Baldwin assesses the Uruguay Round's accomplishments in both traditional and new issue areas. He judges the Round's achievements in the former to run from modest — with respect to establishing criteria and standards for anti-dumping policies — to considerable in the area of subsidies and countervailing duty (CVD) procedures. On the whole, however, much remains to be done in this area and will have to be taken up in the next round of multilateral negotiations.

In the realm of 'new' issues, Baldwin gives the contracting parties high marks for having brought services and agriculture under GATT discipline, for overcoming a number of weaknesses in the area of intellectual property rights protection, and for setting the stage for the gradual elimination of the Multi-Fibre Arrangement. In all these areas, establishment of frameworks, creation of guiding principles and enunciation of future intentions took precedence over actual specific rules-writing. Provisions are often soft and spongy, and important issues are skirted and hence left for future negotiations. A pessimist might see the cup as half empty, as Anderson notes with respect to the limited substantive changes in agriculture. Baldwin does not let us forget, however, what a major accomplishment bringing these important matters under the purview of the WTO really is.

In a companion piece on international institutional or systemic developments, John Jackson examines the World Trade Organisation. He takes note in passing of a fact that is often forgotten, namely, that the GATT neither was nor was intended to be an organisation. It was a trade and tariff agreement to be implemented by the International Trade Organisation (ITO). Since the ITO failed to come into being, the GATT technically never went into force; it was operated by a Protocol of Provisional Application.

The WTO itself is best viewed as a mini-charter, Jackson argues, with an institutional and procedural structure for implementing the Uruguay Round: 'Its text has no substantive rules, but incorporates the Round's substantive agreements as annexes'. This suggests that critics misplace their fire when they blame the WTO rather than the Uruguay Round for substantive changes they do not like. In other words, killing the WTO would not make the substantive changes go away, although it would doubtless impair their implementation.

Jackson praises the WTO for providing more transparency than before, for providing for the first time a legal definition of consensus, and for eliminating the problem of GATT-a-la-carte. He approves of the installation of unified dispute settlement procedures and the establishment of the Trade Policy Review Mechanism (TPRM).

A major concern among some US critics of the WTO was that it presents an intrusion on national sovereignty. Jackson argues that the WTO has no more real power than the GATT and that, in the case of the latter, ambiguous language and prevalence of practices over formal rules provided greater opportunities for misuse of power than will be possible under the WTO. Indeed, Jackson asserts that 'the protection of national sovereignty built into the WTO Charter rules and decision making is substantially enhanced over that of the GATT'.

Not least among the many changes that have taken place in the area of international trade in recent years is the reversal of trade policies in many developing countries from defensive, inward-looking to more open and outwardly oriented ones. To Judith Dean this is nothing less than revolution. She surveys trade policy reforms in various regions, ranging from South and East Asia to Africa and Latin America.

An important and recurring theme is the striking regularity with which trade reforms are endangered by adverse movements in exchange rates. This seems to have been a particularly difficult problem in many African countries, in which real appreciation seems to have been an important cause of reversals in trade reforms. Of course, it would be a mistake to conclude that trade liberalisation cannot and should not be accompanied by a strengthening of the home currency, especially in countries in which trade reforms bring needed investment inflows. Still, the evidence from Africa and other parts of the developing world suggests that the optimism engendered by the 'small revolution in trade reforms' is tempered by the frequency of 'reversals of reform'.

REGIONAL ISSUES

In his paper on trade policy initiatives in the Asia-Pacific region, Paul Wonnacott considers alternative ways of implementing the APEC notion of 'open regionalism', which he defines as strengthening economic relations among members, while also making the region more open to trade and investment with the rest of the world. It is clearly easier to feel good about the idea of open regionalism than to find ways of implementing it, especially if one is to avoid establishing substantial institutional structures as in Europe or resorting to potentially trade distorting rules of origin as in NAFTA.

Wonnacott considers two possibilities. One is a Preferential Trade Area (PTA) combined with reduced barriers to the rest of the world, the other most-favoured-nation (MFN) trade liberalisation in commodity areas with strong elements of potential trade creation. In order to minimise the free-rider problem that accompanies unreciprocated MFN trade liberalisation, Wonnacott considers what he terms the 'predominant supplier' approach, according to which APEC nations would limit MFN tariff liberalisation to product categories in which they are the dominant suppliers.

Upon examining disaggregated trade data, he finds that if APEC adopted MFN tariff liberalisation in all commodities in which members supply 80 per cent or more of world exports, such a policy would cover 19 per cent of APEC exports and 16 per cent of imports. When specific product categories are considered, electronics is a prime candidate for MFN tariff liberalisation on the part of APEC.

Wonnacott considers the alternative of an APEC free trade area (FTA) and finds it to be fraught with problems and potential conflicts. Although he is prepared to argue that APEC nations in general are weakly each other's 'natural' trading partners, he sees no easy way of reconciling the interests of the 'big three' of the Pacific Basin — the US, Japan and China.

Mohamed Ariff looks at cooperative initiatives among the members of the Association of South East Asian Nations (ASEAN) and at their efforts to build their free trade area, the AFTA.

He argues that the arrangement is rather limited in terms of product coverage and the degree of regional integration envisaged. Indeed, it is much less ambitious than NAFTA. But Ariff sees this as something of a virtue, since it may avoid both excessive discrimination in trade policy and the creation of large-scale bureaucratic structures. It is an assessment consistent with the view that the ASEAN countries remain committed to global export strategies. Given the success of their global, export-oriented trade strategies, this is hardly surprising.

TRADE POLICY REVIEWS

One of the innovations of the Uruguay Round of trade negotiations was the creation of the Trade Policies Review Mechanism (TPRM). Under this procedure, the trade policies of member countries are reviewed on a periodic basis. A selection of the trade policy reviews (TPRs) completed in 1993/94 is evaluated in the third section of this issue.

In the TPRM format, the government makes an initial presentation pertaining to the country's trade policies, thereby providing the basis for a panel discussion by experts drawn from other member countries. The review is rounded out by a concluding report of the panel. The basic purpose is to provide information, explanation and discussion of countries' trade policies, and thereby to increase transparency and understanding. It is also a useful means of giving public but informal feedback to governments on issues that may be of concern to their trading partners.

Governments are, of course, unlikely to take a critical view of their own policies; and the review panels will observe standards of civility and diplomacy even when they are being critical, mindful of the fact that their countries, too, will be subjected to the review process. A purpose, therefore, of the evaluations presented in this section of the annual issue is to ensure that sensitive but important policy questions are in fact given proper airing, as well as to fill information gaps, offer relevant background perspectives and provide updates on developments since the completion of individual TPRs.

A good example of the speed with which events can move is the case of Mexico and the peso crisis of late 1994 and early 1995. The peso crisis gives Tim Kehoe an opportunity to focus on the nexus and compatibility between trade policies and trade policy reforms, of which there have been many in Mexico, and exchange rate policies.

As Judith Dean notes in her contribution, unexpected and unwanted real exchange rate movements have caused reversals of trade policy reforms in a number of developing countries. While Kehoe gives the TPR on Mexico high marks in general, he wonders whether and to what extent the panel should have anticipated the exchange rate problem. Should future TPRs pay more explicit attention to the exchange rate policy milieu within which trade policies and trade policy reforms are conducted?

Since trade policy reforms are, in many developing countries at least, often accompanied by reforms of policies pertaining to foreign direct investment (FDI), the question of what constitutes a proper exchange rate policy or a 'correct' exchange rate is not a simple one to answer. Countries whose trade reforms are intended mainly to accommodate export-led growth will prefer current account surpluses and weak and/or depreciating real currency values. The rise in the relative price of tradeables implicit in a real depreciation encourages resource flows into exportables industries.

But countries like Mexico, whose domestic saving rates are deemed inadequate for purposes of desired rates of economic growth and whose trade policy reforms are accompanied by liberalisation of investment policies designed to attract inflows of foreign investment, plan on current account deficits and strong and/or appreciating currencies in real terms. In such an event, the Mexican problem may have been less that the peso appreciated than the extent to which and the reasons for which it appreciated. Kehoe provides a detailed assessment of exchange rate developments since the TPR was completed.

The linkage and interaction between trade policy reforms and exchange rate developments recurs in the cases of both India and South Africa. V.N. Balasubramanyam chronicles the demise of the dirigiste economic policy regime in India and the shift away from import substitution policies. He ascribes an important role in improving the growth performance in India to the 'dismantling of the permit raj', that is, to more than just trade policy reforms. Still, he considers the economic performance of the Indian economy to pale in comparison with many other developed countries.

Average tariff rates are still high in India, licensing controls on consumer goods imports are still pervasive, and the rate of effective protection may actually have risen in the cases of a number of industries in which tariffs on imported inputs have fallen faster and farther than tariffs on imports of competing imported outputs.

The Indian authorities have experimented with various types of exchange rate policies, including a dual exchange rate system, and with foreign exchange controls, raising questions about the extent to which reduction in protection via trade policy reforms is compatible with exchange rate policies and exchange market controls.

Nevertheless, Balasubramanyam views India's accomplishment in the area of trade policy and exchange rate policy reforms as heading the country in the right direction and believes that significant reversals in these policies are unlikely.

The trade and general economic problems of South Africa are, of course, linked to the political turmoil and disruptions the country has experienced until recently and the tasks of restructuring that lie ahead. Indeed, Merle Holden asks whether it is appropriate in view of these difficulties to label South Africa a 'developed' country rather than a country 'in transition', much like the countries and regions of the former Soviet bloc? Such a reclassification would, among other things, allow South Africa more time to make the various policy changes mandated by the Uruguay Round agreements.

Like many other countries, South Africa has been shifting the focus of its trade policies away from import substitution, but its protectionist policies are still very complex and subject to *ad hoc* decisions rather than clear and consistently maintained rules and procedures. It is, thus, often difficult to evaluate the net effect of changes that have recently taken place. The TPR panel expressed serious concerns over the lack of transparency and stability in the country's trade policies.

Two external factors have played a dominant role in the conduct and reform of trade policy in Turkey over the last two decades. These are the stabilisation and structural adjustment programmes of the Bretton Woods institutions and the pursuit of greater integration with the European Community. Sübidey Togan describes both the unilateral policy reform that Turkey has undertaken during the 1980s and 1990s as part of the adjustment programme, and the protracted negotiations that Turkey has had with the EC over a thirty-year period. Although the former have been very significant in transforming a selectively and quantitatively managed trade regime into a more liberal and tariff-based regime, Togan sees Turkish membership of the EC customs union (agreed in March 1995, but still to be ratified) as the critical mechanism for locking in and thereby giving credibility to the economic (and political) reforms initiated during the 1980s.

Australia and the United States are the two genuinely developed countries in the set of TPRs chosen for evaluation in this issue. In many ways, Australia provides an interesting transition between the developing countries, which are just now reforming their trade policies from inward-looking to outwardly-oriented ones, and the United States, which is and has been one of the more open economies.

As Kym Anderson describes it, Australia was for many years an 'outlier' among OECD countries: highly protectionist, largely inward-looking, and with a trade policy regime centred on Britain. It has in recent years liberalised intensively and extensively, has shifted the commodity composition of its trade toward manufactures, and is on the verge of becoming a net services exporter. It has also shifted the country orientation of its trade away from the United States toward East Asia.

In addition to trade policy liberalisation, there have been major reductions in other forms of assistance to tradeables industries. While textiles, clothing, footwear and motor vehicles and parts are remaining, albeit temporary, blemishes, Anderson applauds Australia's '. . . conversion from one of the most protected industrial economies to one of the least protected'.

Among unfinished business as far as general economic reforms are concerned is the labour market. Indeed, Anderson's analysis is a useful reminder of the importance of industry and labour policies for the success of trade policy reforms. The Australian experience may provide one answer to the question of what it takes — or what else it takes — to prevent reversals of trade policy reforms.

One of the major questions pertaining to US trade policy concerns its direction. Is its perspective mainly multilateral and global, which approval by Congress of the Uruguay Round and the WTO would suggest? Or is it mainly regional and plurilateral, as NAFTA and its projected expansion into the rest of the hemisphere, APEC and its plan for the year 2000 and beyond, and Washington's 'aggressive unilateralism' *vis-à-vis* Japan would suggest? Or is it neither or both, that is, driven by whatever suits the political purpose of the moment? These are fundamentally important questions for the international community and the TPR of the US reflects some of them, albeit with diplomatic understatement.

Anne Krueger addresses this issue in her assessment of US trade policy developments and of the US commitment to the WTO and the global trading system. American policy seems at this juncture to be 'more focused on regional arrangements than on implementing the Uruguay Round and strengthening the WTO', thereby raising concerns about a 'lack of US leadership'.

A second key question of interest to Krueger pertains to the degree of openness of the US economy. That it is one of the more open economies is not in doubt, but is it as open and non-protectionist as some like to claim? In addressing this issue, Krueger focuses on the extent and pervasiveness of administered protection in the United States and finds it to be worrisome, indeed. Government procurement practices, maritime shipping, continued use of Section 337 in spite of its violation of GATT Articles, and *ad hoc* administration of rules of origin, are just some of the practices that make the US not only seem less open than its tariff structure would suggest, but seemingly willing to violate GATT 'law' whenever domestic purposes require it.

This first annual review of trade policy by *The World Economy* is launched, therefore, at a time when there are major developments at the multilateral, regional and national level. In the selection of topics for this issue, we have sought to give an appropriate flavour of the developments on all of these fronts. No doubt there are some issues which we have not done justice to. We will need to deal with these in future reviews!

The World Trade Organisation: Watershed Innovation or Cautious Small Step Forward?

John H. Jackson

1. INTRODUCTION

ON 1 January 1995, a new international organisation came into being. Depending on one's perspective, the World Trade Organisation (WTO) is either a modest enhancement of the General Agreement on Tariffs and Trade (GATT) which preceded it, or a watershed moment for the institutions of world economic relations embodied in the Bretton Woods system.

For twelve years, over 100 nations of the world have been participating in the largest and most complex negotiation concerning international economics in history (some would say the largest and most complex negotiation ever). Launched formally under GATT auspices in Punta del Este, Uruguay in September 1986 (after some years of preparation), the Uruguay Round negotiating results were formally signed at Marrakesh, Morocco on 15 April 1994, and ratified by a sufficient number of nations to bring those results into force on 1 January 1995. The results are embodied in a 'document' of some 26,000 pages, most of which are detailed schedules of tariff, services trade, and other concessions. For the first time the GATT system includes major agreements on trade in services, and on trade related intellectual property questions. Some 50 other portions of the agreement address subjects as diverse as anti-dumping, agriculture trade, subsidies, technical standards, textiles, and customs valuation. Included in this agreement are two important institutional measures: the Charter for a WTO, and a new set of dispute settlement procedures, both designed to assist in the effective implementation of the substantive rules established in the agreements.

2. THE GATT AND ITS BIRTH DEFECTS

The GATT was never intended to be an 'organisation'. It was negotiated in 1947

JOHN H. JACKSON is Hessel E. Yntema Professor of Law at the University of Michigan.

and 1948, at the same time as negotiators prepared a Charter for an ITO (International Trade Organisation). The GATT was to be a multilateral trade and tariff agreement, which would depend for its organisational context and secretariat services, on the ITO, but the ITO never came into being because the United States Congress would not approve it. The GATT did not need US Congressional approval because it was negotiated under advance authority granted to the President in the 1945 extension of the Reciprocal Trade Agreements Act (the first such Act was 1934). Because the ITO failed to materialise, the GATT gradually became the institution for international government cooperation on trade matters. In fact, however, the GATT never definitively came into force; instead it was legally applied by a Protocol of Provisional Application originally designed to last only until the ITO came into force.

Despite this inauspicious beginning, the GATT has been remarkably successful during its nearly five decades of history. Partly this is because of ingenious and pragmatic leadership in the GATT, particularly in its early years, as the GATT struggled to fill the gap left by the ITO failure. As decades passed, however, there was recognition that the GATT system was being increasingly challenged by the changing conditions of international economic activity, including the greater 'interdependence' of national economies, and the growth in trade of services. Concern developed that the GATT was too handicapped to play the needed role of complementing the Bretton Woods system as the 'third leg', alongside the IMF and World Bank. Problems and 'birth defects' included:

- Provisional application and Grandfather rights exceptions embraced by the Protocol of Provisional Application.
- Ambiguity about the powers of the Contracting Parties to make certain decisions.
- Ambiguity regarding the waiver authority and risks of misuse.
- Murky legal status leading to misunderstanding by the public, media, and even government officials.
- Certain defects in the dispute settlement procedures.
- Lack of institutional provisions generally, so constant improvisation was necessary.

3. THE WTO

a. Genesis of the WTO

The 1986 Ministerial declaration of Punta del Este, containing the agenda and objectives for the Uruguay Round (UR) negotiation, did not include any explicit call for a new charter or organisation, although it did establish negotiating groups including one for dispute settlement, and another for 'Functioning of the GATT

System', (FOGS). Despite this hesitancy, however, by 1990 there was considerable discussion of the need for an improved organisational structure for effective implementation of the Uruguay Round results. In December 1991, the Uruguay Round Negotiators led by the GATT Director General, Arthur Dunkel, prepared and released a draft text of treaty clauses which covered the entire UR negotiation results up to that point, with indications of work yet to do. This was an important project with many implications. Included in this draft (for the first time), was a tentative draft of a new Charter for an organisation — an MTO or Multilateral Trade Organisation. This draft had a number of flaws, recognised by the US government and others, but through hard work the negotiators were able to revise the draft and iron out most of the flaws. In the December 1993 near final draft, the new organisation was retitled the WTO — World Trade Organisation. This Charter is included in the treaty embodying the results of the Uruguay Round, along with a major text of new procedures and rules for dispute settlement.

b. *What is the WTO?*

With the new WTO Charter, the Uruguay Round results should provide a better institutional structure to fill the gap left in the Bretton Woods structure. Several general characteristics are noteworthy.

First, the charter for the WTO can be described as a 'mini-Charter'. It is devoted to the institutional and procedural structure that will facilitate and in some cases be necessary for effective implementation of the substantive rules that have been negotiated in the Uruguay Round. The WTO is not an ITO (the 1948 ITO draft Charter which never came into force). The WTO Charter text itself does not include substantive rules, but it incorporates the substantive agreements resulting from the Uruguay Round into 'annexes'. In many cases the criticism aimed at the WTO during the implementation debates was really criticism aimed at some of the substantive provisions of the Uruguay Round results, and should not be considered a criticism of the WTO institutional Charter.

Second, the WTO essentially will continue the GATT institutional ideas and many of its practices, in a form better understood by the public, media, government officials and lawyers. To some extent, a number of the GATT 'birth defects' are overcome in the WTO. The WTO Charter (XVI:I) expressly states the intention to be guided by GATT 'decisions, procedures and customary practices' to the extent feasible. The practice of consensus is better defined and for the first time becomes a legal procedure in some important decisions, rather than just a practice.

Third, the WTO structure offers some important advantages for assisting the effective implementation of the Uruguay Round. For example, a 'new GATT 1994' is created to supercede the 'old GATT'. This procedure avoids the constraints of the amending clause of the old GATT which might make it quite difficult to bring the Uruguay Round into legal force. At the same time, the WTO ties together the various texts developed in the Uruguay Round and reinforces the 'single package' idea of the negotiators, namely, that countries accepting the Uruguay Round must accept the entire package (with a few exceptions). No longer will the Tokyo Round approach of side codes, resulting in 'GATT a la Carte' be the norm.

The WTO Charter establishes (for the first time) the basic explicit legal authority for a Secretariat, a Director-General and staff. It does this in a way similar to many other international organisations, and it also adds the obligation for nations to avoid interfering with the officials of the organisation.

Another important aspect of the WTO structure is that it facilitates the extension of the institutional structure to the new subjects negotiated in the Uruguay Round, particularly services and intellectual property. Without some kind of legal mechanism such as the WTO, this would have been quite difficult to do since the GATT itself only applies to goods. The new GATT structure separates the institutional concepts from the substantive rules. The GATT 1994 will remain a substantive agreement (with many of the amendments and improvements developed throughout its history, including the Uruguay Round.) The WTO has a broader context. Similarly, the WTO will be able to apply a unified dispute settlement mechanism, and the Trade Policy Review Mechanism to all of the subjects of the Uruguay Round, for all nations who become members.

Fourth, the WTO Charter offers considerably better opportunities for the future evolution and development of the institutional structure for international trade cooperation. Even though the WTO Charter is minimalist, the fact that there is provision for explicit legal status and the traditional organisational structure, helps in this regard. With the WTO focusing on the institutional side, it also offers more flexibility for future inclusion of new negotiated rules or measures which can assist nations to face the constantly emerging problems of world economics.

c. The Legal Structure of the WTO

The WTO charter is confined to institutional measures, but the charter explicitly outlines four important annexes which technically contain hundreds of pages of substantive rules. The annex structure is important and the different annexes have different purposes and different legal impacts (see Appendix A).

Annex 1: This contains the large texts, termed 'Multilateral Trade Agreements,' which comprise the bulk of the UR results. All these are 'mandatory,' in the sense that these texts impose binding obligations on all members of the WTO. This reinforces the single package idea of the negotiators, departing from the Tokyo Round approach of 'pick and choose' side texts, or 'GATT a la carte.' The Annex 1 texts include:

Annex 1A: GATT 1994, the revised and all-inclusive GATT agreement with related agreements or 'Codes', and the vast 'schedules of concessions' that make up the large bulk of pages in the official treaty text. The schedules for each of the major trading countries, the US, Japan, and the European Union, each constitute a volume of printed tariff listings.
Annex 1B: GATS, is the General Agreement on Trade in Services, with its schedules of specific commitments and Annexes.
Annex 1C: TRIPS, is the Agreement on Trade Related Intellectual Property measures.

Annex 2: This contains the dispute settlement rules, which are obligatory for all members, and which form (for the first time) an integrated and unified dispute settlement mechanism covering the WTO Charter, the agreements listed in Annex 1, Annex 2, and made available for agreements in Annex 4.

Annex 3: This contains the TPRM — Trade Policy Review Mechanism, (in existence since 1988) by which the WTO will review the overall trade policies of each member on a periodic and regular basis, and report on those policies. The approach is not supposed to be 'legalistic,' and questions of consistency with WTO and Annex obligations are not the focus; rather the focus is on transparency and the general impact of the trade policies, both on the country being examined and on its trading partners.

Annex 4: This contains four agreements which are 'optional,' and termed 'Plurilateral Agreements.' This is a slight departure from the single package ideal, but the agreements included tend to deal with subject matter which concerns a small number of countries, or is more 'hortatory' in nature. Clearly this annex, to which addition may be made, provides some important flexibility for the Organisation to evolve and redirect its attention and institutional support for new subjects that may emerge as important during the next few decades. The agreements currently included in Annex 4 cover trade in civil aircraft, government procurement, dairy products, and bovine meat.

Annex 1A is by far the largest and contains the GATT 1994, which is essentially the old GATT as modified by amendments, the Tokyo Round 'codes' as renegotiated in the Uruguay Round, and some new Uruguay Round agreements. In addition to the GATT 1994, Annex 1A includes

agriculture,
sanitary and phytosanitary measures,
textiles and clothing,
technical barriers to trade,
trade-related investment measures,

Article VI (anti-dumping),
customs valuation,
preshipment inspection,
rules of origin,
import licensing,
subsidies and countervailing measures, and
safeguards,

plus a series of 'understandings' which further modify the GATT, and some Ministerial 'decisions and declarations.' The tariff schedules (most of the 26,000 pages), are technically part of this Annex. The relationship of many of these agreements listed above to GATT 1994 is somewhat murky.

Two of these agreements concern what are probably the most contentious of the 'rules of conduct' clauses of the GATT, namely Anti-dumping and Subsidies/Countervailing. One other concerns product standards (technical barriers) also addressed in the Sanitary and Phytosanitary agreement. As noted before, the legal relationship of these various GATT additions to the core GATT agreement itself is not always clear.

As impressive as the Uruguay Round results are, there clearly are a number of 'leftover' issues which the WTO system will need to address during forthcoming years, in addition to overseeing a satisfactory implementation of the UR results. The descriptions above hint at some of these, and other issues can be named. Together these include (1) enhancing and extending liberalisation of trade in agricultural products; (2) future extensive negotiations on services; (3) further elaboration of the rules on subsidies; (4) further market access efforts; (5) further negotiations in the context of trade related investment measures; (6) further negotiations concerning rules of origin; (7) greater integration of developing countries as well as monitoring the WTO/GATT rules to ensure fair treatment of those countries; (8) attention to the problems of anti-dumping rules and their compatibility with some of the Uruguay Round results; and (9) the problem of integrating the 'economies in transition' (e.g. China, Russia, etc.) into the WTO system.

4. DECISION MAKING AND THE WTO: THE 'SOVEREIGNTY' ISSUES

The governing structure of the WTO follows some of the GATT 1947 model, but departs from it substantially. At the top there is a 'Ministerial Conference' which meets not less than every two years. Next there are not one, but four 'Councils.' These include one 'General Council,' which seems to have overall supervising authority, can carry out many of the functions of the Ministerial Conference (MC) between MC sessions, and presumably meets at least as often as the GATT 1947 Council (monthly with exceptions). In addition, however, there is a Council for each of the Annex 1 agreements, namely, a Council for Trade in Goods, a Council for Trade in Services, and a Council for Trade-Related Aspects of Intellectual Property Rights.

There is also a 'Dispute Settlement Body — DSB' to supervise and implement the dispute settlement rules in Annex 2. The WTO Charter provides that the 'General Council shall convene as appropriate to discharge the responsibilities of the DSB.' In the same manner there is a TPR Body for the TPRM.

There have been some allegations that the WTO Charter is an important intrusion on 'national sovereignty.' Apart from the general problems of how to define 'sovereignty' in a world that is increasingly interdependent, the WTO contains an elaborate matrix of decision-making procedures bounded by important constraints. Basically, there are five different techniques for making decisions or formulating new or amended rules of trade policy in the WTO: amendments to the agreements, decisions on various matters, 'interpretations,' waivers, and finally the negotiation and implementation of new agreements. (See Appendix B.)

A careful examination of the WTO Charter suggests that apart from the addition of many new subjects to the substantive annexes, the WTO has no more real power than that which existed for the GATT under the previous agreements. This may seem surprising, but in fact the GATT treaty text contained language that was quite ambiguous, and could have been misused (but fortunately was not) to provide rather extensive powers. For example, in Article 25 of the GATT the Contracting Parties acting by majority vote were given the authority to take joint action 'with a view to facilitating the operation and furthering the objectives of this agreement.' This is very broad and ambiguous language.

Under the WTO Charter, although majority of one-nation-one-vote is the fall-back where consensus cannot be achieved, considerably more attention has been given to the question of decision-making in a number of different contexts, and certain restraints have been added, such as increasing the voting requirements for certain actions (to three-quarters of the members for many waivers and for formal interpretations), and a provision in the amending clauses that a country will not be bound by an amendment which it opposes if the amendment would 'alter the rights and obligations of the members.' Likewise, the waiver authority is more constrained and will be harder to abuse. Furthermore, formal 'interpretations,' 'shall not be used in the manner that would undermine the amendment provisions.' Thus there are more legal grounds than under GATT 1947 to challenge any potential over-reaching on the part of the trade system's institutions. The protections for national sovereignty built into the WTO Charter rules on decision-making are substantially enhanced.

Regarding the practice of 'consensus', as established for several decades in the GATT, several characteristics are worth noting. In the GATT, there is no explicit indication of a 'consensus practice', and the word 'consensus' is not used. The reason that the consensus practice developed was partly the uneasiness of governments about the loose wording of GATT decision-making powers, particularly that in GATT Article XXV. Partly because of this uneasiness, the practice developed of avoiding strict voting. Instead, the Contracting Parties have for several decades taken virtually all of their decisions by 'consensus'. Even when a formal vote was required (such as for a waiver), there would generally be a negotiation for a consensus draft text before such text was submitted to capitals for the formal vote.

In the practice of GATT, however, the word 'consensus' was not defined. In the legal sense, if some sort of 'consensus' could not be achieved, the fallback was the loose voting authority of the GATT. In the WTO Charter, however, consensus is defined (at least for some purposes) as the situation when a decision occurs and 'no member, present at the meeting when the decision is taken, formally objects to the proposed decision.' It should be noted that this is not the same as unanimity, since consensus is defeated only by a formal objection by a member present at the meeting. Thus, those absent do not prevent a consensus, nor does an abstention prevent a consensus. Furthermore, the practice in GATT and surely also in WTO is that some countries which have difficulty with a particular decision, will nevertheless remain silent out of deference to countries with a substantially higher stake in the pragmatic economic consequences of a decision. Thus the consensus practice itself involves some deference to economic power. This has certainly been the practice in the GATT, and the WTO Charter provides that the WTO shall be guided by such 'customary practices'.

The WTO is considerably more explicit about the situation where consensus fails. In a few instances, a decision must be by consensus and there is no fall-back to a majority vote. (For example, adding plurilateral agreements to Annex 4, Article X:9: and amendments to the dispute settlement procedures in Annex 2.) In many other situations, when consensus fails there is an explicit fall-back vote, such as three-fourths of the membership. It is considered quite difficult to achieve such a heavy fall-back vote as three-quarters of the membership (not three-quarters of those voting), since often twenty five per cent of the membership is not involved in a particular decision and may not show up at the meeting. Thus the protections of national sovereignty built into the WTO Charter rules on decision-making are substantially enhanced over that of the GATT.

The amending authority (Article X) is itself quite intricate and ingenious. It obviously has been carefully tailored to the needs of the participating nations related to each of the major multilateral agreements (GATT, GATS (Services), and intellectual property). Amendments for some parts require unanimity. Other parts require two-thirds (after procedures in the Ministerial Conference and Councils seeking consensus for amendment proposals). In almost all cases, as mentioned above, when an amendment would 'alter the rights and obligations', a member who refuses to accept the amendment is not bound by it. In such a case, however, there is an ingenious procedure (partly following the model in GATT) whereby the Ministerial Conference can by three-quarters vote of the members require a holdout member to accept the amendment, or withdraw from the agreement, or remain a member with explicit consent of the Ministerial Conference (i.e. grant that member a waiver). It is therefore very hard to conceive of the amending provisions being used in any way to force a major trading country such as the United States, the European Union or Japan, to accept altered rights or obligations. As stated above, the spirit and practice of GATT has always been to try to accommodate, through consensus negotiation procedures, the views of as many countries as possible, but certainly to give weight to views of countries who have power in the trading system. This is not likely to change.

There still exist some risks in the voting system and practice under the WTO could be crucial in defining and constraining these risks. For example, bloc voting could develop and there have been hints that the European Union with its number of votes (equal to the number of its members who are also Members of the WTO) and the votes of members of a series of association and affiliation agreements (all totalling more than a majority of GATT and, now, WTO members) could be tempted to use this voting strength in a way to achieve some of its trade policy goals (such as a waiver or selection of officers.)

5. DISPUTE SETTLEMENT PROCEDURES

One of the many achievements of the GATT, despite its 'birth defects,' has been the development of a reasonably sophisticated dispute settlement process. The original GATT treaty contained very little on this, although it did specifically provide (in Articles 22 and 23) for consultation, and then submittal of issues to the GATT Contracting Parties. As time went on, however, the practice began to evolve more towards a 'rule oriented' system. For example, in the late 1950s the practice introduced a 'panel' of individuals to make determinations and findings and recommend them to the Contracting Parties. Before that, disputes had been considered in much broader working parties comprised of representatives of governments.

During the next several decades, the Contracting Parties utilised the panel process more and more. Increasingly, the reports began to focus on more precise and concrete questions of 'violations' of treaty obligations. At the end of the Tokyo Round in 1979, the GATT Contracting Parties adopted an understanding on dispute settlement which embraced some of these concepts, and embodied the practice concerning dispute settlement procedures which had developed during the previous decades.

In the 1980s, the dispute settlement panels were for the first time assisted by a new legal section of the GATT Secretariat. The panels began to write reports that were much more precise and better reasoned, (and much longer!). Many countries, including the United States (which has been the largest single applicant for dispute settlement procedures in the GATT) found it useful to take issues to panels as part of their broader approach to trade diplomacy.

However, as might be expected given the history of GATT, there were a number of defects and problems in the dispute settlement process. Some of the problems were gradually overcome through practice in the GATT. But in the Uruguay Round December 1994 text, there is a major new section concerning dispute settlement procedures, the 'Understanding on Rules and Procedures Governing the Settlement of Disputes.'

The new text solves many, although not all, of the issues that have plagued the GATT dispute settlement system. It establishes a unified dispute settlement system for all parts of the GATT/WTO system, including the new subjects of services and intellectual property, thus, precluding procedural controversies. It provides that all relevant parts of the Uruguay Round legal text can be considered in a particular dispute case, and it reaffirms the right of a complaining government to a panel process. Finally, it establishes a unique new appellate procedure. Thus, a panel report will be deemed adopted by the new DSB, unless it is appealed by one of the parties to the dispute. If appealed, the dispute will go to an appellate panel. After the appellate body has ruled, its report will go to the DSB, but in this case it will be deemed adopted unless there is a consensus *against* adoption, and presumably that negative consensus can be defeated by any major objector. Thus the presumption is reversed, compared to the previous procedures, with the ultimate result that the appellate report will come into force as a matter of international law in virtually every case. The opportunity of a losing party to block adoption of a panel report will no longer be available.

6. THE WTO AS A BRETTON WOODS PARTNER

The combination of events and institutional developments of the last few years, with the NAFTA in North America, the EC evolution towards deepening and broadening integration, the extraordinarily elaborate Uruguay Round results, as well as developments in China and East Europe, probably amount to the most profound change in international economic relations, institutions and structures, since the origin of the Bretton Woods System itself in the immediate post-war period. Inevitably of course, this raises the question of the role of the new WTO as part of the 'new Bretton Woods System,' as a partner to the IMF — International Monetary Fund, and the World Bank (IBRD).

It is therefore significant that for the first time we will have an explicit treaty-charter agreement establishing an international organisation for trade, which can take its place beside the previously mentioned Bretton Woods Organisations. This may seem a mere formalism, but it can have importance in orienting public and official perceptions and understandings. It could have a healthy influence in increasing the prestige of the trade organisation and treaty system, and clearly that is one of the hoped-for results. No longer will government officials or the press have to run through the slalom of legal obstacles provided under the previous system, with its 'provisional application,' and its convoluted multiple dispute settlement procedures, as well as the difficult web of treaties that applied. The new structure carries forward much complexity, but in terms of general understanding, the new WTO Charter should be considerably better. Furthermore, there are at least some indications in this structure of the need for the organisation to pay attention to its 'public image.' In order for an organisation which has such a potentially profound impact on economic affairs to succeed it must give some attention to how it is understood by public constituencies in different cultures and economic systems.

An important defect of the previous system (a Bretton Woods system without an international trade organisation) was perceived by many to be its lack of 'coherence.' This meant the lack of appropriate coordination and discussion between national government officials and international organisational officials who concentrated on monetary and lending questions, on the one hand, and those involved in the somewhat 'messier' problems of trade in goods (involving many different interest groups and political/economic forces), on the other hand. One of the purposes of a new WTO is clearly to assist in providing this coherence, partly by establishing a higher profile, understandability, and prestige for the WTO, its organisation officials, and national government officials accredited to it. If managed appropriately, there should be a considerably greater interchange among the three Bretton Woods institutions, possibly through certain joint committees, or at least through more attention to some issues such as how trade matters affect balance of payments or other monetary questions; and vice versa how monetary affairs, including exchange rate changes, can have great effects on trade policy.

Indeed, in recent years there has been a number of circumstances which have poignantly demonstrated the importance of the connection between monetary and trade policy. The bilateral trade tensions between the United States and Japan and the ensuring dramatic exchange rate shifts, are one such example. The desires and advantages of some of the newly privatising, or 'marketising' economies (Russia and other Republics, China, etc.) also amply demonstrate this link, as economists and policy makers stress the need for floating exchange rates in order for trade relations to be successful. Likewise, problems of Latin American exchange rates, debt structure, and investment flows confirm the importance of this link.

Even in the GATT there was recognition of the monetary – trade link in several articles. Countries who were GATT Contracting Parties but not Members of the IMF had an obligation under GATT to enter into some sort of monetary framework agreement. Likewise, the GATT had provisions for trade measures linked to balance of payment difficulties.

A number of issues that are left over for future work will have important implications for the work of the World Bank and possibly the Fund. For example, anti-dumping and subsidy rules have often been contentious. Apparently there have occasionally been recommendations to developing countries to use these rules in a way that would seem less than optimal by trade specialists. Hopefully the new institutional structure will create an environment of better coordination and mutual understanding between trade specialists and monetary specialists.

Likewise agriculture and food policy deserve much more attention, and so also do policies relating to commodities and commodity agreements. All of these can be substantially affected by monetary movements, particularly for some smaller countries.

Dispute resolution procedures are an important attribute of an international treaty 'regime,' and are looked upon as an essential component of effectively implementing treaty obligations so as to produce the degree of credibility for those obligations that makes them operate successfully in international economic relations. It is inevitable that some monetary issues will find their way into some disputes resolved through these procedures.

Other monetary and financial links to trade policy include:

- effects of exchange rate shifts on trade rules regarding financial services,
- methods of financial adjustment costs caused by liberalising new trade rules,
- questions whether and when trade barriers and other distorting measures (such as subsidies) affect exchange rates or inhibit the ability of the monetary system to adjust,
- the question of the responsibility of a balance of payments global *surplus* country to contribute to 're-balancing',
- the question of use of trade measures to offset BOP difficulties,
- calculations of anti-dumping margins and subsidy impacts in the context of exchange rate shifts, and
- effects of debt on trade and monetary imbalances (and vice versa).

7. RELATION TO DOMESTIC LAW OF THE US AND OTHER NATIONS

There is some confusion about the effect of a WTO and its actions on US domestic law. The Congress has provided in its implementing legislation that the WTO and the Uruguay Round agreements will not be self-executing in US law; thus they do not automatically become a part of it. Neither do the results of panel dispute settlement procedures automatically become part of US law. Instead the US implemented the international obligations through legislation adopted by the Congress. Likewise the US (like most countries) must implement the results of a dispute settlement panel through legislation or other domestic legal action which will incorporate the decision into domestic law. In a case where the US feels that it is important to deviate from the international norms, knowing that it may be acting inconsistently with its international obligations, the US government has that power under its constitutional system. This can be an important constraint if matters go seriously wrong. Such power however, should not be lightly used. The same legal situation is also present in many other members of the WTO, often with an even more stark 'dualist' approach of their constitutions, which always require some domestic legal action such as legislation or regulation for an international treaty norm or dispute settlement result to be officially incorporated into their domestic jurisprudence.

In addition, it should be noted that governments as members of the WTO have the right to withdraw from it with a mere six months notice (XV:I). This is a drastic action which would not likely be taken, but it does provide some checks and balances to the overall system.

Clearly, several nations are so important to the success of the WTO and the trading rules, that as a practical matter they cannot be ignored. Indeed, some of the more specific rules of the WTO will reinforce deference to their position. Thus, even without formal 'weighted voting' or 'veto power', there is differential voting weight in practice, embellished by the practice of 'consensus' decisions.

The question has been raised whether the new GATT/WTO dispute settlement procedures of the Uruguay Round results will require fundamental changes in the Section 301 statutes, which provide a procedure allowing individual enterprises to compel the US government to investigate alleged foreign practices that harm US commerce. These are mostly targeted on US exports, but also apply to matters such as intellectual property, subsidised imports, service trade, etc.

It appears that very few statutory changes to US Section 301 were needed, at least to the 'regular 301' (compared to Special 301 and other similar statutory provisions, such as those on telecommunications). Some alterations to some time limits, or transition measures are provided, but the basic structure of 301 is not necessarily inconsistent with the Uruguay Round results. It is argued that Section 301 as appropriately used in its current statutory form, is a constructive measure for US trade policy, and for world trade policy. Section 301 calls for cases presented under the 301 procedural framework to be taken to the international dispute settlement process that pertains to the case. Likewise, Section 301 in its present formulation does not *require* the Executive Branch to ignore the results of the international dispute settlement process. Thus the Executive appears to have the discretion to apply actions under Section 301 in a manner consistent with the proposed new rules of the Uruguay Round dispute settlement understanding.

However, the procedures of the new dispute settlement understanding will provide moderately more pressure on all member governments to conform to the results of a dispute settlement process. Partly this is because the new dispute settlement procedures include a segment dealing explicitly with the question of responses available to a complaining state, when a defending member of WTO does not conform to its obligations after a dispute settlement procedure. Of course, a nation can still refuse to conform. For example, this could mean that despite a ruling against the United States on a complaint brought by the United States, the President might be tempted to take action that he is authorised to take under Section 301. Such action could be in violation of international obligations. The mere existence of the possible hypothetical authority to take such action would not necessarily be a violation.

A critical provision in the Uruguay Round text concerning dispute settlement in this regard is Article 23. Article 23.1 requires members of the WTO to use the dispute settlement procedures whenever they seek redress of a violation of obligations or other nullification or impairment with respect to matters covered by the WTO Agreement. It also states that members shall 'abide by, the rules and procedures of this understanding.' Thus, several instances where the United States in the 1980s took unilateral and independent action without proceeding through the GATT, would be inconsistent with the new rules. However, they were also inconsistent with the old rules, to the extent that actual trade restraining measures were applied at the border which violated the GATT (such as an increase in bound tariffs).

8. REFLECTIONS AND PERSPECTIVES: FUTURE PROSPECTS

A safe answer to the question asked in the title of this article, is 'both.' That is to say, the new WTO and the results of the Uruguay Round are both a modest step forward with regard to the institutional structure, and a watershed for the international economic system. The modest step can be seen in the WTO Charter as described above. The watershed, however, is the mere fact of creating a definitive institutional arrangement, combined with the extraordinary expanse of the Uruguay Round substantive negotiations. Clearly this marks a considerable departure from the hesitancy, tentativeness, and 'provisional' nature of the GATT system. It puts in place a structure that will necessarily have to face an increasing number of problems during the next few decades.

Almost any reflective consideration of the rapidly increasing international economic interdependence leads to recommendations for increasing international cooperation in order to cope with the problems of interdependence. No longer can nations effectively implement their national economic regulations because of international constraints and implications. However, the more one turns to international cooperation institutions, the more it begins to be clear that attention must be paid to the 'constitution' of these international institutions, just as extensive attention is given to national level 'constitutions'.

This raises issues about 'governance', such as preventing abuse of power, effectively channelling important information to decision makers, giving constituencies the opportunity to be heard and to have weight of influence on the decision-making processes. These concepts inevitably lead to questions about the appropriate distribution of power over economic affairs in the world, and the degree to which power should be located in an international institution, or a national/federal institution, or in sub-federal or even very local governmental units. The word 'subsidiarity' is sometimes used to describe these general concepts of distribution of power, and the opposing goals of keeping government decisions at levels as close as possible to affected constituents while empowering higher levels of government to take measures that affect broader segments of society.

The WTO as an institution continues to require attention in several respects. First, an important question is whether the new dispute settlement procedures will work effectively. There will indeed be temptations of some member nations, probably the largest, to ignore or undermine the results of dispute settlement procedures when those procedures do not entirely suit their interests. The dispute settlement procedure will lose credibility, and thus will fail in its primary purpose of establishing and maintaining a creditable 'rule oriented' system.

Second, the decision-making and voting procedures of the WTO, although much improved over the GATT, still leave much to be desired. It is not clear how the consensus practice will proceed, particularly given the large number of members. It may be necessary at some point to develop certain practices about voting to constrain misuse of the various voting rules.

Third, with a likelihood of well over 120 nation members, the WTO must soon face up to its internal procedures for effective governance and administration. This suggests the need for some sort of steering group to guide and advise the Director-General, and other officers of the WTO, in developing priorities for agenda and secretariat work, as well as initiatives to meet new problems in the world. The question of such a steering group has been controversial in the past; every country that suspects it would not be a member of such a group, tends to oppose its establishment. However, without such a group informal mechanisms arise that may be even more exclusive and biased to certain types of economic structures than would otherwise be desired by the membership. For example, the 'quad' group consisting of the US, the EU, Japan and Canada, has been very influential of the GATT system. Surely that influence will continue, but the question is will those four governments be joined by a broader group of representative governments while still maintaining a number small enough to be an effective guiding mechanism for the WTO.

Fourth, an important institutional problem will be how to integrate into the WTO new or emerging subjects which arise in the future, such as the problem of environment and trade rules. The amending rules of the WTO may (as they did in

GATT) turn out to be too rigid and difficult to fulfill. If that is the case, how will new subjects be integrated into the system? As mentioned above, it may be that new 'plurilateral agreements' under Annex 4 will be a major device for this, but the more that occurs, the more we will go back to the old GATT difficulty of 'a la carte' choices.

Fifth, there is the broad and important issue of enhancing the public understanding of the WTO and its work. This leads to the subject of 'transparency', commonly understood to mean adequate information and openness of the procedures, advocacy, meetings, etc., so that the media and scholarly endeavours can assist in informing the world public about the operation of the WTO.

Sixth, there has already been much comment about the 'agenda' after the Uruguay Round, for the World Trading System. One question often raised is whether there should be another 'round', or whether the procedures for pursuing future subjects should try to avoid rounds which tend to be complicated and cumbersome. The arguments in favour of rounds, however, may still prevail, namely that a larger round gives more opportunity for trade-offs between different subjects, and raises the issues to the highest level of national governments where definitive decisions can usually be made, (whereas lower level officials and technicians would not be able to make such compromises).

Many participants will have great influence on the way the WTO responds to those issues, but the most significant influence will likely be that of the new Director-General of the WTO. His guidance and diplomacy will shape the early years of the Organisation in ways that will have a profound impact on the longer term shape of its 'constitution.'

Without necessarily providing a complete inventory of substantive subjects issues to be faced in the future by the organisation (in addition to the so-called 'left over issues' mentioned in Section 3.*c* above), the following seem to be appropriately included on most lists:

(i) A series of subjects, already newly facing the organisation:

- Competition policy in relation to trade rules.
- Non-market economies, state trading, and economies in transition and their relation to the trading rules (e.g., China, Russia, etc.).
- Product (and service) standards and the use of science, raising the question of harmonisation or other techniques for facilitating trade flows.
- Cultural, social policy, and structural impediments to trade.

(ii) There are also a series of subjects called 'link issues', which are subjects that are often separately considered, but which have important interlinkages with trade. These include:

- Environmental rules and trade policy.

- Labour standards and rules and trade policy.
- Human rights and trade policy (including economic sanctions).
- Monetary policy and its relation to trade policy.
- Arms control and non-proliferation issues and their relation to trade policy.

(iii) Apart from these subjects for a post-Uruguay Round agenda, there are certain basic GATT concepts that need to be reconsidered and possibly altered so that they will be more effective in the future economically interdependent world. These include:

- The most-favoured-nation clause (and problems of the free rider).
- Regionalism and its relation to the multilateral system.
- Reciprocity and whether this concept can effectively handle the problems of rule making.
- National treatment and the need for minimum standards that go beyond non-discrimination or 'equal' treatment.
- Anti-dumping rules (as previously mentioned) and the question of whether these rules are in reality 'safeguards' or 'escape clause' measures, rather than unfair trade measures.

In short, we have put in place an 'evolutionary watershed' structure of institution and rules to round out the international economic system, but any close look quickly reveals that there is much more to do.

APPENDIX A

Annexes to the WTO

List of Annexes

ANNEX 1

ANNEX 1A: Multilateral Agreements to Trade in Goods
- General Agreement on Tariffs and Trade 1994
- Agreement on Agriculture
- Agreement on the Application of Sanitary & Phytosanitary Measures
- Agreement on Textiles and Clothing
- Agreement on Technical Barriers to Trade
- Agreement on Trade-Related Investment Measures
- Agreement on Implementation of Article VI of the General Agreement on Tariffs and Trade 1994
- Agreement on Implementation of Article VII of the General Agreement on Tariffs and Trade 1994
- Agreement on Preshipment Inspection
- Agreement on Rules of Origin
- Agreement on Import Licensing Procedures
- Agreement on Subsidies and Countervailing Measures
- Agreement on Safeguards

ANNEX 1B: General Agreement on Trade in Services and Annexes

ANNEX 1C: Agreement on Trade-Related Aspects of Intellectual Property Rights

ANNEX 2

Understanding on Rules and Procedures Governing the Settlement of Disputes

ANNEX 3

Trade Policy Review Mechanism

ANNEX 4

Plurilateral Trade Agreements
- Agreement on Trade in Civil Aircraft
- Agreement on Government Procurement
- International Dairy Agreement
- International Bovine Meat Agreement

APPENDIX B

Decision Making Authority in the WTO

WTO Decision Making

ORDINARY DECISIONS: ARTICLE IX:1

The WTO Charter specifies that the GATT practice of decision making by consensus is to be continued for the WTO Ministerial Conference (MC) and General Council (GC), but when consensus cannot be achieved, decisions will be made on the basis of the majority of votes cast, with each member having one vote, unless otherwise provided.

INTERPRETATIONS: ARTICLE IX:2

The MC and GC have exclusive authority to adopt interpretations of the WTO Charter and the Annex 1 Multilateral Trade Agreements. Interpretations of the Annex 1 agreements are to be based on a recommendation of the Council for that agreement and require an affirmative vote from three-quarters of the overall WTO membership. Interpretations are not to be used to undermine Article X's amendment procedures.

WAIVERS: ARTICLE IX:3

The MC may waive an obligation under the WTO Charter and the Annex 1 Multilateral Trade Agreements. If consensus cannot be reached, the grant of a waiver requires an affirmative vote of three-quarters of the overall WTO membership. In the case of Annex 1 agreements, the waiver request is to be submitted to the relevant Council (e.g., Goods, Services or TRIPS), which will submit a report to the MC. Article IX:4 provides that any waiver granted shall specify the exceptional circumstances justifying it and a termination date. Waivers are subject to annual MC review.

AMENDMENTS: ARTICLE X

Amendments to the WTO Charter and the Annex 1 Multilateral Trade Agreements may be proposed to the MC by members or Councils. If consensus cannot be reached, the approval of an amendment for submission to the members requires a two-thirds vote of the overall WTO membership. Generally, amendments come into force on acceptance by two-thirds of the members. If it has been determined that the amendment will not affect member rights and obligations, it comes into force for all members at that time. Otherwise, amendments come into force only for those members accepting them, unless by a three-quarters vote of the overall WTO membership, it is decided that if a member does not accept the amendment it shall be free to withdraw or remain a member with permission of the MC. (In the case of GATS, amendments to certain provisions come into force on a two-thirds vote. For the other provisions, they come into effect for those approving them, but are subject to the same three-quarters vote procedure.)

Amendments to certain rules take effect only upon acceptance by all members: WTO decision making and amendment rules (Arts. IX, X); GATT Arts. I (MFN) & II (Tariff Schedules); GATS Art. II:1 (MFN); TRIPS Art. 4 (MFN).

Amendments to Annexes 2 (Dispute Settlement) & 3 (TPRM) can be made by MC action alone (without member acceptance), but for Annex 2, MC approval must be by consensus. Art. X:8.

Negotiating Other Agreements: Article III:2

The WTO is to provide a forum for negotiations on agreements contained in its annexes. It may also provide a forum for other negotiations on trade relations and a framework for the implementation of the results of such negotiations, by decision of the MC.

Annex 4: Plurilateral Agreements

Decision making and amendments under these agreements are governed by the rules contained in each agreement. (Arts. IX:5, X:10). The MC may add trade agreements to Annex 4 on the request of the members party to the agreement. Art. X:9.

APPENDIX C

Some References to Works of the Present Author Containing More Detail

Restructuring the GATT System (The Royal Institute for International Affairs, Chatham House, London, January 1990).

The World Trading System: Law & Policy of International Economic Relations (The MIT Press, 1989).

'The General Agreement on Tariffs and Trade in United States Domestic Law,' *Michigan Law Review*, **66** 249 (December 1967).

World Trade and the Law of GATT, 'Treatise on a Legal Analysis of the General Agreement on Tariffs and Trade' (Bobbs-Merrill Company, December 1969).

Legal Problems of International Economic Relations — Cases, co-authored with W.J. Davey and A. Sykes, 3rd. ed. (West Publishing Company, 1995).

Chapter on United States, in Volume 'The Effect of Treaties in Domestic Law', F.G. Jacobs (University of London) and S. Roberts (King's College, London), (eds.), (London, Sweet & Maxwell 1987, proceedings of United Kingdom National Committee of Comparative Law Conference in London).

'Status of Treaties in Domestic Legal Systems: A Policy Analysis', *The American Journal of International Law*, **86**, 2, 310–340 (April 1992).

'World Trade Rules and Environmental Policies: Congruence or Conflict?' *Washington & Lee Law Review*, **49**, 4, 1227–1278 (Fall 1992).

'Regional Trade Blocs and GATT', *The World Economy*, **16**, 2, 121–131 (March 1993).

'Managing the Trading System: The World Trade Organization and the Post-Uruguay Round GATT Agenda' Ch. 3, 131–152 in P.B. Kenen (ed.), *Managing the World Economy: Fifty Years After Bretton Woods* (Institute for International Economics, September 1994).

Merchandise Trade in the APEC Region: Is There Scope for Liberalisation on an MFN Basis?

Paul Wonnacott

1. INTRODUCTION

THE APEC region (Asia-Pacific Economic Cooperation) includes many of the world's most rapidly growing economies.[1] Exports have been one of the building blocks in their impressive growth; access to relatively open markets has played a central role, together with high saving rates, imaginative entrepreneurship, and hard work. By providing further international economic cooperation, APEC may help to provide the basis for continuing prosperity and growth.

One of the concepts underlying APEC is *open regionalism*, a somewhat puzzling term, but one which represents a relatively simple idea: economic relations may be strengthened among member nations, while at the same time the region also becomes more open to trade and investment with other parts of the world.

In line with this objective, APEC has taken a number of preliminary steps, and is considering additional initiatives. Some of the steps are quite undramatic, but very constructive; for example, steps to make the customs clearance process simpler, faster, and more predictable. Other possible initiatives will require fundamental policy issues to be addressed; a possible investment code is a prime example.

The purpose of this paper is to consider how the concept of 'open regionalism' might be applied to merchandise trade. While international investment and

PAUL WONNACOTT is from the Institute for International Economics and Middlebury College. He is indebted to Gautam Jaggi for his assistance.

[1] The APEC members are Australia, Brunei, Canada, Chile, China, Hong Kong, Indonesia, Japan, Korea, Malaysia, Mexico, New Zealand, Papua New Guinea, the Philippines, Singapore, Taiwan, Thailand, and the United States.

service trade have become increasingly important in recent decades, merchandise trade remains at the heart of international economic relations.

There are two ways to apply the concept of open regionalism to merchandise trade in the APEC area. One is to consider a Free Trade Area (FTA) or even a Customs Union (CU) among the participants, while ensuring strict adherence to GATT Article 24 and scrupulously avoiding any increase in barriers to outside countries. Openness might be taken further, by having members of a prospective FTA agree to unilaterally reduce barriers on outside countries as they phase out internal barriers among themselves.[2] In addition, of course, the FTA members could participate actively in any future multilateral GATT negotiations to reduce trade barriers and other obstacles to international commerce.

An alternative to the FTA approach is to stay within the core of the GATT; that is, adherence to the Most Favoured Nation (MFN) principle in GATT article 1. This would mean that any reductions in tariffs or other trade barriers negotiated within APEC would also be extended to imports from other, non-APEC nations. This paper will focus on the MFN approach.

A difficulty which immediately arises is that a negotiation within APEC for reductions in trade barriers, which would then be extended on an MFN basis to non-member countries, would give a 'free ride' to outside countries; they would benefit from APEC's reductions in barriers without being required to reduce their own barriers.

2. A WAY AROUND THE FREE RIDER PROBLEM? THE PREDOMINANT SUPPLIER APPROACH

There are several ways of dealing with the free rider problem. One would be to use the APEC forum simply for preliminary discussions on the next steps in world trade liberalisation, as a catalyst to prepare for multilateral negotiations within the WTO. In this case, all the actual negotiations would occur within the WTO framework, and the APEC countries would face no special free rider problem.

A second possibility — the one considered in this paper — would be to focus an APEC negotiation on the products where the free rider problem would be minimised. In an extreme case, where the only source of actual or prospective supply is within the APEC area, the free rider problem would evaporate: there would be no outside supplier to get the free ride. In general, the greater the

---

[2] A proposal along these lines has been made by Prime Minister Mahatir. Bhagwati (1994, p. 36) has made a somewhat similar proposal in customs unions, suggesting that GATT article 24 be strengthened by requiring that the common external tariff be set at the lowest rate of any of the members before the establishment of a customs union.

concentration of supply within the APEC area, the smaller the free rider problem is likely to be.

Table 1 shows products — using the Standard International Trade Classification (SITC) — where APEC nations supply 70 per cent or more of world exports, as indicated in the final column.[3] In this column, intra-EU trade is excluded, on the ground that it is becoming more like intra-national than international trade. For comparison, the second last column includes intra-EU trade as part of international trade. Where there is a large discrepancy between the two columns — for example, the difference of over 14 per cent in motorcycles (No. 15) — intra-EU trade is relatively large, and EU suppliers might become important suppliers into the APEC markets if APEC nations substantially reduced their trade barriers. Perhaps most notable in this regard is trucks (No. 73), where EU countries could expect to benefit significantly from unilateral cuts in the trade barriers of APEC countries — most notably, the 25 per cent US tariff. Thus, a large percentage in the final column should be taken as an indication — but not proof — that the free rider problem is small.

The products in Table 1 may be grouped into a number of major categories. One is electronic equipment, including TV recorders, TV cameras, receivers, and picture tubes (Nos. 4, 5, 12, 23, and 57), radios (Nos. 9, 14, and 38), sound recording equipment (No. 19), microcircuits and transistors (Nos. 21 and 32), and computers (No. 26). Another is textiles (Nos. 1, 2, 3, 28, etc.). A third is transportation equipment: motorcycles (No. 15), bicycles (No. 22), and trucks (No. 73). A fourth is a list of agricultural and raw materials — rubber (No. 7), corn (No. 13), vegetable oil (No. 25), coal (No. 27), animal oils and fat (No. 52), tin (No. 53), etc. Finally, there is a group of products that does not fit into any of the above categories; for example, cameras, other photo equipment, and optical instruments (Nos. 18, 24, 89), toys (No. 56), stringed musical instruments (No. 59), tugs and special vehicles (No. 62), and luggage and handbags (No. 79). (Because some data are also included in broader categories — e.g., portable radios in No. 9 are also included in radios in No. 14 — care should be taken whenever adding up the dollar numbers in the first three columns.)

Of these major categories, electronic equipment is probably the best candidate for the top of the list for possible discussion of liberalisation. Not only do most of

---

[3] Table 1 is based on United Nations trade data for 1991. Almost all 3 digit categories were included in the data used to develop Table 1 (the major exceptions being a number of 'other' categories, each composed of products with little apparent close relation). Four digit categories were not dealt with comprehensively; they were chosen primarily when the corresponding 3 digit category indicated that APEC countries were the predominant suppliers. Five digit data were considered even more selectively.

There is a fair amount of noise in these data; the decimals in Table 1 should not be taken seriously, but are simply a way of ranking close categories. Anyone interested in trivial inconsistencies in the data might consider lines 50, 54, and 55.

Data in the UN's 'Other Asia NES' category are used for Taiwan.

TABLE 1
Products for which APEC Countries Provide the Predominant Supply of World Exports

Rank (No.)	*SITC (Rev. 2)*	*Description*	*APEC Exports US$ Millions*	*World Exports US$ Millions*	*World Exports Excluding Intra-EU Trade US$ Millions*	*APEC Exports as a Percentage of World Exports*	*APEC Exports as a Percentage of World Exports, Excluding Intra-EU Trade*
1	6551	Knitted, etc. synthetic fabric nonel.	957	957	957	100.0	100.0
2	6553	Knitted, etc. fabric, elastic.	179	179	179	99.9	99.9
3	2613	Raw silk not thrown	512	542	516	94.5	99.1
4	76381	TV image, sound recorders, etc.	8,810	9,459	8,959	93.1	98.3
5	76482	Television cameras	6,293	7,180	6,479	87.6	97.1
6	7638	Other sound apparatus, etc.	13,838	15,599	14,376	88.7	96.3
7	232	Natural rubber, gums	3,728	3,919	3,875	95.1	96.2
8	763	Sound recorders, phonographs	13,523	15,349	14,086	88.1	96.0
9	7622	Portable radio receivers	4,667	5,075	4,900	92.0	95.3
10	261	Silk	436	496	459	88.0	95.0
11	7631	Electric gramophones, etc.	457	526	486	86.9	94.1
12	7612	Monochrome TV receivers	563	649	606	86.8	92.9
13	044	Maize unmilled	6,300	8,564	6,846	73.6	92.0
14	762	Radio broadcast receivers	10,166	12,197	11,084	83.3	91.7
15	7851	Motorcycles, etc.	3,388	4,409	3,721	76.9	91.1
16	7525	Automatic data proc. peripheral units	20,091	26,662	22,313	75.4	90.0
17	7768	Electronic component parts, crystals	5,161	6,066	5,739	85.1	89.9
18	8811	Cameras still, flash equipment	4,298	5,231	4,786	82.2	89.8
19	89831	Prepad sound recording media	6,357	9,289	7,099	68.4	89.5
20	7512	Calculating, accounting, etc. machinery	2,173	2,697	2,441	80.6	89.0
21	7764	Electronic microcircuits	39,982	49,856	44,946	80.2	89.0
22	7852	Cycles, etc. non motorised	2,036	2,756	2,290	73.8	88.9

TABLE 1
Continued

Rank (No.)	*SITC (Rev. 2)*	*Description*	*APEC Exports US$ Millions*	*World Exports US$ Millions*	*World Exports Excluding Intra-EU Trade US$ Millions*	*APEC Exports as a Percentage of World Exports*	*APEC Exports as a Percentage of World Exports, Excluding Intra-EU Trade*
23	7761	TV picture tubes	3,375	4,849	3,805	69.6	88.7
24	75182	Photo, thermocopy apparatus	3,503	6,290	3,983	55.7	87.9
25	424	Fixed vegetable oil nonsoft	3,066	3,833	3,488	80.0	87.9
26	7522	Digital computers	7,058	9,783	8,059	72.2	87.6
27	322	Coal, lignite, peat	12,527	15,344	14,306	81.6	87.6
28	8443	Undergarments, not knit, of women	951	1,166	1,087	81.6	87.5
29	7762	Other electronic tubes, etc.	2,223	2,723	2,541	81.6	87.5
30	6871	Tin, alloys unwrought	807	975	925	82.8	87.3
31	785	Cycles, etc. motorised or not	8,010	11,266	9,227	71.1	86.8
32	776	Transistors, valves, etc.	50,463	65,865	58,673	76.6	86.0
33	268	Wool (excluding tops), animal hair	3,697	4,831	4,301	76.5	86.0
34	32	Coal, coke, briquettes	13,053	17,161	15,444	76.1	84.5
35	246	Pulpwood, chips, woodwaste	897	1,188	1,061	75.5	84.5
36	23	Rubber, crude	5,485	7,946	6,501	69.0	84.4
37	759	Office, ADP machine pts, accessories	35,432	55,236	42,076	64.1	84.2
38	7621	Motor vehicle radio receivers	2,759	3,895	3,277	70.8	84.2
39	6531	Cont. synthetic weaves nonpile	7,821	10,770	9,356	72.6	83.6
40	752	Automatic deata processing equipment	45,062	70,836	54,151	63.6	83.2
41	75	Office machines, ADP equipment	84,998	135,557	102,356	62.7	83.0
42	2614	Silk worn cocoons, waste	91	121	110	75.4	83.0
43	7853	Invalid carriages, parts of cycles	2,805	4,297	3,413	65.3	82.2
44	881	Photo apparatus, equipment, nes.	5,588	7,912	6,802	70.6	82.1

TABLE 1
Continued

Rank (No.)	*SITC (Rev. 2)*	*Description*	*APEC Exports US$ Millions*	*World Exports US$ Millions*	*World Exports Excluding Intra-EU Trade US$ Millions*	*APEC Exports as a Percentage of World Exports*	*APEC Exports as a Percentage of World Exports, Excluding Intra-EU Trade*
45	223	Seeds for other fixed oils	292	429	358	68.2	81.6
46	247	Other wood rough, squared	4,351	6,069	5,359	71.7	81.2
47	8942	Toys, indoor games, etc.	7,553	11,799	9,355	64.0	80.7
48	76	Telcomm., sound equipment	73,582	106,664	91,317	69.0	80.6
49	751	Office machines	6,548	11,482	8,126	57.0	80.6
50	0411	Durum wheat, etc. unmilled	527	1,310	654	40.2	80.5
51	7511	Typewriters, check writers	715	1,132	896	63.1	79.7
52	411	Animal oils and fats	610	1,058	766	57.7	79.7
53	687	Tin	862	1,157	1,084	74.5	79.5
54	0412	Other wheat, etc. unmilled	7,304	12,184	9,228	60.0	79.2
55	041	Wheat, etc. unmilled	7,831	13,534	9,921	57.9	78.9
56	894	Toys, sporting goods, etc.	13,557	21,007	17,473	64.5	77.6
57	761	Television receivers	9,347	17,224	12,050	54.3	77.6
58	289	Precious metal ores, waste nes.	637	1,050	826	60.7	77.2
59	8981	Pianos, other string instruments	420	661	546	63.5	77.0
60	7611	Colour TV receivers	8,482	16,277	11,145	52.1	76.1
61	045	Cereals nes. unmilled	923	1,379	1,216	67.0	76.0
62	7938	Tugs, special vehicles, etc.	1,507	2,150	1,990	70.1	75.7
63	6534	Discon. synthetic blended fabric nes.	3,483	6,019	4,602	57.9	75.7
64	7523	Digital central processors	10,134	20,135	13,401	50.3	75.6
65	7521	Analog. hybrid computers	316	554	418	56.9	75.6
66	2665	Discon. synthetic fibre uncombed	1,538	2,774	2,039	55.5	75.4

TABLE 1
Continued

67	764	Telecomm. equipmt., parts, access. nes.	40,547	61,577	53,780	65.8	75.4
68	037	Fish, etc., prepared, preserved, nes.	3,652	6,177	4,866	59.1	75.1
69	287	Base metal ores, conc nes.	7,394	10,634	9,855	69.5	75.0
70	211	Hides, skins, excl. furs, raw	2,116	3,851	2,830	55.0	74.8
71	8983	Sound recording tape, discs	9,338	17,490	12,490	53.4	74.8
72	898	Musical instruments, parts	10,664	19,664	14,283	54.2	74.7
73	7821	Lorries, trucks	18,556	33,883	24,878	54.8	74.6
74	122	Tobacco, manufactured	7,122	13,177	9,560	54.1	74.5
75	685	Lead	511	954	686	53.6	74.5
76	7528	Off-line data processing equipment	2,876	5,297	3,869	54.3	74.3
77	7763	Diodes, transistors, etc.	5,489	8,129	7,407	67.5	74.1
78	634	Veneers, plywood, etc.	5,344	9,004	7,213	59.3	74.1
79	831	Travel goods, handbags	5,774	8,926	7,852	64.7	73.5
80	8941	Baby carriages, parts, nes.	261	489	355	53.3	73.3
81	222	Seeds for soft fixed oil	5,717	9,373	7,819	61.0	73.1
82	22	Oil seeds, oleaginous fruit	5,922	9,769	8,144	60.6	72.7
83	655	Knitted, etc. fabrics	3,782	6,786	5,232	55.7	72.3
84	871	Optical instruments	2,522	4,158	3,499	60.6	72.1
85	7712	Calculating, accounting, etc. machinery	4,741	8,021	6,579	59.1	72.1
86	653	Woven man made fib. fabric	12,484	22,896	17,338	54.5	72.0
87	291	Crude animal materials, nes.	1,375	2,480	1,911	55.4	72.0
88	8947	Other sporting goods, fair amusm.	3,904	6,162	5,432	63.4	71.9
89	8710	Optical instruments	2,633	4,268	3,664	61.7	71.9
90	251	Pulp and waste paper	8,804	13,783	12,318	63.9	71.5
91	78	Road vehicles	149,237	319,654	209,589	46.7	71.2
92	6536	Discon. regen. textile fabric nes.	1,205	2,136	1,701	56.4	70.9
93	274	Sulphur, unrstd. irn. pyrte.	786	1,211	1,116	64.9	70.5
94	6532	Discon. synthetic textile fabric nes.	815	1,532	1,159	53.2	70.4
95	77	Electric machinery nes., etc.	109,624	198,167	155,906	55.3	70.3
96	6552	Other knit etc. fabric nonel.	3,423	6,434	4,879	53.2	70.2

Source: Calculated from United Nations Comtrade data.

the major, highly-competitive world producers have their headquarters and primary production facilities in the APEC countries, laying the basis for efficient intra-industry trade within the APEC region, but electronics also represents an industry where protection may backfire, making firms comfortable with their domestic market, losing out in the rush for technological improvement. Looking to the world market seems absolutely indispensable for a healthy electronics industry. (It is possible to produce cars whose design is 30 years out of date, as Brazil has demonstrated. But, for most electronic products, it would be preposterous to produce goods 15 years out of date.) It is perhaps undiplomatic, but true, to observe that much of the European electronics industry is playing catch-up. A lack of a true common market, and a general lack of outward orientation, has perhaps been the major reason why this very advanced technological continent has been lagging in the most technologically dynamic of all industries.

3. WHAT'S AT STAKE: SIGNIFICANCE OF PREDOMINANT SUPPLIER GOODS IN THE TRADE OF APEC COUNTRIES

Gains from regional negotiations on some or all of the products in Table 1 would depend on the importance of these products in the trade of the APEC nations. Table 2 presents the dollar figures for trade in these products, plus the shares of trade which they represent.

Specifically, the first part, panel A of Table 2 shows the imports of all the APEC partners of the goods above various cut-off levels. For example, the first column shows that, for the products in which APEC nations provide 85 per cent or more of world exports (excluding intra-EU trade), Australia's APEC partners (that is, all APEC countries other than Australia) imported $111 billion in 1991 from all sources, including both APEC and non-APEC countries. Thus, in the event of an APEC agreement to cut tariffs on this group of products, Australia would have improved access to markets worth $111 billion. That does not, of course, tell us how much Australia itself would benefit; the other APEC exporters would also have better access to these markets, as would outside suppliers, since cuts in trade barriers would be on an MFN base. In other words, the first column of Panel A simply shows the market to which Australia, along with everybody else, has improved access; it provides little focus on the interests of Australia itself. Similar figures for other APEC members are presented in the second and following columns of Panel A.

Panels B and C provide much more focused information on the stakes for individual APEC members; they show the shares of each of the APEC members' exports and imports made up of products above various cut-off percentages in

Table 1. Thus, for example, 18 per cent of Australia's exports, and 5 per cent of its imports, are made up of products which lie above an 85 per cent cut-off line in Table 1.

One thing stands out strongly from Panels B and C. There would be very little to be gained from a negotiation which covered only the products where APEC countries provide 90 per cent or more of world exports. Such products make up only 3 per cent of total APEC exports. Any serious negotiation would have to go down at least to the products where APEC countries provide 85 per cent of exports; going down this far would include products which make up 10 per cent of APEC exports. Indeed, the last column of Table 2B would suggest that 80 per cent might be a good cut-off; at this level, the percentage of APEC exports covered rises to 19 per cent.

Not surprisingly, the APEC nations as a whole have some comparative advantage in the products in which they are principal exporters; at the 80 per cent level, these make up 19 per cent of APEC exports, compared to 16 per cent of imports. However, even though export shares are somewhat higher than import shares, regardless of how high the cut-off percentage is chosen, import shares are almost as high in each case as export shares (Table 2, Panels B and C, last column). This indicates that not only are the APEC nations the predominant suppliers of these products; they are also the predominant importers.

The data in Panels B and C of Table 2 suggest that some countries might be much more enthusiastic about selective liberalisation than others. The countries with the biggest export-import discrepancy are Malaysia (45 per cent of exports compared to 23 per cent of imports would be liberalised, if liberalisation went down to the 80 per cent level), Japan (27 per cent vs. 13 per cent), Philippines (29 per cent vs. 18 per cent), and Thailand (22 per cent vs. 12 per cent). On the other hand, Chile, Mexico, Canada and New Zealand are more heavy importers than exporters. For the United States, the shares of imports and exports are the same (16 per cent) at the 80 per cent cut-off, and very similar regardless of what cut-off is chosen. Hong Kong and Singapore are somewhat special cases; as entrepots with open trading systems, they have the strongest general interest in reductions in trade barriers.

Rather than having a cut-off at a specific percentage, an alternative might be to look at major product categories appearing in Table 1, most notably the electronic equipment sector. Most of the 'non-European' countries of APEC (i.e., those not settled predominantly from Europe) are net exporters of these products; Hong Kong and Indonesia are exceptions (Table 2, Panels E and F). But, regardless of existing trade patterns, electronic products are promising candidates for liberalisation. Unlike heavy manufacturing, such as automobiles, electronics are relatively footloose; they migrate easily to new production locations. If remaining barriers were cut by APEC nations, new producers would not enjoy substantial protection in their domestic markets; but, they would be in a

TABLE 2
Importance of Products in which APEC Countries are the Principal Suppliers

*Products Above**	*Australia*	*Canada*	*Chile*	*China*	*Hong Kong*	*Indonesia*	*Japan*	*Korea*	*Malaysia*	*Mexico*	*New Zealand*	*Philippines*	*Singapore*	*Taiwan*	*Thailand*	*United States*	*APEC*
Panel A: Potential Market: Imports by APEC Partner Countries of Specified Goods, 1991 (US$ Billions)*																	
70%	480	444	489	472	453	486	431	469	477	476	488	487	466	470	482	298	
75%	248	237	252	244	232	251	214	238	244	248	252	250	236	240	248	164	
80%	224	215	229	222	208	228	198	216	221	225	228	227	212	217	225	146	
85%	111	107	112	109	101	112	96	103	107	111	112	111	103	104	110	78	
90%	30	29	30	29	26	30	27	29	30	30	30	30	28	29	30	17	
Panel B: Share of Products in Country's Exports, 1991 (Per Cent)																	
70%	28	40	21	30	15	26	57	44	54	18	17	40	48	44	34	34	39
75%	25	12	16	15	7	11	28	27	48	4	11	34	40	30	27	18	21
80%	19	8	3	13	7	8	27	25	45	3	10	29	40	25	22	16	19
85%	18	3	0	6	4	7	15	16	30	1	7	21	18	10	10	7	10
90%	0	0	0	3	0	4	7	4	9	0	0	1	6	1	5	2	3
Panel C: Share of Products in Country's Imports, 1991 (Per Cent)																	
70%	28	39	26	30	38	20	25	27	40	30	32	34	38	34	25	38	34
75%	13	13	11	14	21	9	17	19	26	10	15	22	27	20	13	18	17
80%	12	12	10	12	21	6	13	17	23	9	12	18	26	19	12	16	16
85%	5	5	4	6	11	3	7	11	15	3	4	13	14	13	6	7	8
90%	2	1	2	2	4	0	2	2	1	2	1	0	4	2	0	3	2

TABLE 2
Continued

Group	Australia	Canada	Chile	China	Hong Kong	Indonesia	Japan	Korea	Malaysia	Mexico	New Zealand	Philippines	Singapore	Taiwan	Thailand	United States	APEC
Panel D: Potential Market: Imports by APEC Partner Countries of Specified Goods, 1991 (US$ millions)*																	
Electronic Equip.	172,657	164,713	176,455	171,976	160,715	175,978	163,649	168,043	169,162	173,458	176,118	174,898	160,772	167,731	172,919	105,884	
Textiles	15,258	15,056	15,545	13,907	10,319	15,344	14,401	14,849	15,086	15,289	15,528	15,148	14,673	15,105	15,196	13,843	
Transportation Equip.	131,263	111,658	134,006	128,788	132,533	133,127	128,027	133,607	132,636	128,357	133,960	134,255	133,335	131,567	132,714	61,271	
Agr. & Raw Materials	68,679	66,383	68,985	66,121	66,494	67,817	40,417	61,118	68,059	67,032	68,918	68,464	67,724	64,122	68,244	59,687	
Misc.	244,514	230,974	250,823	244,875	226,590	250,038	227,697	239,391	242,380	246,573	250,190	249,171	234,111	239,537	246,245	150,427	
Panel E: Share of Products in Country's Exports, 1991 (Per Cent)***																	
Electronic Equip.	2	5	0	6	8	1	24	24	31	3	1	24	37	22	16	12	15
Textiles	6	0	0	3	1	3	1	6	1	0	6	1	1	4	2	0	1
Transportation Equip.	2	21	0	8	1	1	23	5	2	11	1	1	1	4	1	8	10
Agr. & Raw Materials	19	11	19	7	2	10	1	1	14	2	10	9	3	2	9	8	6
Misc.	2	7	1	12	12	13	27	26	27	5	2	27	34	32	20	17	19
Panel F: Share of Products in Country's Imports, 1991 (Per Cent)***																	
Electronic Equip.	10	10	7	8	16	4	6	11	21	7	11	16	25	15	11	14	12
Textiles	1	0	1	3	5	1	1	1	1	1	1	4	1	1	1	0	1
Transportation Equip.	8	19	10	9	2	6	3	1	6	13	9	4	2	5	5	14	9
Agr. & Raw Materials	1	2	3	5	3	5	12	10	3	4	4	6	2	8	3	2	5
Misc.	17	17	10	10	25	6	10	15	25	10	16	19	26	19	14	20	17

Notes:
* Products above these levels in Table 1.
** Imports by all other APEC countries, from all sources, including non-APEC countries.
*** Include only items in SITC categories where APEC exports exceeded 70 per cent of World exports in Table 1.

position to sell into the open markets of their APEC partners. Indeed, because of rapid technological change, adopting and keeping up with world-class technology is an indispensable part of success in this industry. Furthermore, electronics are a group of products where liberalisation within a small region — for example, the ASEAN nations — holds out much less promise than liberalisation within a much larger region (such as APEC and, *a fortiori*, the world). One reason is that access to large markets is important, while geographical proximity is relatively unimportant; transportation costs do not loom large because most electronic products have a high value for their size and weight.

If we go beyond electronic equipment in Table 2, Panels E and F, things look less promising for APEC liberalisation of broad categories of goods. Textiles have been one of the most thorny categories for trade negotiations, and there would likely be substantial concern about the potential free ride of suppliers, like India, who maintain high restrictions on their own textile imports. Although specific textile products might be chosen for liberalisation from Table 1, it would probably be best to consider broad liberalisation within the textile area within the encompassing framework of the GATT. Similarly, broader negotiations — in this case, specifically including Europe — would seem to be the most appropriate approach to a comprehensive liberalisation of the transportation equipment category.

4. WHAT'S AT STAKE: POST URUGUAY ROUND TARIFFS

The potential gains from liberalisation of products in which APEC countries provide the principal supplies clearly depend not only on the volume of trade in those products, but also on the trade barriers that will remain after the Uruguay Round cuts are put into effect. Post-Uruguay Round tariff rates for the top 50 categories in Table 1 are shown in Table 3.

For many of these products, tariffs will already be very low in a number of the APEC countries at the end of the Uruguay Round reductions. Hong Kong stands out, with its zero tariffs across the board. For most products, Japanese tariffs will be zero, and discussions with Japan will continue to focus on structural impediments to trade. The United States will likewise have very low tariffs — less than 5 per cent — on most of the products.

There will, however, still be high tariffs of 20 per cent or more in many of the products in a number of countries — Korea, Mexico, the Philippines, and Thailand. The last two of these — the Philippines and Thailand — are two of the countries who conspicuously export more 'principal supplier' goods than they import (as noted in the discussion of Table 2). Thus these two countries, which would face the prospect of the greatest tariff cuts from liberalisation of products in Table 1, would also be in a very strong position to gain from the liberalisation.

In the electronic products category — which the previous section suggested was a primary target for liberalisation — tariffs are still above 10 per cent in a number of categories in about half the countries. Thus, there is scope for significant liberalisation in this category, in which freer commerce is particularly important. Several countries might be at the top of the list to consider significant liberalisation in this area — namely, the countries which have significant surpluses in electronics products, yet maintain high tariffs on some of these products: Korea, Malaysia, the Philippines, and Thailand.

5. AN ALTERNATIVE: AN APEC FREE-TRADE ASSOCIATION?

If consideration is given to the possibility of a Free-Trade Association (FTA) in the APEC area, then one of the central issues will be the relationships among the three largest economies — China, Japan, and the United States. Needless to say, these three countries do not always look on questions the same way; here, we consider the prospects of an APEC-wide FTA from the viewpoint of the United States.

From the US viewpoint, participation in a FTA which includes China and Japan would offer better access to very large markets, but it would also raise major problems. The inclusion of Japan, at least within the foreseeable future, would raise concerns in the United States that the elimination of the already-low Japanese tariffs could be negotiated, but the more important non-tariff barriers represented by the distribution system and the Keiretsu (for example) would likely survive any FTA negotiation. In other words, it would heighten US concerns regarding an 'uneven playing field.' In the long run, this concern may weaken as Japanese non-tariff barriers are worn away. But the recent rocky trade negotiations between the two nations underline just how different are the perceptions of the two countries over what constitutes a 'level playing field;' this difference in perceptions is likely to persist for an extended period.

China would be likely to raise even stronger worries, over competition from low-wage workers. There can be mutually advantageous trade between nations at quite different stages of development, but free trade with China — with its huge size and very low wages — would be unlikely to survive a political debate within the United States; trade policy would be faced with the 'Ross Perot' problem, writ large.

On the other hand, if the United States were to raise the possibility of an FTA with East Asian countries excluding Japan and China, these two nations would likely object; we would be fishing in their pond. (A prospective agreement with Australia and New Zealand might be an exception.) The United States might similarly object to broad arrangements which exclude them, but include Japan and/or China.

TABLE 3
Post Uruguay Round Tariff Levels (Product rankings from Table 1)

Rank (No.)	SITC (Rev. 2)	Post-Uruguay Round Average Tariffs[1] of: Australia	Canada	EU	Hong Kong	Japan	Korea	Malaysia	Mexico	New Zealand	Philippines	Singapore	Thailand	US[2]
1,2	6551, 6553[a]	18.30	14.00	7.95	0.00	7.89	30.11	20.00	35.00	27.50	30.00	10.05	30.00	10.77
3	2613	—	0.00	—	—	—	51.33	—	—	—	—	—	—	0.00
4	76381	Data unavailable for SITC 76381. See rank 6 for tariffs in SITC 7638.												
5	76482	15.02	0.00	4.77	0.00	0.00	20.01	5.00	35.00	0.00	19.98	10.00	4.88	2.10
6	7638	4.43	4.98	7.10	0.00	0.00	25.67	27.09	33.34	18.74	49.84	2.69	30.03	0.17
7	232	2.34	0.00	0.02	0.00	0.00	13.00	1.80	35.00	2.31	20.05	0.07	30.22	0.00
8	763	6.75	4.82	6.15	0.00	0.00	22.63	25.28	33.59	22.78	49.84	2.09	30.04	0.18
9	7622	14.95	2.09	5.70	0.00	0.00	12.50	4.76	35.01	17.78	50.00	10.17	29.87	1.89
10	261	—	0.00	—	—	—	51.20	—	0.00	—	—	12.50	—	0.09
11	7631	Very low trade. See rank 8 for tariffs in SITC 763.												
12	7612	15.02	5.72	7.48	0.00	0.00	14.74	25.00	35.00	10.00	50.00	0.00	30.00	5.00
13	044	1.18	0.73	0.00	0.00	14.06	368.90	0.00	189.14	—	50.00	9.09	73.06	0.19
14	762	15.01	0.78	7.92	0.00	0.00	14.54	14.34	35.00	31.58	50.00	10.00	30.00	1.62
15	7851	2.87	0.00	6.12	0.00	0.00	68.40	60.00	35.00	0.00	27.17	15.09	—	0.81
16	7525[b]	4.64	0.00	0.93	0.00	0.00	12.41	0.00	35.00	0.00	20.00	1.40	20.00	0.98
17	7768	12.02	0.00	3.18	0.00	0.00	0.00	0.00	35.11	8.20	20.00	0.73	35.00	0.53
18	8811	0.88	2.94	3.77	0.00	0.00	19.88	0.94	35.92	6.94	26.55	0.00	33.88	0.54
19	89831[c]	2.58	2.84	1.67	0.00	0.00	10.90	7.12	35.00	5.63	11.82	0.26	30.00	0.15
20	7512	5.26	0.00	3.89	0.00	0.00	12.95	4.94	35.00	4.54	10.34	7.05	29.92	1.34
21	7764	2.00	0.00	7.00	0.00	0.00	0.00	1.84	35.00	0.00	20.00	10.00	35.00	0.00
22	7852	15.03	13.20	14.99	—	0.00	12.50	7.14	35.02	20.06	50.00	0.00	33.33	9.37
23	7761	0.47	6.10	12.51	0.00	0.00	25.00	5.17	35.00	20.00	20.00	9.44	35.08	3.71
24	75182	0.84	0.00	5.61	—	0.00	23.30	19.86	35.00	9.89	19.95	9.30	40.15	2.32
25	424	0.56	6.20	5.80	0.00	1.45	25.22	0.00	45.00	—	41.67	9.88	27.27	0.23
26	7522	6.00	0.00	2.45	0.00	0.00	20.00	0.00	35.00	0.00	20.00	0.00	20.00	0.98
27	322	0.00	0.63	0.00	—	0.00	—	0.00	35.02	0.00	—	0.00	—	0.00
28	8443	37.33	17.99	11.93	0.00	7.23	—	11.11	35.04	34.48	—	10.14	33.33	11.57
29	7762	10.30	5.45	2.68	0.00	0.00	15.34	4.94	35.00	0.00	20.06	10.03	34.78	3.43

TABLE 3
Continued

Rank (No.)	SITC (Rev. 2)	Post-Uruguay Round Average Tariffs[1] of: Australia	Canada	EU	Hong Kong	Japan	Korea	Malaysia	Mexico	New Zealand	Philippines	Singapore	Thailand	US[2]
30	6871	—	0.02	0.00	0.00	0.00	10.45	5.00	35.14	0.00	10.42	10.53	—	0.00
31	785	3.53	1.85	5.86	0.00	0.00	36.91	18.52	35.00	4.78	28.28	4.32	38.46	4.41
32	776	2.50	0.35	6.28	0.00	0.00	0.63	0.27	35.00	0.09	20.00	6.66	34.99	0.30
33	268	—	0.09	1.76	0.00	0.00	2.00	3.33	15.00	—	—	—	0.00	2.00
34	32	0.00	0.00	0.00	0.00	0.02	1.38	1.94	14.59	0.00	13.87	0.00	25.00	0.00
35	246	0.00	0.00	0.00	0.00	0.00	4.97	—	35.02	0.00	—	—	—	0.00
36	23	2.34	0.02	0.02	0.00	0.00	12.98	1.80	35.00	2.25	20.19	1.19	30.22	0.00
37	759	7.17	0.00	0.16	0.00	0.00	13.19	0.39	35.00	0.41	10.23	0.27	20.04	0.26
38	7621	15.79	0.00	10.85	0.00	0.00	15.99	20.51	35.00	30.43	50.00	10.00	30.47	2.34
39	6531[d]	26.62	14.00	8.00	0.00	6.08	13.00	20.05	35.00	5.56	30.00	9.99	30.02	13.89
40	752	4.64	0.00	0.93	0.00	0.00	12.41	0.00	35.00	0.00	20.00	1.40	20.00	0.98
41	75	5.57	0.07	0.73	0.00	0.00	12.75	0.51	35.02	0.26	15.30	0.79	20.24	0.91
42	2614	—	0.00	—	—	—	51.04	—	0.00	—	—	12.50	—	0.74
43	7853	5.02	2.12	2.76	0.00	0.00	12.36	12.50	34.97	11.32	21.68	0.00	39.13	2.65
44	881	4.11	2.59	3.24	0.00	0.00	6.51	8.86	35.44	9.64	20.65	0.58	37.88	0.71
45	223	0.99	2.53	0.38	—	0.00	50.00	9.09	25.44	—	40.09	8.89	39.47	0.04
46	247	—	0.00	0.00	0.00	0.03	4.79	20.29	34.98	0.00	10.00	10.01	4.83	0.00
47	8942	14.91	0.45	2.55	0.00	2.45	11.09	5.02	35.00	27.57	50.00	0.00	30.23	0.00
48	76	11.73	2.21	3.69	0.00	0.00	15.30	9.63	34.50	22.61	21.22	6.98	19.62	1.71
49	751	2.11	0.86	4.06	0.00	0.00	13.30	10.61	35.12	5.53	14.05	7.72	31.02	2.05
50	0411	—	—	—	—	—	8.87	5.03	40.00	—	—	—	—	2.82

Notes:
— Value of trade in the SITC is less than $500,000.
[1] Tariffs are weighted according to 1988, 1989, or 1991 imports of the country from the US in the specified SITC.
[2] Tariffs are weighted according to total US imports from all countries in the USTR database in the specified SITC.
[a] This line shows tariff rates on SITC 655 rather than SITC 6551 and 6553, which were not available.
[b] This line shows tariff rates on SITC 752 rather than SITC 7525.
[c] This line shows tariff rates on SITC 8983 rather than SITC 89831.
[d] This line shows tariff rates on SITC 653 rather than SITC 6531

Source: USTR.

TABLE 4
Trading Patterns: Ratio of Trade Share to Share of Gross Product, 1989

	Importer:					
	US	*Canada*	*Other Americas*	*Japan*	*Developing Asia*	*EC*
Exporter:						
United States	—	5.2	1.3	1.1	1.7	0.6
Canada	2.9	—	0.4	0.6	0.6	0.4
Other Americas	1.5	0.6	2.0	0.6	0.5	0.5
Japan	1.1	0.9	0.5	—	3.1	0.5
Developing Asia	0.8	0.5	0.2	1.5	3.3	0.5
EC	0.3	0.3	0.3	0.3	0.5	2.5

Source: Summers (1991)

This, then, is a fundamental problem: would it be possible to reconcile the interests of the big three of the Pacific Basin in any free-trade area?

If this very knotty problem were simply set aside, and the question asked about the economic advisability of an APEC FTA, a major research project would be required to reach an answer. This would have to range from the potential trade creation and trade diverting effects — which are difficult to estimate — to the even more complex question of the probable dynamic effects of an FTA. Short of such a project, the concept of 'natural' trading areas is worth considering. The idea is that if countries already trade disproportionately with one another *prior to the establishment of preferential arrangements*, they represent a 'natural' trading area; there is a presumption (but no certainty) that a CU or FTA among such members is likely, on balance, to be trade creating and beneficial.

Perhaps the most interesting summary data on this issue have been presented by Summers (1991), reproduced as Table 4. The basic idea is that, if trade between countries exceeds what one would expect on the basis of their gross products, then they are natural trading partners. The numbers in Table 4 represent the following ratio: Country A's share of B's exports, divided by A's share of World GDP excluding B's GDP.

If countries are chosen at random, the expected value of this expression is one. If the expression gives a number of more than one, A takes a greater share of B's exports than can be explained by the size of A's economy (relative to the size of the economies of all other purchasers of B's exports). A imports a disproportionate amount from B; A is a natural trading partner of B.[4] High numbers in Table 4 may be due to geographical proximity — close countries tend

[4] What is relevant here is A's share of total output of all the countries that buy B's imports — that is, all countries except B. (B's purchases of B's goods are neither exports nor imports; they are domestic trade.) That is why B's GDP is subtracted in calculating the numbers in Table 4.

to trade intensively with one another;[5] they may also be due to other factors, such as complementary products or factors of production. (For example, industrial countries may import large quantities of oil from far-off lands.)

Table 4 suggests that strong natural trading relationships exist between the United States and Canada [ratios of 5.2 (for Canada's share of US exports) and 2.9 (for the US share of Canada's exports)], among the developing countries of Asia (3.3), and within the EC (2.5).

One must, however, be careful in interpreting these data, because natural trading areas should be identified by the trade patterns *before* the establishment of any preferences; that is, trade patterns in a world in which every country grants MFN treatment to every other country, and there are no preferences or penalties to distort trade. However, this condition was not met in 1989. Most conspicuously, the EC nations had had a common market for many years. The high volume of trade among them was certainly due, at least partly, to the preferences among them; it is not clear just from Table 4 that they really are natural trading partners. (There are, however, *a priori* reasons — most notably, their physical proximity — to believe that they are natural partners, although not to the degree suggested by Table 4.)

To a much smaller extent, the strength of the natural ties between the United States and Canada are also overstated. Since the time of the Auto Pact of 1965, most automotive products have passed duty-free between the two countries.

Where does Table 4 leave us with respect to an APEC FTA? Most of the intra-APEC ratios are above 1, suggesting that the APEC nations[6] are, at least weakly, natural trading partners — with the notable exception of Canada in its trade with Japan and the developing nations of Asia, which in each case yield ratios less than one. This suggests that, if the problem of the three large countries diminishes with time, and if the multilateral approach to liberalisation through the GATT/WTO loses steam, the case for an APEC FTA will be strengthened.[7]

6. CONCLUSIONS

For the foreseeable future, however, I conclude that MFN is a more promising approach within APEC than an FTA. While this is not in line with the declaration at the recent APEC summit, it is consistent with a recent working paper of the World Bank (1994, pp. 48, 50). Of the four options studied for East Asia, they

[5] In addition to GNP — which is taken into account in Table 4 — Frankel, Wei, and Stein (1994) investigate the effects of a number of other determinants of trade: GNP per capita, distance, and whether the trading partners have a common border.

[6] The 'developing Asia' numbers should be taken as tentative; they include countries not in APEC.

[7] For additional discussion of 'natural' trading areas, see Bergsten (1991); Frankel, Wei, and Stein (1994); Krugman (1991 and 1994); and Wonnacott and Lutz (1989).

ranked regionwide MFN liberalisation first, better than unilateral or small-group liberalisation on an MFN basis, a small free-trade area, or a regionwide FTA. (The working paper did not consider an APEC-wide FTA.)

The present paper has suggested a way in which the MFN approach may be pursued, focusing on products where APEC countries are the predominant suppliers, and where, as a consequence, the granting of a 'free ride' to non-APEC nations is a relatively small problem. The data presented point toward the electronics industry as a particularly promising one for the APEC countries to consider liberalisation, with the lower trade barriers being extended to outside countries on an MFN basis.[8] The broad question of APEC priorities has, however, not been addressed. Consequently, I do not have recommendations as to the sequencing of topics — where, for example, the priorities lie among liberalisation of merchandise trade, and other issues such as common standards, intellectual property, etc. The purpose of this paper has not been to issue a call to action, but to pursue a much more modest agenda: if we want to reduce barriers to merchandise trade among the APEC nations, how might we go about it?

REFERENCES

Bergsten, C.F. (1991), 'Commentary — The Move to Free Trade Zones,' in *Policy Implications of Trade and Currency Zones* (Symposium sponsored by the Federal Reserve Bank of Kansas City).

Bhagwati, J. (1994), 'Regionalism and Multilaterialism: An Overview,' in J. De Melo and A. Panagariya (eds.), *New Dimensions in Regional Integration* (Cambridge: Cambridge University Press).

Frankel, J. with S.-J. Wei and E. Stein (1994), 'APEC and Other Regional Economic Arrangements in the Pacific,' Working paper 94-1 (Washington: Institute for International Economics).

Garnaut, R. and P. Drysdale (1994), 'Asia Pacific Regionalism: The Issues' in Garnaut and Drysdale (eds), *Asia Pacific Regionalism* (Pymble, Australia: Harper Educational).

Krugman, P. (1991), 'The Move to Free Trade Zones,' *Federal Reserve Bank of Kansas City Review* (December).

Krugman, P. (1994), 'Regionalism versus Multilateralism: Analytical Notes,' in J. De Melo and A. Panagariya (eds.), *New Dimensions in Regional Integration* (Cambridge: Cambridge University Press).

Summers, L. (1991), 'The Move to Free Trade Zones: Comment,' *Federal Reserve Bank of Kansas City Review* (December).

Wonnacott, P. and M. Lutz (1989), 'Is There a Case for Free Trade Areas?' in J. Schott (ed.), *Free Trade Areas and US Trade Policy* (Washington, DC: Institute for International Economics).

---

[8] Elsewhere (Wonnacott and Wonnacott 1981 and 1992) we have argued that a common proposition — that countries can gain everything by unilateral tariff reduction that they can get from an FTA (terms-of-trade and economies of scale aside) — is invalid; it overlooks fundamental FTA gains from access to foreign markets. Nevertheless, I would look favourably on the extension of MFN in the products in which APEC countries constitute the principal suppliers, because the free rider problem is not great.

Wonnacott, P. and R. Wonnacott (1981), 'Is Unilateral Tariff Reduction Preferable to a Customs Union? The Curious Case of the Missing Foreign Tariffs,' *American Economic Review*, **74**, 3.

Wonnacott, P. and R. Wonnacott (1992), 'The Customs Union Issue Reopened,' *The Manchester School*, **60**, 2.

World Bank (1994), 'Building on the Uruguay Round: East Asian Leadership in Liberalisation,' Discussion paper (Washington, 14 April).

The Prospects for an ASEAN Free Trade Area

Mohamed Ariff

1. INTRODUCTION

ASEAN (Association of Southeast Asian Nations) now represents a twenty-seven-year old, mature regional grouping. The primary purpose of ASEAN has always been political. It was a product of the Cold War, designed essentially to ward off the communist threat. Interestingly, the end of the Cold War has not rendered ASEAN apolitical. Geopolitical and security considerations still continue to play a dominant role in ASEAN, now that there are many contentious territorial claims in the region and its neighbourhood.

All this notwithstanding, ASEAN is paying much attention to economic matters as well. But, economic cooperation among ASEAN countries is widely seen as a means, not an end. Be that as it may, ASEAN has not been very successful in its attempts at regional economic cooperation. The evolution of ASEAN economic cooperation seems to have gone through three distinct stages. In the first stage, starting from the Bangkok Declaration of 1967 till the Bali Summit of 1976, the political foundations of economic cooperation were laid, defusing tensions, resolving conflicts and building confidence. The second stage, spanning a period of 15 years from 1976 to the Fourth Summit of January 1992 in Singapore, was a period of experimentations in regional economic cooperation schemes, a sort of learning by doing through trial and error. ASEAN regional economic cooperation has entered the third, advanced stage with the launching of AFTA (ASEAN Free Trade Area) in January 1993.

It is important to stress at the outset that ASEAN is not a homogeneous grouping. There are important differences among its members in terms of size, historical legacy, industrial experience and level of development (Table 1). However, a common denominator for all of them is that they are all trade-dependent market economies with a global orientation. The latter is reflected by the fact that intra-ASEAN trade accounts for only a small proportion of the total (Table 2).

MOHAMED ARIFF is Professor and Dean in the Faculty of Economics and Administration, University of Malaya.

TABLE 1
ASEAN Basic Economic Indicators, 1992

	GDP (US$b)	*Population (million)*	*GDP/capita (US$)*	*Exports/ GDP (%)*	*BOP (US$b)*	*Debt Service Ratio (%)*
Brunei*	3.9	0.3	13,160	60.8	1.4	—
Indonesia	124.5	191.1	650	25.0	−3.0	31.4
Malaysia	55.8	18.8	2,980	69.8	−1.8	7.4
Philippines	52.9	64.3	820	19.4	−4.4	23.9
Singapore	46.0	2.9	16,080	133.8	6.4	—
Thailand	104.8	58.2	1,800	30.5	−2.2	16.3

Notes: * 1990 data.

Source: Asian Development Bank (1993); International Monetary Fund (1993); and Ministry of Finance, Malaysia (1994).

TABLE 2
Direction of ASEAN Trade Flows 1985–90 (Percentage)

	1985	*1990*	*Growth 1985–90*
Intra-ASEAN	19.7	17.1	14.8
East Asia	33.8	34.4	17.7
NAFTA	18.7	18.2	16.7
EC	11.5	14.8	23.4
Rest of the World	16.2	15.0	15.5
Total	100.0	100.0	17.3
US$ billion	135.5	301.6	

Source: IMF, Direction of Trade Statistics 1991.

An attempt is made in this article to take a close look at AFTA. The focus is on the anatomy, mechanics and dynamics of AFTA, with a view to assessing its prospects. As the prospects of AFTA would critically hinge on the extent to which the regional arrangement would fit into the trade strategies of ASEAN countries, an effort is made to cast AFTA in broad perspectives.

2. STRUCTURE

AFTA, like any other free trade area, entails elimination of tariff and non-tariff barriers among member countries in a preferential fashion. Under this arrangement, individual ASEAN countries are free to pursue their own independent trade policies towards non-members, and the question of common extra-regional tariffs does not therefore arise, unlike in a customs union.

The original AFTA timetable called for tariffs to be slashed down to 0–5 per cent within fifteen years and all non-tariff barriers to be dismantled among the ASEAN countries within eight years beginning from 1 January, 1993. It was envisaged that tariffs on all products will be reduced to 20 per cent within eight years before they get trimmed further to 0–5 per cent in seven years hence. This trade liberalisation was planned to proceed along two lines. Under the 'Fast Track', tariffs of 20 per cent or less were to be scaled down to 0–5 per cent within seven years and tariffs of over 20 per cent to 0–5 per cent in ten years. Under the 'Normal Track', the timeframe for these two categories of tariffs was ten years and fifteen years, respectively.

It is significant to note that the above timetable has been subsequently shortened from fifteen to ten years. It was decided at the Fifth Meeting of the AFTA Council, held in Chiengmai, Thailand, on 21 September, 1994, that the AFTA process should be completed by 1 January, 2003, instead of 1 January, 2008. Under the new arrangement, fast-track tariff reductions will be completed by 1 January, 1998, in the case of tariffs of 20 per cent or less and 1 January, 2000, in the case of tariffs exceeding 20 per cent. The corresponding new normal-track deadlines are 1 January, 2000, and 1 January, 2003, respectively.

The AFTA tariff cuts are based on the CEPT (Common Effective Preferential Tariff) formula. The CEPT scheme represents a sector-by-sector approach, aimed at equalising the intra-ASEAN tariff rates. Fifteen products of considerable commercial importance have been identified for accelerated tariff reduction under the CEPT scheme.[1]

All this, however, is subject to an exception clause which allows 'sensitive' items to be excluded from the AFTA excercise. The number of items under 'temporary' exclusion ranges from zero in the case of Singapore to 1,654 in the case of Indonesia (Table 3). Temporary exclusion originally meant that these products would be either placed in the Normal Track after the eighth year or, failing which, they will be placed in the Fast Track at a later date. In addition to the temporary exclusion list, there is a permanent exclusion list which initially comprised not only items of security importance such as guns and ammunitions under General Exception, but also raw agricultural products.

The AFTA Council, at its Fifth Meeting in Chiengmai, has decided to gradually transfer the products in the Temporary Exclusion List to the Inclusion List in five equal instalments of 20 per cent annually within five years beginning on 1 January, 1995, instead of reviewing the Temporary Exclusion List at the end of the eighth year. It is also heartening to note that agricultural products are now admitted into the CEPT scheme, instead of being placed under General Exception.

---

[1] CEPT products for accelerated tariff reduction consist of vegetable oils, cement, chemicals, pharmaceuticals, fertilisers, plastics, rubber products, leather products, pulp, textiles, ceramics and glass, gems and jewellery, copper cathodes, electronics, and wooden and rattan products.

TABLE 3
AFTA Inclusion and Exclusion Lists

Country	*HS Digit Level*	*Inclusion*			*Exclusion*		
		ATRP	*NTRP*	*Sub-Total*	*Temporary*	*General Exception*	*Unprocessed Agricultural Prod.*
Brunei	9	2,472	3,498	5,970	208	243	22
Indonesia	9	2,816	4,539	7,355	1,654	50	324
Malaysia	9	3,166	5,611	8,777	627	—	541
Philippines	8	1,033	3,418	4,451	714	28	398
Singapore	9	2,205	3,517	5,722	—	120	—
Thailand	6	1,736	2,777	4,513	118	26	390

Notes: ATRP = Accelerated Tariff Reduction Programme.
NTRP = Normal Tariff Reduction Programme.

Source: ASEAN Secretariat, Jakarta.

The number of items in the Inclusion list ranges from 4,451 offered by the Philippines to 7,355 put up by Malaysia (Table 1). In all cases, the number of normal-track items exceeds that of fast-track ones. Overall, a little more than one-third of the items in the Inclusion List belong to the Fast Track. It is also of interest to note that about 72 per cent of the fast-track items have low tariff rates of 20 per cent or less (Ariff, 1994).

It is noteworthy that the products covered by the Inclusion List, in value terms, account for about 85 per cent of intra-ASEAN trade (ASEAN Secretariat, 1994) and that the trade value of the fast-track CEPT products represents some 37 per cent of intra-ASEAN imports (Kumar, 1992).

Since individual ASEAN countries are at varying levels of economic development, some form of differential treatment was accorded in the implementation of the AFTA scheme. While Malaysia and Singapore were scheduled to implement both the Normal Track and Fast Track programmes in 1993 and Brunei in 1994, Indonesia and Thailand were allowed to join the Fast Track in 1995 and the Normal Track in 1998 and 1999, respectively, with the Philippines joining both tracks in 1996. It is encouraging to observe, however, that all member countries had commenced tariff reductions under the CEPT scheme by 1994.[2]

The decision by the AFTA Council to incorporate the agricultural sector into the CEPT scheme augurs well for the AFTA process, given the importance of

[2] Singapore and Thailand began their tariff reductions in 1993. Indonesia and the Philippines effected their tariff reductions on 1 January, 1994. Malaysia began implementation on 28 July, 1994 with retroactive effect going back to 1 January, 1994. Brunei's tariff reductions became effective as of 1 June, 1994.

trade in raw materials. Other measures to expedite the AFTA process include (a) harmonisation of tariff nomenclature, customs procedures and customs evaluation, to be completed by the end of 1995 and (b) establishment of an AFTA unit within the ASEAN Secretariat in January 1995 to coordinate and manage AFTA, monitor its progress and handle private sector queries.

3. EVALUATION

AFTA is by no means a new idea. It was thought of even in the early days of ASEAN, way back in the late 1960s, but the ASEAN countries were not ready for it then. Dramatic changes in the international scene and domestic fronts in recent times have rendered the idea palatable to ASEAN countries in the 1990s. The end of the Cold War, the deepening and widening of regional economic integration in Western Europe, the establishment of NAFTA (North American Free Trade Area) and the rising tide of economic regionalism in the Third World represent important external factors favouring a deepening of ASEAN. To be taken seriously by the international community in the post-Cold War era, ASEAN needed AFTA.

Equally important are the internal factors, including the spate of economic reforms since the mid-1980s which made ASEAN more amenable to bold intra-regional trade liberalisation initiatives. Interestingly, Indonesia which was not in favour of an ASEAN free trade area in the past, fearing that the Indonesian market would be flooded with a one-way flow of goods from its neighbours, has changed its mind and become more confident, having learnt from its own experience that liberalisation can pay handsome dividends and having emerged as an exporter of manufactures. Indonesia, being the 'Big Brother' in the ASEAN family, tends to set the pace for the ASEAN. It is clear that AFTA can go only as far as or as fast as Indonesia would like it. This is not surprising, since Indonesia accounts for over one-half the ASEAN market.

There are no doubts about the feasibility of AFTA, given the downtrends in the tariff levels of ASEAN countries. It is of relevance to note that tariffs in ASEAN are low by developing country standards.[3] Average tariff rates in Brunei and Singapore are already close to zero, while the tariff rates in the other four ASEAN countries (ASEAN-4) have been declining through unilateral and multilateral trade liberalisation. For example, Indonesia's tariff range has shrunk from 0–225 per cent in early 1985 to 0–60 per cent in 1993 with unweighted tariff rates falling by almost half from 37 per cent to 20 per cent

[3] Unweighted average nominal tariffs in ASEAN-4 are as follows: 21.68 per cent for Indonesia; 15.64 per cent for Malysia; 25.96 per cent for the Philippines; and 43.83 per cent for Thailand (*Asian Business*, 1992).

TABLE 4
Average Unweighted Tariff by Product
(Percentage)

Product	*Indonesia*	*Malaysia*	*Philippines*	*Thailand*	*Average*
Pulp	9	3	7	5	6
Textiles	19	6	26	30	20
Vegetable Oils	13	1	21	10	11
Chemicals	4	0	7	10	5
Pharmaceuticals	5	0	9	8	5
Fertilisers	0	0	3	0	1
Plastics	15	13	17	25	18
Leather	3	9	19	24	14
Rubber Prod.	9	8	23	22	15
Cement	15	55	30	5	26
Ceramics & Glass	20	15	20	18	18
Gems & Jewellery	11	5	24	0	10
Electronics	24	15	18	25	21
Furniture	50	24	33	80	47
Total	14	11	19	19	16

Source: Kumar (1992).

(Pangestu, 1994). Malaysia has abolished or reduced its tariffs unilaterally on 4,200 items between 1988 and 1994, in addition to multilateral tariff reductions on 7,218 items under the Uruguay Round. It should not be difficult for ASEAN to implement the CEPT scheme, since the nominal tariff rates on CEPT products average less than 20 per cent for ASEAN-4 (Table 4). The 'real' tariff rates may well be considerably lower than the 'official' tariff rates, due to extensive circumvention of trade barriers. Moreover, there appears to exist considerable tariff redundance, given the competitiveness of ASEAN products in the marketplace.

To be sure, tariff reductions alone cannot ensure the success of AFTA. Non-tariff barriers (NTBs), such as quotas, health standards, safety regulations and customs procedures, also constitute obstacles to intra-regional trade flows. Accordingly, Article 5A of the CEPT Agreement makes the removal of all quantitative restrictions mandatory upon enjoyment of tariff concessions and demands that all other forms of NTBs be phased out within five years after the concessions come into effect.

All this however cannot ensure increased intra-ASEAN trade. To be effective, trade liberalisation must be accompanied by investment liberalisation as well, since trade and investment are interlinked. It is no coincidence that ASEAN countries' major trading partners are also their main sources of foreign direct investment (FDI). FDI projects tend to generate much trade through imports of capital and intermediate goods and exports of components and finished products.

However, unlike NAFTA, AFTA does not go beyond the realm of trade, although there is now talk of 'AFTA-Plus'.

The operationalisation of the AFTA scheme may present difficulties. In particular, the rules of origin for determining the eligibility of products for preferential treatment themselves may act as a barrier. For one thing, it is not easy to ascertain product origins, given the ever increasing internationalisation of production processes. For another, extensive documentation will raise transaction costs. A saving grace, however, is that ASEAN has adopted a fairly mild 40 per cent minimum cumulative regional content for AFTA without any backward reduction for obtaining a 'net' aggregate cumulative regional content.[4]

The local content calculations are not fool-proof. It is possible for traders to manipulate profit margins in such a way as to overstate local value added. Thus, for example, a firm may add a 40 per cent profit margin to an imported item and re-export it as a CEPT product (Razak, 1993). Likewise, bulk cargo from a non-member country may take a circuitous route via Singapore or Brunei for relabelling to gain preferential access into other ASEAN countries.

To plug such loopholes, the ASEAN Federation of Textile Industries and the ASEAN Chambers of Commerce and Industry have suggested the criterion of 'substantial process transformation'. This, however, would not only raise the question of how substantial is 'substantial' but also interfere with the important role of entrepot trade.

The AFTA formula allows an importing member country to deny CEPT preference, if the exporting member country has excluded the same product in its CEPT scheme or if the CEPT tariff offered by the latter does not satisfy Article 4.2 of the CEPT Agreement which provides for automatic preferential access only in cases of tariff rates of 20 per cent or less in the exporting country. Such reciprocity conditionality will tend to undermine the usefulness and efficacy of the AFTA exercise.

Differences in the customs tariff classifications do pose some practical difficulties, as the number of tariff lines vary between 5,318 in Thailand to 11,746 in Malaysia, with Thailand and the Philippines maintaining tariff lines at HS (Harmonised System) Code 6-digit and 8-digit levels, respectively, and all other ASEAN countries operating at 9-digit level. However, it is encouraging to note that ASEAN is currently working on a common digit level classification for all its members.

[4] For example, Country A's item worth US$40 with US$16 local content qualifies for CEPT preferences in Country B where it is further transformed with US$60 value-added, of which local content is just US$1 so that this item, valued at US$100 is eligible for CEPT preference in Country C, as it is deemed to have US41 (41 per cent) ASEAN content, notwithstanding the fact that the 'net' cumulative regional content is only US$17 or 17 per cent of the value of the item (Azahari, 1993).

The dismantling of NTBs will prove to be more difficult than reductions in tariffs, since non-tariff barriers tend to be much less transparent than tariffs. It is not easy to monitor progress in this area, although the ASEAN Secretariat has instituted a system of direct notification and reverse notification by affected parties.

The question of safeguards against material injury inflicted on domestic manufacturers by import influxes remains nettlesome. For it is extremely difficult in practice to demarcate between fair and unfair trade. The CEPT Agreement allows AFTA members to temporarily suspend their concessions as a 'safeguard' measure, but it is unclear what is the trigger point and how long is 'temporary'.

Another area of concern is the absence of dispute settlement provision in the CEPT Agreement. Under the current ad hoc arrangement, the Senior Economic Officials Meeting (SEOM) will serve as the first avenue for trade disputes which may be taken to higher levels if necessary, i.e. the AFTA Council and AEM (ASEAN Economic Ministerial Meeting). It would be difficult for ASEAN to set up a formal dispute settlement machinery, as it is accustomed to an informal, casual approach that would not fit neatly into a legalistic framework.

The distribution of costs and benefits of AFTA among its members is a difficult issue. Net gains, if any, are likely to be unevenly distributed, given the heterogeneity of the grouping. It is widely assumed that Singapore would gain most, as it is the most developed member accounting for nearly half of intra-ASEAN trade. But, this is an overstatement in view of the fact that Singapore is a small city-state economy with a high degree of specialisation. Malaysia ranks second in terms of contributions to intra-ASEAN trade, accounting roughly for one-quarter. Of particular relevance is the fact that Malaysia is the biggest exporter of CEPT products (Table 5). This does not necessarily mean that Malaysia will gain most from AFTA. For it is unlikely that CEPT exports will increase sharply under AFTA, since the biggest importer (Singapore) is unlikely to import more given its low initial tariffs. Besides, it is difficult to assess the impact of AFTA on Singapore's imports, since most of these are re-exported. In any case, it would be wrong to associate 'gains' with exports and 'losses' with imports, as importing countries also benefit from cheaper goods.

The low-tariff countries are at an advantage *vis-a-vis* high tariff ones: the former have nothing much to offer by way of tariff cuts but stand to gain from the tariff cuts of the latter. While there is nothing 'unfair' about all this, there is a tendency in the ASEAN circle to view trade liberalisation as a lopsided affair, which may not bode well for AFTA. It is also feared that some countries would use AFTA for dumping their products. It is this fear that is largely responsible for the 0–5 per cent rather than zero tariff targeting.

It would be uneconomical to keep tariffs at five per cent, as customs revenue based on such low tariff rates may not even meet the cost of tariff collection and

TABLE 5
Profile of CEPT Trade, 1990

Country	*Country Share of CEPT Imports (%)*	*CEPT Imports as Share of Intra-ASEAN Imports (%)*	*Country Share as Source of CEPT Imports (%)*
Indonesia	3.6	18.3	7.8
Malaysia	12.5	21.1	60.0
Philippines	2.3	17.0	2.8
Singapore	73.6	55.8	17.8
Thailand	8.0	17.8	11.5
Total	100.0	37.2	100.0

Note: Brunei's share is negligible.

Source: Kumar (1992).

administration. Besides, free trade area by definition implies zero tariffs. There is clearly a need for AFTA to seek other solutions for dumping instead of maintaining tariffs at five per cent.

4. PROGNOSIS

Intra-ASEAN trade is unlikely to assume a greater significance under AFTA than it presently does. At present, intra-regional trade accounts for only one-fifth of total ASEAN trade, much of which is attributed to the role of Singapore as an entrepot port. If Singapore is excluded, the ratio will be much less, around one-tenth. The ASEAN countries have traditionally been open economies with strong extra-regional trade linkages. We must hasten to add that trade statistics understate intra-ASEAN trade flows, since 'illegal' and 'informal' trade among ASEAN countries are not captured by these numbers.

The ASEAN countries do realise that they owe their economic progress to the multilateral trading system and value their extra-regional commercial connections. It is quite obvious that the ASEAN market is no substitute for the lucrative markets of North America, Western Europe and Northeast Asia. It is therefore in ASEAN's interest to ensure that AFTA does not render ASEAN inward-looking. It is thus not surprising that the ASEAN countries seem more willing to reduce their tariffs unilaterally than intra-regionally.

The fact remains that the ASEAN economies do not really need AFTA. They can do quite well on their own, if their past performance is anything to go by. AFTA is considered useful primarily because it can help strengthen ASEAN. And, ASEAN is considered important, because it can ensure geopolitical stability, security and harmony in the region so that the ASEAN countries can concentrate on their economic pursuits without being distracted by conflicts and tensions. This means that they are even prepared to pay a price for it. Needless to say, they would like to keep the 'price' as low as possible. Hence the need to ensure that AFTA will not render their economies less outward-looking than they are.

ASEAN has made it clear that the purpose of AFTA is not to increase intra-regional trade. Its main objective is to make ASEAN products internationally competitive. It is hoped that AFTA will enable and encourage local firms in the ASEAN countries to export their products to other markets in the region before they can venture out into the extra-regional market. In other words, AFTA can serve as a 'training ground' for these firms so that they can learn to compete among themselves first before competing with others in the international arena. It may be surmised from all this that AFTA is an exercise in competition rather than an experiment in cooperation.

Nonetheless, intra-ASEAN trade will increase in absolute terms under AFTA. It appears that AFTA will be more trade-creating than trade-diverting, given the fairly price-elastic demand and supply for most manufactures and the relatively low MFN tariffs in the ASEAN countries (Ariff, 1992). Simulation exercises have also shown that trade creation[5] will clearly exceed trade diversion[6] under AFTA (Imada, Montes and Naya, 1991).

Foreign investments in the ASEAN region are likely to grow under AFTA. Free trade in the ASEAN market of 350 million people should render the region attractive for FDI which in turn would strengthen ASEAN's external linkages. The expanding investment networks of the multinationals (MNCs) are likely to generate much intra-industry and intra-firm trade within the region and without. However, it would be naive to think that foreign investors, under AFTA, will rush into ASEAN as an offshore regional base for exports to other parts of the world. For they already enjoy duty-free imports so long as their products are exported, and this means that AFTA will not make any difference to them unless they can cater to the ASEAN market as well. The fairly liberal regional content rule of AFTA should enable them to do so.

As alluded to earlier, free trade among the ASEAN countries should bring about a more efficient allocation of resources which would make ASEAN products competitive in the world market and render the region more attractive to

---

[5] Trade creation refers to a shift from a high-cost domestic source to a low-cost foreign source. Trade creation is positive, because it enables a country to source a product more cheaply from a partner through trade than to produce it domestically.

[6] Trade diversion refers to a shift from a low-cost world source to a high-cost partner source. Trade diversion is negative, because it amounts to shifting the source of imports from a more efficient third country to a less efficient partner.

foreign investors. The upshot of all this would be 'growth dividends' emanating from the AFTA exercise, with ASEAN economies growing faster than they otherwise would.

At the microeconomic level, however, there will be both winners and losers in the AFTA game, depending on the competitiveness of their businesses in terms of the comparative advantage of their respective countries (Ariff, 1993). The likely winners include Indonesian manufacturers of cement, chemicals, pharmaceuticals, plastics, rubber products, textiles and vegetable oils, Malaysian manufacturers of ceramics, chemicals, electronics, fertilisers, plastics, rubber products and vegetable oils, Philippine manufacturers of cement, copper cathodes, electronics, pharmaceuticals and pulp, and Thai manufacturers of jewellery, rubber products and textiles. Among the likely losers are Indonesian electronics and fertiliser manufacturers, Malaysian cement manufacturers, textile firms and jewellery makers, Philippine ceramics and glass manufacturers, textile firms and vegetable oil producers, and Thailand's cement, glass, fertilisers, plastics and vegetable oil concerns.

5. CONCLUSION

AFTA is no big deal, judging by the product coverage of the Inclusion List, the size of the exclusion list and the mechanism of trade liberalisation. It certainly pales in comparison with NAFTA which represents a comprehensive package with liberalisation going beyond merchandise trade to services trade and investment regulations, and regional programmes extending beyond trade to environment and intellectual property rights.

The preceding observation is by no means a criticism. For it is not in the interest of ASEAN to emulate NAFTA or any other grouping. All regional groupings are unambiguously discriminatory even if no new barriers are erected against non-members. Regional trading arrangements are clearly inferior to the multilateral trading system, the first-best option. Unilateral trade liberalisation can confer greater benefits than preferential trade concessions. The former, quite unlike the latter, allows a country to enjoy trade creation without having to suffer any trade diversion. Seen in these terms, the low-key AFTA scheme does make much economic sense. This will also ensure that documentation, paperwork and red tape are kept at a minimum so that increases in transaction costs, if any, do not neutralise the margin of preference under AFTA. A deeper regional integration will have serious cost implications for the ASEAN countries.

In fairness, AFTA should be judged not by what goes into it but by what comes out of it. Without a doubt, AFTA represents the most important trade initiative that ASEAN has ever taken since inception. AFTA can bring about important changes in the structure of production and trade in the ASEAN countries. A new pattern of specialisation and complementarity, with each country carving a niche for itself, is likely to emerge in the ASEAN region.

In the final analysis, AFTA's success will be measured not by the amount of intra-ASEAN trade it will generate but by the competitiveness of ASEAN products in the world market and the degree of integration of ASEAN with the global economy.

REFERENCES

Ariff, M. (1992), 'ASEAN Free Trade Area (AFTA): Problems and Prospects,' MIER National Outlook Conference (Malaysian Institute of Economic Research, Kuala Lumpur, December).

—— (1993), 'AFTA: An Outward-looking Free Trade Agreement', PITO Economic Brief No. 14 (East-West Center, Hawaii).

—— (1994), 'AFTA = Another Futile Trade Area?' (Inaugural Lecture, University of Malaya, Kuala Lumpur, 3 February).

ASEAN Secretariat (1994), 'Joint Press Statement: Fifth AFTA Ministerial Council Meeting at Chiengmai on 21 September 1994' (Jakarta).

Asian Business (1992), July issue, 26.

Asian Development Bank (ADB) (1993), *Asian Development Outlook 1992* (Manila).

Azahari, N. (1993), 'The CEPT Scheme: Mechanisms of Implementation', *Forum* (The Federation of Malaysian Manufacturers, Kuala Lumpur).

Imada, P., M. Motes, and S. Naya (1991), *A Free Trade Area: Implications for ASEAN* (Institute of Southeast Asian Studies, Singapore).

IMF (1993), *Direction of Trade, 1992* (New York).

Kumar, S. (1992), 'ASEAN Free Trade Area — Issues for policy', paper presented at the ASEAN Roundtable (Institute of Southeast Asian Studies, Singapore).

Razak, A. (1993), 'Latest Development on AFTA and CEPT', *Forum* (The Federation of Malaysian Manufacturers, Kuala Lumpur).

US Trade Policy and the GATT Review[1]

Anne O. Krueger

1. INTRODUCTION

THE United States has the most open trade policy in the world. The US supports the open multilateral trading system, has a 'most-favoured nation' (mfn) policy and has been a leader in multilateral trade liberalisation. The United States has entered into preferential trading arrangements with Israel and under NAFTA, and extends preferences to the Caribbean Basin countries and the Andean group. The United States demands quantitative indicators of Japan's 'progress' to meet targets put forth by Americans, and bargains bilaterally over trade practices seen to harm American exports. The United States resorts to anti-dumping and countervailing duty (administered protection) measures more than almost any other country, and is thus much more protectionist than appears at first sight. The United States uses measures such as 'Super-301' to threaten its trading partners in bilateral negotiations unless they conform with US mandated practices that are not covered under GATT.

All of these statements are true, and the tensions between them reflect the underlying realities of US trade policy. According to the official view, the United States pursues a 'multi-track' approach, under which it supports the multilateral system but seeks to go further in 'prying open' markets and guarding against 'unfair' trade practices. An alternative and less charitable view might be that the US uses whatever route — unilateral administered protection, bilateral bargaining, preferential trading arrangements, or the open multilateral system — suits the particular purpose (and responds to the protectionist pressures) of the

---

ANNE O. KRUEGER is from Stanford University. This article was written for *The World Economy* in its annual review of developments in the world trading system. The author is indebted to Sven Arndt for helpful comments on an earlier version of the article, and to Roderick Duncan for valuable research assistance.

[1] This article is concerned with US trade policy, and takes as its point of departure the GATT (1994) *Trade Policy Review* of the United States. That *Review* is in two volumes. References in parentheses in the text are to the published volumes, dated June 1994. The Roman numeral indicates the volume and the arabic number the page on which the discussion is based.

moment.

To be sure, like any other government policy, American trade policy is subject to conflicting political pressures, and the outcome reflects that fact. But there is also a sense in which the crosscurrents in US trade policy go far beyond that — both because US pronouncements often appear to be at odds with US practices and because the importance of the US in the international economy results in a systemic impact of American adherence to, or departures from, the open multilateral system.

In this review, I attempt first to sketch out the main outlines of these various facets of policy, starting with the main strands that have characterised the past decade. Then, attention turns to the ways in which policy has changed in the past two years, with emphasis on the increasing resort to preferential arrangements. A third section then provides a critical evaluation of US trade policy and considers the extent to which the GATT Trade Policy Review appropriately portrays US policy.

2. KEY FEATURES OF US TRADE POLICY

There is little doubt that after World War II the US economy was the most open of any industrialised country. It was also the predominant trading nation in the initial postwar period. And, as Europe and Japan rebuilt and the NICs began their rapid development, the US was their major market.

Moreover, at US initiative and with US hegemony, successive rounds of multilateral trade negotiations from the 1940s through the 1960s under the aegis of GATT greatly reduced tariff rates of the industrial countries while Europe and Japan were simultaneously removing their quantitative restrictions on trade. US leadership was unequivocal in support of an open multilateral system, and of trade liberalisation, under GATT. That system provided the world with an environment highly conducive to rapid economic growth. Although the rest of the world was much more highly protective than the United States in the immediate postwar years, even US tariffs averaged 26 per cent on dutiable imports in 1946, and fell to an average of 5.2 per cent by 1992 (II, p. 82).[2].

Until the 1970s, there was bipartisan support for the open multilateral stance of US trade policy.[3] Since that time, however, protectionist pressures for

[2] Smoot-Hawley tariff rates continue to apply to countries for which the United States does not grant MFN privileges (I, p. 44).

[3] Democrats and Republicans alike supported open multilateral trade. When the US and Britain had been negotiating over the postwar structure of the international trading system (under a Democratic President and Administration), the US had opposed *any* preferential trading arrangements, but the UK insisted upon them because of their desire to maintain Commonwealth Preferences. Even the US labour movement supported free trade, as reflected in statements of the AFL-CIO leadership. See Baldwin (1985) for an account.

departures from the open multilateral system have intensified. Successive trade acts have weakened the standards to be applied in anti-dumping and countervailing duty cases, shifted administrative duties from the relatively free-trade oriented Treasury Department to the more industry-sympathetic Department of Commerce, and even in 1988 introduced 'Super-301' under which the United States could unilaterally find other countries' trade practices as 'unfair' (even when they were not illegal under GATT) and impose trade sanctions if the offending country did not reach a satisfactory settlement with the US Trade Representative (USTR).

US trade policy started out in the 1940s motivated both by foreign policy considerations and economic considerations (with memories of the Great Depression in the aftermath of the Smoot-Hawley tariffs), but there was no inconsistency between them. Over time, an increasing number of derogations from the GATT system took place as trade policy motivations were increasingly complex and ad hoc: outright protectionist pressures (as, for example, in the case of textiles and apparel), a desire to 'pry open' foreign markets (as in the case of semiconductors — see Irwin, forthcoming, for an account), concern about the economic fortunes of countries considered of special interest to the US (the Caribbean Basin Initiative), worries over the environment (the tuna-dolphin case), drug trafficking (Andean preferences), workers' rights (suspension of GSP in several countries), and a variety of other 'exceptions' to multilateral MFN and open trade arose. Even when the United States reversed official policy[4] and announced that it would welcome negotiations leading to free trade agreements (FTAs) among 'like-minded' trading partners that would go beyond agreements achievable through GATT and constitute even closer economic relations (GATT-plus arrangements), the apparent motivation was to put pressure on other countries further to open their trade.

Had these same measures been taken by a small country, its economists and citizens could justly have criticised them both because of the direct economic costs and because of the tendency for departures from open multilateral principles to induce pressures for still further departures. When the United States took these measures, it was vulnerable to those criticisms, but in addition, its importance and leadership role in the multilateral system made its actions even more suspect. And the fact that the US has considerable bilateral bargaining power in trade, at least in the short run, made its bilateral moves even more suspect.

Basic US trade law is found in a number of pieces of legislation. The most recent 'trade bill' was the 1988 Omnibus Trade and Competitiveness Act (which

[4] The United States itself followed MFN policies with all its trading partners. A first break was acceptance of the developing countries' demand for the Generalised System of Preferences (GSP). In the early 1980s, unilateral duty exemptions were extended to the Caribbean Basin Initiative countries.

contained the notorious Super 301 discussed below, provisions for USTR's evaluation of other countries' standards of intellectual property rights protection, as well as provisions weakening standards for anti-dumping and countervailing duty findings, and many other measures basic to US trade policy). The 1990 Farm Bill (which expires in 1995 and will be revised), budgetary rules,[5] and the Export Enhancement Act of 1992 (under which US exports of some agricultural commodities are subsidised), are also fundamental to US trade policy.

As of the 1994 GATT report, US trade policy needed characterisation under a number of headings: tariffs, quotas and other nontariff barriers, administered protection, and preferential arrangements are the most significant.[6] In addition, there are a variety of other measures that have consequences for trade patterns and are reviewed in the GATT document.

a. *Tariff Rates*

For most US trading partners, US trade is carried out on an MFN basis.[7] MFN tariffs have been greatly lowered since the infamous Smoot-Hawley tariff days.

There were 8,995 eight-digit tariff items in the Harmonised Tariff Schedules of the United States in 1992, of which over 99 per cent were 'bound' under GATT. Twenty two per cent of imports (by value — 15 per cent by number of items) entered the US duty-free, 64 per cent (by value) entered under ad valorem tariffs, and 12 per cent entered under specific tariffs. Eleven and a half per cent of all eight-digit items (by number — 5.3 per cent by value of imports) were subject to tariff rates greater than 15 per cent. There are tariff rate quotas on certain items (such as some dairy products, sugar, oranges and brooms) under which tariff rates are lower until the quota is reached, and higher thereafter.

b. *Other Barriers to Imports*

There are also outright quotas. The two major sets of quotas are those on textiles and apparel, on one hand, and on agricultural commodities, on the other. Under the Multifibre Arrangement (MFA) for textiles and apparel, quotas restricting imports were set for 38 countries and 147 commodity categories

---

[5] These rules do not permit any action which will reduce federal government revenue without its replacement by alternative taxes. It was this provision of the law which held up passage of NAFTA while the estimated $12 billion of 'lost revenue' was made up by other tax changes.

[6] There are sections in the GATT report on many other aspects of trade policy, including state trading, standards, environmental and other technical requirements, import cartels, countertrade, export prohibitions, export controls, and so on. Some of these have intended or unintended consequences that result in trade barriers, but by and large they are not quantitatively significant relative to the measures reviewed here. The interested reader can refer to Volume 1 for particulars.

[7] Exceptions in 1994 were Cuba and the Federal Republic of Yugoslavia. (I. p. 29).

(p. 69).[8] It has elsewhere been estimated (Hufbauer and Elliott, 1994 pp. 88–89) that the tariff equivalent of all protective measures (especially the MFA) is 23 per cent for textiles and 48 per cent for apparel).[9]

Agricultural protection is set primarily by the US Department of Agriculture to reinforce domestic agricultural programmes; it nonetheless is strongly protective, with particularly high protection for tobacco (a tariff rate of up to 354.9 per cent, along with domestic content requirements) and sugar (up to 75 per cent, along with quotas) (Table AV.2). The net producer subsidy equivalent for all US agriculture in 1992 was 28 per cent, about one percentage point more than it had been in 1990 and 1991 (I, p. 129). The highest PSEs were for wool, milk, sugar, rice and wheat.

Anti-dumping and countervailing duties are also maintained against a variety of agricultural products (including a 100 per cent AD on New Zealand kiwi fruit). Phytosanitary standards are the subject of concern by several US trading partners, and regarded as deterring imports (I, p. 134).

There were also voluntary export restraint arrangements on a number of items, including meat (from Australia and New Zealand) and some machine tools, although these were being phased out (II, p. 37). Although these were the only arrangements reported to be in effect, it was also true that the Japanese continued to restrict the number of automobiles that would be exported to the United States, despite formal American opposition to the continuation of these quotas (I, p. 80).[10]

c. *Administered Protection*

'Administered protection' is among US trade policy practices to which foreign governments object most strenuously. They have protectionist consequences which, although difficult to measure, are thought by many to be among the most egregious of American practices.

Provisions to guard against imports sold 'below cost' and/or receiving foreign government subsidies are permissible under GATT (and subsequently WTO) rules.[11] Anti-dumping (AD) and countervailing duty (CVD) provisions of US

---

[8] Under the Uruguay Round agreement, the MFA is to be phased out over ten years. Although the phase-out is 'end-loaded', with a high fraction of the reduction coming in the last year, quotas are to be increased substantially in earlier years. When the MFA is dismantled, it will represent highly significant trade liberalisation.

[9] There were 20 anti-dumping orders and countervailing duty orders in effect at the time of the GATT review (I. p. 164). The GATT also noted that there were virtually no GSP preferences extended for textile and apparel products.

[10] The Japanese adoption of the quotas was 'voluntary', although there is no doubt that there were American political pressures to restrict auto imports at the time. For an account, see Nelson (forthcoming).

[11] There are two very good appendices to Chapter IV of Volume 1 which provide a brief outline of the legal processes involved in US anti-dumping and 301 procedures.

trade law are thus, at least broadly, GATT/WTO-consistent.

However, in administration, US AD and CVD measures have become 'the protectionist's weapon of choice'.[12] Threats of AD and CVD actions have been instrumental in inducing other countries to impose voluntary export restraints: the steel industry has filed as many as 200 complaints in a single year! Procedures are biased against foreign companies in estimating either their costs or their selling prices in the US and home markets.[13] In the two years covered by the GATT review, an average of 60 AD investigations had been launched each year, contrasted with about 40 annually in the 1980s, (I, p. 60), and there were 268 AD orders in effect as of June 1993.

Preliminary affirmative findings occur in more than 90 per cent of cases filed, and thereafter any would-be exporter to the US must deposit sums equivalent to the amount that is then estimated until a final determination is reached. The Chairman's report for the GATT Panel stated diplomatically that:

> Participants noted that increased recourse to anti-dumping and countervailing actions was a source of apprehension, as such actions could lead to unpredictability and increased cost. The use of the 'best information available' method for determining dumping margins had become frequent, rather than exceptional. In addition, many cases accepted at the preliminary stage were finally rejected, or margins sharply reduced . . . (II, p. 4).[14]

The Chairman noted especially the protective effect of AD measures for the US steel industry (II, p. 50.

d. Intellectual Property Rights

Section 337 of the trade bill[15] prohibits imports of articles that infringe a valid US patent or trademark.[16] By the end of 1992, there were 51 exclusion orders

---

[12] See the papers in Boltuck and Litan (1991) for a good exposition.

[13] There are a large number of biases. Those foreign firms accused of dumping are required to complete a huge questionnaire and return it on tape in a format specified by the Department of Commerce within 60 days. Many firms, especially small ones, do not have the accounting systems to provide the necessary data. When the respondent does not provide all the information requested, the Department of Commerce is entitled to base its findings on 'best available evidence', which is often 'constructed cost' (using an eight per cent mark-up for 'necessary profit') or the plaintiff's estimate of the defendant's costs. Even when data are supplied, the method for estimating whether foreign selling price is the same as the price sold in the American market is highly biased (by rejecting low prices in foreign markets and high prices in American markets). See Boltuck and Litan (1991) for a full account.

[14] The US responded that '. . . the discretion available to the Department of Commerce was limited where exporters did not co-operate with investigations' (II, p. 5).

[15] This section was originally included in the 1930 Tariff Act.

[16] The act also makes importation illegal if other 'unfair' practices are involved. These include imports which 'have the effect or tendency to destroy or substantially injure a domestic industry, to prevent the establishment of such an industry, or to restrain or monopolise trade and commerce in the United States (I, p. 74).

under 337. Of those, 33 involved patent violations, of which 25 were with Taiwan (I, p. 75).

In 337 cases, which like AD and CVD are also undertaken by the International Trade Commission, there is a strong inducement for the foreign party against whom the complaint is lodged to settle before the ITC has completed its investigation. Of the 25 investigations 'completed' in the two years ending December 1992, 13 were terminated on the basis of settlement agreements, one by a consent order, and six were terminated on a 'no violation' or dismissal basis (I, p. 75).

In 1989, a GATT panel found that 337 was in violation of the GATT articles. At the time of the 1994 Report, the US had made no changes in that section. (I, p. 75). Inactions in response to GATT rulings lead some to question the US commitment to the open multilateral system, and to doubt the American claims that they have the most open market in the world.

e. *Other Significant Trade Practices*

There are a number of other ways in which US trade policy practices have discriminated against foreign-source goods. US government procurement, for example, has been subject to Buy-American provisions. Even after the adoption of the Government Procurement Code in the Tokyo Round, the US awarded only 11.9 per cent of eligible government purchases to foreign suppliers in 1990, with comparable figures for other countries being 97.9 per cent in Hong Kong, 98 per cent in Israel, 21 per cent in the EC, and 14.8 per cent in Japan (I, p. 86).

Administration of rules of origin in the US is especially ad hoc. Although rules of origin are most important for NAFTA, other rules of origin apply for imports eligible for GSP treatment, for marking (indicating the origin of the product), for AD and CVD procedures, and for government procurement requirements. It is possible that a product could be classified as originating in one country for marking purposes, another country for GSP treatment, another country for application of anti-dumping rules, and so on (I, p. 53ff). Simplification of rules of origin (and moving to a single standard for all purposes) would remove a significant administrative barrier to imports.

The Jones Act in maritime services greatly protects US shipping, and prohibits foreign shipping between US ports. Protection for maritime services is estimated to be equivalent to a tariff of about 85 per cent (Hufbauer and Elliott, 1994, p. 85).

On the export side, starting in the mid-1980s, the US added to its agricultural programme and began subsidising agricultural exports under the Export

Enhancement Program (EEP).[17] Exporters of some agricultural commodities are compensated for the difference between the price at which the commodity (primarily wheat) is sold in the world market and their purchase price for the commodity. By 1993, $5.3 billion of subsidies under EEP had financed $18 billion of exports (I. p. 133). In the diplomatically-cautious phraseology of the GATT Review:

> . . . The practice of competitive subsidization between the United States and certain trading partners continues to have particularly disruptive effects on world trade in wheat, and on farm income in other countries that do not subsidize their agriculture to the same extent. Recently, the number of complaints regarding the effects of the EEP has grown rapidly, and two formal disputes concerning wheat trade were active during the period under review (I, p. 134)

3. SIGNIFICANT DEVELOPMENTS SINCE 1992

Of the many US trade policy actions in the two years covered by the GATT Report, three deserve special attention: the conclusion of the Uruguay Round, the NAFTA agreement, and the decision to pursue 'quantitative indicators' with Japan.[18]

a. *Conclusion of the Uruguay Round*

The Uruguay Round agreement represented significant advances in the world trading system with respect to some of the issues discussed above — intellectual property rights protection, agricultural protection, and the phase-out of the MFA being perhaps the most notable. There were other issues on which some progress was made but which, from the perspective of economists, were disappointing. Most notably, the anti-dumping and countervailing duty provisions of the WTO have been strengthened (to reduce harrassment filing and to increase the minimal amount that must be found before anti-dumping or countervailing duties are

---

[17] There were altogether five programmes in effect that contributed to export subsidies at the time of the GATT review. These included the Marketing Promotion Programme, PL 480 food aid, a short and medium term export credit programme, a Dairy Export Incentive Programme and the Export Enhancement Programme. (See I, p. 131.)

[18] Since June 1994, the date the *Report* was published, two other trade policy issues have also assumed importance. These are the trade relationship with China (including disputes over intellectual property rights, conditions for WTO entry, and extension of MFN) and the decision to finance the development of flat-panel screens. This latter is to a large extent a departure from earlier US policy under which development of specific technologies and products has not been supported by US subsidies. To be sure, defence procurement and support for such activities as Sematech have been somewhat similar.

These actions, and especially the flat-panel decision, raise a host of issues, and would require considerably more discussion than space permits here. They also occurred after the *Report* was compiled.

imposed), but by much less than had been hoped. Administered protection will remain a major concern. Likewise, there is no significant improvement in measures protecting maritime shipping.

US policies with respect to the Uruguay Round are not discussed in the *Report*, nor is the stance of the US prior to signing the agreement in Marrakesh. While it behoves an international organisation not to appear self-serving in trade policy reviews, any overview of US trade policy that does not examine policies with respect to the support (or absence thereof) of the open multilateral system is somewhat lacking.

In the US case, the Uruguay Round was ratified, but not until a period during which debate about US sovereignty[19] and other aspects had raised questions about its ultimate fate. Moreover, since the ratification, US attention in trade policy matters seems to have been more focused on regional arrangements than implementing the Uruguay Round agreement and strengthening the WTO. There is certainly a case to be made that lack of US leadership has detracted from the implementation of the WTO, but it is (probably appropriately, given what would appear to be the self-serving nature of any such criticism) not made in the GATT *Report*.

Moreover, prior to signing at Marrakesh, the United States and France jointly announced their determination to obtain a commitment of members to convene to agree on labour standards and environmental protection as a necessary condition for their signature on the Uruguay Round accord. This announcement naturally sent shivers through the economics ministries in developing countries where relatively abundant unskilled labour is an integral part of their comparative advantage. While there are legitimate environmental concerns, there is no question that the issue has been seized by those wanting protection for other reasons. Moreover, there are significant questions as to the manner in which environmental issues are appropriately tied to trade issues, with considerable potential for capture by protectionists.

The issue of labour standards is perhaps even a more direct threat to the international trading system. Since anything that raises labour costs above the levels that would result in well-functioning labour markets imposes costs on those deprived of work in poor countries, it is questionable how much of an international standard there should be.[20]

Yet, despite the importance of these issues, the matter is not addressed in the GATT *Report*.

---

[19] The 'loss of sovereignty' issue was raised by many of the same parties who had earlier claimed US right to act unilaterally because the issues were not covered under GATT.

[20] This applies to proposals for prohibitions or restrictions on child labour, as well as other issues. In very poor countries, restricting child labour can result in forcing parents into even more reprehensible practices and/or leaving children in even worse situations.

b. Preferential Trading Arrangements

The NAFTA accord, and its ultimate passage by the US Congress, was certainly the trade policy issue that received the most public attention in the two years under review. The GATT *Report*'s secretariat provides a summary of the key features of the NAFTA agreement (I, p. 31–3) followed by summaries of the US — Canada and US — Israel FTAs, as does the US government submission (II, pp. 31–35).

As is well known, all tariffs and virtually all other trade barriers between the three countries are to be phased out over a period of at most 15 years.[21] Provisions are included for liberalisation of trade in services (primarily national treatment) and investment rules. Rules of origin, safeguards provisions, intellectual property rights, and government procurement are briefly described. The labour and environmental side agreements are also described, including the roles of the two Commissions established to oversee those agreements. The *Report* of the US Government provides the US International Trade Commission's estimates of the likely impact of NAFTA (II, pp. 34–5).

Interestingly, while the NAFTA document affirms the rights and obligations of each party under GATT, it also provides that, in the event of any inconsistency, NAFTA provisions should prevail (I, p. 31).

The summaries are useful, but descriptive. There are grounds for concern that regional arrangements could be trade diverting (the 200 pages of rules of origin are perhaps an omen), and could in the longer term undermine the open multilateral system. Moreover, subsequent to the GATT *Report*, the US undertaking at APEC for regional free trade by 2010 (2020 in the case of developing contries) raises a host of questions.[22] In the Chairman's Concluding Remarks, there is an allusion to concerns:

> While action by the United States in support of the multilateral system was recognized, there were preoccupations concerning some of its trade policy initiatives. The ratification of the North American Free Trade Agreement was welcomed. However, some felt the agreement could lead to net trade diversion. The pursuit, through bilateral and unilateral means, of market-opening in other nations was seen by many as potentially counterproductive and disruptive to the multilateral trading system . . . (II. p. 3).

---

[21] Canada did not negotiate with the United States with respect to agriculture, wanting instead to use the Uruguay Round for that purpose. So there is a bilateral accord on agriculture with respect to Mexico.

[22] It is not entirely clear in the text of the APEC documents whether the 'free trade' to which ministers committed themselves (without, however, any formal plan or timetable as to how this could be achieved) was free trade *vis-a-vis* the world, or preferential free trade. If APEC free trade is to be a preferential trading arrangement, questions arise as to the trading relationship between countries in APEC and those in NAFTA. Chile already has a free trade agreement with Mexico, is negotiating with the US, and has announced its intention to join any APEC arrangement! The issue of overlapping free trade areas will certainly arise if the APEC commitment is fulfilled and NAFTA enlarged.

The issues that arise with respect to overlapping preferential arrangements were not raised in the *Report*, but should constitute a focus of concern for those committed to the strengthening of the WTO and the open multilateral system.[23] At the time of writing in the winter of 1995, WTO remains without a head, and the budget of the WTO for its first year is set at $84 million with a professional staff of 200.[24]

c. *Unilateral/Bilateral Trading Relationships*

Over the past decade, the United States has increasingly resorted to bilateral bargaining over trade issues with some of its major trading partners. It was already mentioned that 'Super-301' was part of the 1988 Trade Bill, and empowered USTR to designate countries as 'unfair traders', pinpointing the unfair practices, and negotiating a settlement, or in its absence, imposing punitive duties on imports from that country.[25]

While the VERs (I, p. 79) and AD and CVD actions actually taken are reported in the GATT document, there is no discussion or analysis of the bilateral approach. In 1993, the Clinton Administration began talks with Japan, seeking 'quantitative indicators' of Japanese progress with regard to market opening for commodities designed by the Clinton administration. Bilateral negotiations were also conducted with a number of other countries, including as already noted China.[26] The negotiations with Japan have continued, with threats of sanctions on several occasions, and agreements announced on all but one of the sectors where action was demanded.

There are ample grounds to question the US resort to bilateral bargaining, rather than reliance on a multilateral mechanism, in pursuit of its trading objectives.[27] Only in the Chairman's report is there an allusion to these practices:

---

[23] For a set of papers raising the issues that arise with respect to overlapping preferential trading arrangements, see the papers in Schott (1989).

[24] By contrast, the International Labour Organisation has 1,700 professionals. See *Financial Times* (editorial page, 22 February 1995).

[25] The Section 301 (unfair trade) actions in the two years covered by the *Report* (oilseeds, Canadian liquor, EC's third country meat directive, China's market access, Indonesian pencil slats) are briefly described in Vol. I, Appendix IV.2. The same appendix lists Special 301 (intellectual property rights) actions.

[26] The International Trade Commission's annual *Operation of the Trade Agreements Program* does provide an overview of trade relations with key trading partners and the issues that were addressed in bilateral negotiations.

[27] These include: the obvious fact that those negotiations take place outside the GATT framework; the failure of the US to provide reciprocal market opening as would happen in the GATT/WTO framework; the tendency to choose commodities in which the US has a special interest and, on occasion, to seek or to receive preferential access for US products and firms. See Krueger (1995).

> . . . concern was expressed that the United States should not resort to managed trade, particularly in the form of numerical targets, to address bilateral trade difficulties but should use the present GATT and future WTO mechanisms to the fullest extent (II, p. 3).

The US response included a defence of its bilateral and unilateral measures as designed to obtain 'market-opening'. (II, p. 4). Although as practised, resolution of bilateral issues has often favoured the United States (see Krueger, 1995), there are even more fundamental reasons for seeking a multilateral approach.[28] These include the infeasibility of avoiding 'third-country' effects, both as alternative sources of supply and as injured parties when the US product is favoured by the outcome.[29] When, for example, the US negotiated with Korea over the opening of its insurance market, the Koreans permitted entry of US companies prior to admission of firms from other countries. Over the years, Australia has vigorously protested against a number of US trade arrangements with Japan and Taiwan.

4. THE GATT REVIEW: AN ASSESSMENT

The first thing to be said is that the GATT document is a highly useful summary of US trade policy. Moreover, the entire 'surveillance' process instituted by GATT increases the transparency of trade policies of all member countries. As such, it is greatly to be applauded.[30]

The second thing to be said is that GATT is an international institution, dependent on its members for support (and funding). The language of any report issued by GATT (or other international organisations) must necessarily be somewhat muted in its critiques. In that regard, the value of the process of surveillance should not be judged entirely by the contents of the *Report*. There is undoubtedly value in the process of review. Even though the Chairman's summary — quoted above to provide a flavor — is diplomatically phrased, it nonetheless enables the reader to glimpse some of the discomfort which US representatives must have felt at the lapses in US trade policy. Quite aside from the value of the document, the discussion of trade policy based on a systematic presentation may be important.

Turning then to the document itself, the analysis presented above should already have indicated that there are some issues — systematic presentation of AD and CVD processes, delineation of the NAFTA agreement, policies toward

---

[28] For a thorough critique, see Irwin (1994).

[29] Even when the US negotiates 'market opening' on a multilateral basis, it nonetheless focuses on products in which it believes there is likely to be most benefit to the US. On several occasions, however, US firms have been extended preferential treatment. See Krueger (1995) for examples.

[30] The only obvious omission, by way of format, is the absence of an index. That would have been very helpful for this reviewer, and probably would increase the value of the document enough to warrant the resource cost.

imports in individual sectors of the economy — on which the GATT *Report* provides a very valuable survey.

As a critical overview of US trade policy, however, it falls short, and perhaps necessarily so for the reasons already mentioned. Issues surrounding the relationship between regional FTAs and the multilateral trading system, and between overlapping FTAs, are not discussed. Nor (except for the Chairman's brief statement quoted above and the delineation of AD, CVD, and 301 actions), are the worrying tendencies for increased resort to 'demands' from individual trading partners for market opening, increased reliance on AD and CVD actions, and the variety of other departures from open multilateral practices in which the US has engaged.

There is a role for academic research and analysis here. The GATT/WTO Secretariat is clearly limited to reporting 'objectively'. As such, it can estimate, or reproduce estimates of, rates of protection, producer subsidy equivalents, and the like. At present, there are no accepted measures with which to estimate the extent of unilateral bargaining, resort to GATT-inconsistent measures, or other derogations of the GATT system. If measures of such departures from multilateralism can be devised, it would provide increased transparency of trading practices in the United States and elsewhere, and enable increased scrutiny. At any event, critical evaluation of politically-contentious issues such as trade policy is a task more appropriately left largely to the academic and policy community: in a sense, GATT/WTO must remain 'impartial' and above the fray if it is to play its appropriate role as an international institution.

The practice of holding Trade Policy Reviews should be enthusiastically welcomed by all those concerned with the protection and preservation of the open multilateral trading system. The GATT Secretariat, limited in numbers of personnel as it has been, has done an impressive job of marshalling the available evidence and bringing increased transparency to trade policy.

REFERENCES

Baldwin, R.E. (1985), *Political Economy of US Import Policy* (MIT Press, Cambridge, MA).

Boltuck, R. and Robert E. Litan, editors. 1991. *Down in the Dumps. Administration of the Unfair Trade Laws* (Brookings Institution, Washington, DC).

GATT (1994) Trade Policy Review — United States (Geneva, GATT Secretariat).

Hufbauer, G. and K.A. Elliott (1994). *Measuring the Costs of Protection in the United States* (Institute for International Economics, Washington, DC).

Irwin, D. (1994), *Managed Trade. The Case against Import Targets* (American Enterprise Institute, Washington, DC).

Irwin, D. (forthcoming), 'The Political Economy of the Semiconductor Agreement', in A.O. Krueger (ed.), *The Political Economy of US Trade Protection* (University of Chicago Press, Chicago).

Krueger, A.O. (1995), *US Trade Policy: A Tragedy in the Making* (American Enterprise Institute, Washington, DC).

Nelson, D. (forthcoming), 'The Political Economy of US. Auto Protection', in A.O. Krueger, (ed.), *The Political Economy of US Trade Protection* (University of Chicago Press, Chicago).
Schott, J.J. (1989) (ed.), *Free Trade Areas and US Trade Policy* (Institute for International Economics, Washington, DC).

India's Trade Policy Review

V.N. Balasubramanyam

1. INTRODUCTION

THE dirigiste economic regime, which India clung to with surprising tenacity for more than four decades, appears to be tottering if not dead. It will remain a puzzle that the regime should have survived for so long despite its manifest inefficiency and the inequities it perpetuated, all of which were incisively analysed time and again (Bhagwati and Desai, 1970; Bhagwati and Srinivasan, 1975; and Lal, 1988), and brought to the attention of policy makers. The economic reforms launched in 1991 may not have made a bonfire of the extensive controls over trade and investment, the main planks of the dirigiste regime along with the presence of a substantial public sector, but that the reforms should have been attempted at all is in itself a cause for satisfaction. Are the reforms likely to be sustained? Will they gather momentum over the years and usher in a market-based economy? Why were the reforms not much more extensive in scope and why was a swift sharp shock not administered?

The GATT's review of India's trade policy (GATT, 1993) provides a reference point for discussing these issues. The review is in two volumes. The first volume prepared by the GATT secretariat provides a concise account of recent economic trends and trade performance, a detailed account of trade policy objectives and instruments, and a comprehensive analysis of trade and trade policies relating to the major sectors of the economy. The second volume contains the Report by the Government of India and the minutes of the Council meeting which includes comments on India's trade policy reforms by members of the council. These two volumes provide the basis for analysing India's recent policy reforms.

2. WHY THE REFORMS?

India's achievements to date cannot be belittled. As the GATT's trade policy review (TPR) notes, during the decade of the sixties and the seventies the annual average growth rate of GDP was around 3.6 per cent and increased to around

V.N. BALASUBRAMANYAM is from the Department of Economics, Lancaster University.

6 per cent per annum over the past decade. Although income inequalities and the absolute level of poverty are high, the incidence of poverty has steadily declined. Other social indicators such as literacy rates and life expectancy also show improvement over the years. And as often noted, India possesses a highly trained pool of scientists and engineers. Even so, India's achievements on both counts of efficiency and equity not only pale in comparison with that achieved by most other developing countries (Figure 1), but are also well below the aspirations of her policy makers. A telling indictment of India's dismal performance is the fact that even at the end of the decade of the 1980s the percentage of population considered to be poor exceeded a quarter of the total population.

What went wrong? There are a number of controversial explanations. Controversy and dispute is the stuff of the immense literature on each and every aspect of India's economy. There are colourful debates on whether or not India should have accorded pride of place to the objective of growth and self-sufficiency, and whether or not growth trickles down to the poor and alleviates poverty. There are also a number of studies on India's agriculture, including the green revolution and its impact on equity and efficiency, scores of studies on India's industrialisation and extensive analysis of India's foreign trade policies and performance. The inescapable conclusion which most of these studies reach is that the interventionist economic regime, with import substitution and self-sufficiency as its objectives, is largely responsible for India's poor economic performance.

The inefficiencies and inequities perpetrated by these policies have been analysed and documented extensively. It is sufficient to note here that the highly diversified and largely inefficient industrial structure India possesses, the steady erosion of India's share in world exports, a pronounced policy-induced bias against agriculture, and low growth in employment and incomes are all mostly a consequence of the import substitution policies pursued in the name of self-sufficiency.

The euphoria with which the recent attempts at liberalisation have been greeted is in a sense a huge sigh of relief that the policy makers have at last accepted the verdict on the dirigiste regime passed by the analysts of India's economic policies and performance. It is often asked why it took so long for India's policy makers to accept the verdict. To say that the policy makers and their advisors were impervious to the inefficiencies and inequities of the policies they had put in place would amount to an insult to their intelligence and intellectual abilities. It is just that they were loath to accept that the grand design they had put in place had failed and were able to put their undeniable intellectual prowess to rationalising and defending it. As Bhagwati (1993) puts it:

> India has suffered because her splendid economists were both able and willing to rationalise every one of the outrageous policies the government was adopting: by ingeniously constructing the models designed to yield the desired answers.

FIGURE 1
A Comparison of GDP Per Capita in India and Other Developing Countries, 1960–88

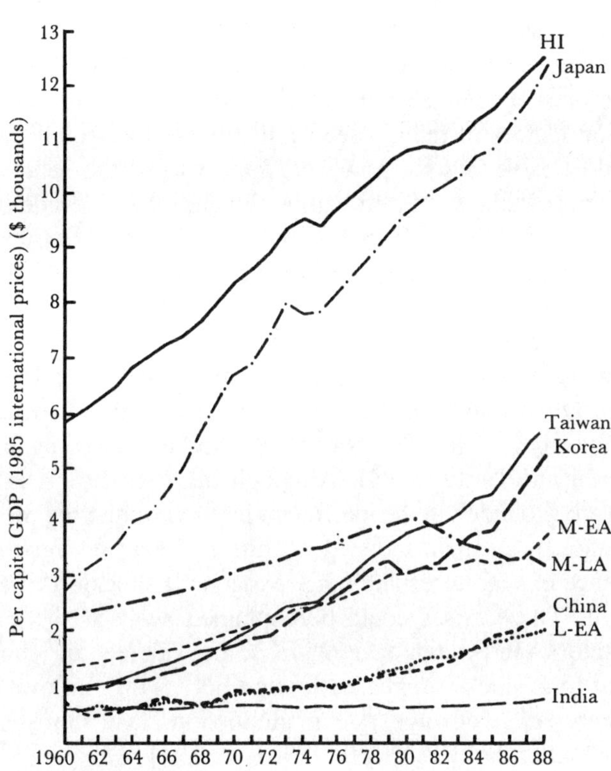

Key:
HI High-income countries.
M-EA Middle-income countries in East Asia.
M-LA Middle-income countries in Latin America.
L-EA Low-income countries in East Asia.

Source: J.N. Bhagwati, *India in Transition: Freeing the Economy.*

Beyond this, as often noted, the policies handsomely rewarded businessmen by providing them with lucrative sheltered markets and the bureaucrats by catering to their yen for power and the exercise of power.

How and why was the mould broken? Several explanations have been offered. These include the lessons offered by the outward-looking model of development successfully pursued by the fast-growing East Asian economies, growth in consumer awareness and increasing dissatisfaction with the interventionist policies on the part of the electorate, and the collapse of dirigiste regimes and the surge towards market-oriented policies the world over. No doubt all of these were motivating factors in India's determined move towards liberalisation. The immediate and decisive factors, however, appear to be the nature and extent of the economic crisis India was faced with at the end of the decade of the eighties, and the presence of a Prime Minister and his Finance Minister who had the prescience to recognise that nothing less than a dismantling of the dirigiste regime would do to meet the crisis and restore economic stability.

Economic crises are nothing new in India. The economy has in fact lurched from one crisis to another, the most significant of these occurring in the mid-sixties, the early seventies and the late seventies, all of which have been incisively analysed in a recent book on the Indian economy by the Oxford economists Joshi and Little (1994). Although the periodic crises the economy experienced were grounded in the inefficient interventionist regime in place, they were exacerbated by drought-induced decline in food and agricultural output, increased defence expenditures and other exogenous shocks such as increases in the price of oil. These crises could be explained away as the consequence of exogenous factors and contained with some degree of success through management of food stocks, increased foreign borrowing, inflows of funds from non-residents abroad, exchange rate manipulation, and short-term fiscal and monetary stabilisation policies.

The crisis at the end of the decade of the eighties, however, could not be explained away as yet another hiccup induced by droughts and exogenous shocks. Indeed, during the decade of the eighties the economy registered an impressive five per cent rate of growth, there were no major droughts and there was also a strong growth in exports. The crisis at the end of the decade of the eighties which compelled the policy makers to institute widespread reforms was mostly macroeconomic in origin. In the year 1990–91, inflation exceeded ten per cent, a rate to be considered high in relation to past trends; the public debt to GNP ratio was around 60 per cent, a near doubling of the ratio in 1980, fiscal deficit increased to ten per cent of GDP from eight per cent in 1985–85; the deficit on the current account of the balance of payments rose from three billion dollars in the mid-eighties to more than seven billion dollars, around three per cent of GDP; the gap between domestic investment and savings grew from 1.5 per cent of GDP in 1980 to around 3.3 per cent by the end of 1990, and this was reflected in the current account deficit referred to earlier. The current account deficit was financed partially through reductions in official reserves, as a consequence of which foreign currency reserves could finance no more than two weeks of imports in June 1991.

This state of affairs was not entirely due to the current account deficit, it was also in part due to the Gulf War, which not only pushed up oil prices but also led to the loss of several million dollars of workers' remittances from the Middle East. This was compounded by the trend towards withdrawal of deposits by non-resident Indians during the first half of 1991, triggered by the fact that well before then India's credit rating was under review by external agencies and it had in fact collapsed.

The crisis at the end of the eighties served to highlight the fragility of an economy subject to recurring crises which could be just about contained with foreign borrowing and inflows of remittances. Such borrowing and remittances could be relied upon only because of fiscal prudence and low inflation rates exhibited in the past; but once the grip on public finances was loosened, the fragility of the economy, weakened by years of interventionist policies, was exposed. And in the vastly changed international economic environment, which is not only characterised by increased competition for aid and private capital flows but also by a general loss of faith in state-managed capitalism, India could no longer rely on external assistance and short-term fire-fighting tactics to cope with the crisis. The immediate cause of the crisis was no doubt macroeconomic in nature, but the growth in the gap between savings and investment was a consequence of low growth over the years which in turn had its origins in the inefficient microeconomic trade and investment policies grounded in the inward-looking import substitution philosophy justified by the objective of self-sufficiency. Both the magnitude of the crisis and the realisation that in the absence of reforms India could not hope to attract external capital, appear to have convinced the policy makers of the need for reform.

3. THE REFORMS

The reforms introduced in 1991 include those relating to controls on domestic investment, exchange rate and tariff reforms, measures relating to foreign direct investment and measures designed to promote privatisation of public sector enterprises. In addition, the government introduced measures designed to curb the budget deficit and control the money supply. The Trade Policy Review (TPR), volume 1, provides an exhaustive account of most of these measures, especially those relating to trade and tariffs, including details on most of the categories of trade. Here we note only the major measures of reform.

a. Controls

India's industrial policy structure with its extensive controls, which required entrepreneurs to obtain licences from the government for almost each and every aspect of their business including establishment of enterprises, expansion of investment and access to foreign exchange, raw materials and imported technology, familiarly known as the permit raj, has been mostly dismantled. Industrial licensing is abolished for all except a list of environmentally sensitive industries. Large and dominant firms are no longer required to obtain permission to expand their investments. The number of industries reserved for the public sector is reduced from 17 to 6 and the private sector is allowed participation in the reserved list. Access to technology is much freer than before. These domestic de-licensing reforms, which remove stifling restrictions on entrepreneurship and more importantly remove opportunities for bribery and corruption, should count as a significant departure from the interventionist regime.

b. Tariffs and Controls on Trade

Reforms in this category include reduction of tariffs and liberalisation of import licensing requirements. As the TPR notes, tariffs have been lowered using mainly a 'tops down' approach; peak applied tariffs have been reduced from 355 per cent to 85 per cent. The effective tariff rate (actual tariff rates which takes into account tariff exemptions) on manufacturing was reduced from 126 per cent in 1990–91 to 73 per cent by the end of the fiscal year 1993–94; on agriculture the average tariff rate was lowered from 113 per cent to 43 per cent and on mining from 100 to 70 per cent. The reform package also allows for tariff concessions on imports of capital goods by user industries, especially exporters. The scheme permits imports of both new and second-hand capital goods at a concessional rate of 15 per cent, with the proviso that the manufacturer should increase direct exports above the average level in the preceding three years, by an amount equivalent to four times the value of capital goods imported.

Another significant trade policy reform is the liberalisation of the import-licensing system. Until 1991 imports were subject to a complex licensing system consisting of 26 commodity lists covering all merchandise. The export and import policy reform of 1992 replaced the 'positive' list with a consolidated 'negative' list of goods subject to licensing; all items not on the list can be imported without licence. The negative list consists of all consumer goods including consumer electronic goods, drugs and pharmaceuticals, chemicals and allied items, and items relating to the small-scale sector. Items in the negative list are subject to import licences and the *actual user* condition, which requires the approved importer of the goods also to be the end user of the goods.

Yet another move towards liberalisation relates to the reduction in the number of the so-called canalised items or items which could only be imported by state-trading agencies. The rationale for the grant of this monopoly to the state-trading agencies was that they could obtain improved terms of trade through handling of bulk transactons. Available evidence, cited in the TPR, suggests that the measure only served to restrict competition and any benefits in terms of scale economies the system provided were outweighed by bureaucratic inefficiencies.

c. Exchange Rate Reforms

Changes in the exchange rate regime complemented the mid-1991 trade reforms. Until 1991 the rupee was tied to a weighted basket of currencies of India's major trading partners. The first move towards reform of the exchange rate regime was a 24 per cent devaluation of the rupee from Rs 21 per dollar to Rs 25.95 dollars. Subsequently, in March 1992, the government introduced a dual exchange rate regime designed to liberalise foreign trade. While the system allowed most current account and capital account transactions to take place at the market-determined exchange rate, certain key imports including those transacted by government departments were to be transacted at the official rate which exceeded the market rate. Also, forty per cent of receipts from exports was to be converted into rupees at the official rate, with the remainder to be converted at the market rate. During the period of the dual rate regime, the spread between the two rates is reported to have been around 16 to 17 per cent. The dual exchange rate, as stated earlier, was designed to liberalise trade, by subsidising imports, and initiate a move towards convertibility of the rupee. Nonetheless, the system penalised exporters to the extent that they subsidised imports. The system, however, did not last long. The Finance Minister, in his 1993–94 budget, announced unification of the exchange rate with market forces determining the rate. The combination of the earlier devaluations and the unification measure resulted in a real effective depreciation of the rupee of around 20 to 25 per cent between July 1991 and March 1993.

Another move towards reform of the exchange rate regime is the relaxation of controls over foreign exchange transactions. Significant among these is the abolition of the advance deposit scheme on imports of non-capital goods.

d. Reforms Relating to Foreign Direct Investment

India is not a major recipient of foreign direct investment (FDI). Both controls over trade and the complex set of regulations governing inward investment and technology flows have deterred foreign investors from investing in India. As the TPR reports, during the period 1985–87 FDI in India amounted to a meagre 0.2 per cent of capital formation, compared with 25.5 per cent in Singapore, 15.2 per cent in Hong Kong, 14.4 per cent in Indonesia, 8.7 per cent in Malaysia and 1.4 per cent in Korea. The liberalisation of rules and regulations relating to FDI counts as a significant move towards integrating India with the world economy — the primary objective of the reforms. Significant departures from the earlier restrictive regime include the abolition of the requirement that FDI inflows should be accompanied by technology transfers, automatic approval of FDI up to foreign equity participation of 51 per cent in a range of industries in 34 sectors, and automatic approval of technology transfer agreements, subject to limits on royalty and lump-sum fee payments. Also, an attraction to foreign investors is the undertaking that approval of projects will be given within two weeks of notification of intent to invest.

4. IMPACT OF THE REFORMS

The policy makers can derive much satisfaction from the performance of the economy since the inception of the reforms in 1991. Growth of real GDP was around four per cent and exchange reserves increased from $1.5 billion in July 1991 to around $15 billion by the end of 1993–94, and are projected to reach $20 billion by the end of 1994–95. The deficit on the current account has shrunk from $10 billion in 1990–91 to less than a billion. From virtually negligible amounts, FDI in India increased to $577 million in 1993 and is expected to reach a figure of $2 billion by the end of this year. The number of foreign investment approvals has increased from around 650 in 1990 to more than 1,500. Inflation has been contained to less than ten per cent and the stock markets are buoyant, with foreign purchases of equity amounting to around $3.5 billion in 1993–94. Since the reforms, exports have grown at around 20 per cent per annum and imports have declined by around eight per cent per annum. The most significant achievement of the reforms, however, is the atmosphere of change and optimism which they have created.

5. THE SCOPE AND CREDIBILITY OF REFORMS

'The Tiger Steps Out', 'Elephant in a Race with the Tigers of Asia', 'it resembles guerrilla warfare, with the aggressors a small band of technocrats fighting the rest of the bureaucracy and almost all the politicians', are some of the headlines with which the world's press has greeted India's reforms. They capture the enormity of the task shouldered by the policy makers and the distance India has still to go.

The discussants at the GATT meeting on the TPR express similar views. One issue which surfaces repeatedly in the discussion relates to the depth of the cuts in tariffs and the extent of the reforms. Although the peak levels of tariffs have been reduced, average import tariffs continue to be much higher than those in other developing countries such as Thailand, Korea and Indonesia. Additionally, the dispersion of tariffs around the average is high, with the index of dispersion for effective tariffs at around 42, which is a ten point increase over the dispersion level in 1990–91. There is also a substantial escalation of tariffs by stage of processing; the unweighted average import tariff rate of 75 per cent on semi-processed products is one and a half times higher than that on unprocessed products. This escalation, in combination with the virtual ban on imports of consumer goods, amounts to substantially high rates of effective protection for processing industries. The TPR does not provide estimates of effective rates of protection, but its comment on the likely levels is worth citing here:

> In terms of effective protection, it is difficult to judge precisely what the effect of India's reform programme has been on manufacturing assistance. This is partly because, although tariffs have been cut substantially on output, the reduction of tariffs on inputs, including capital goods, has also received special treatment under the reform programme. Thus, it is conceivable that effective assistance to many industries may have actually increased under the reform, as reductions in output assistance may have been more than compensated for by falls in input assistance. Moreover, most of the goods experiencing substantial cuts in tariff assistance, namely consumer goods, remain covered by comprehensive import licensing requirements (GATT, 1993, p. 157, vol. 1).

The so-called negative list, which covers items for which import licences are required, covers an enormous range of industries. The table in the TPR which lists these items runs to nearly seven pages, and most of the items listed are also subject to the actual user condition which further restricts competition. The ostensible justification for the preservation of the licensing system continues to be 'balance of payments reasons' which, without being cynical, may be interpreted as meaning necessary for political reasons. In this case the technocrats have conceded victory to the politicians. It is also worth noting that the tariff system continues to be complex, with all sorts of exemptions and concessions which render the system less than transparent.

The protection structure including tariffs and licences continues to favour manufacturing and imposes relatively high input costs on agriculture, despite the input subsidies the latter receives. In addition, the web of controls over exports of a range of agricultural products places the agricultural sector at a disadvantage. The discussion of the impact of the reforms on the agricultural sector and its performance is one of the highlights of the TPR.

The TPR also provides an extensive discussion of India's export promotion measures, including the now defunct cash compensation schemes, income tax exemptions accorded to exporters, subsidies on input prices and assistance with marketing. The seven export processing zones (EPZs) in India should also be counted as part of the export promotion package. A highly pertinent issue, raised by one of the discussants at the GATT meeting, is whether, given India's rich endowments of labour, these measures are necessary for the growth of India's exports. The short answer to the question is — yes, they are necessary insofar as the policy regime continues to be biased in favour of domestic markets and against exports. Admittedly, the reforms have done away with much of the policy-induced bias against exports. Even so, the extent of domestic market protection which is in place requires a counterweight in the form of export promotion measures. Whether or not the government is wise in establishing seven export zones, with all the attendant subsidies and infrastructure costs they entail, is also open to question. Thus far, the contribution of the zones to India's exports of manufactures is around four per cent. A cost–benefit analysis of the zones would make for a valuable study. Here again, the logic underlying the establishment of the zones must be that they are required to lure both foreign and domestic producers away from the protected domestic markets towards export markets.

Reforms covering FDI appear to be both timely and extensive in relation to the controls it was subjected to prior to the reforms. Both the growth in the number of approvals and actual inflows of FDI suggest that foreign investors are responding to the policy initiatives of the government. Whether or not this momentum of FDI in the country will be maintained will depend upon the continuation of the liberalisation of the trade regime, the speed with which decisions on applications are taken and the continued favourable stance towards private sector participation in economic activity. In this context, the comment by Goh Chok Tong, Prime Minister of Singapore, is worth noting:

> Many potential investors in India are holding back because they are unsure whether the commitment to reform is deep-seated and widely supported across party lines, and because many rules are not transparent. India needs to convince them that it is serious in wanting to open up.

While many observers of the Indian scene may share the scepticism expressed by Mr Goh, it is worth pondering whether South Korea and not Singapore should be the role model for India. The former country has relied mostly on technology licensing agreements rather than FDI for its requirements of foreign technology and know-how, and the amount of FDI it has allowed is low in comparison with other Asian tigers. India, like South Korea, possesses a large pool of trained engineers and technicians, and may be well placed now to benefit from technology licensing agreements, much more so than in the past when India favoured licensing agreements as opposed to FDI as a method of importing foreign technology and know-how. It is also worth pondering whether or not the volume of FDI in consumer goods industries that India has attracted in recent years is in response to the protection they enjoy and whether or not such investments are socially beneficial. As always, India's economic policy experiments open up a number of issues, such as the ones posed here, for research.

Three other issues noted by both participants at the GATT meeting and observers of the Indian scene are in general worth noting. The first of these relates to the promotion of efficiency and privatisation of India's public sector enterprises, which number well over a thousand, account for 13 per cent of GDP and are renowned for their economic inefficiencies, their dependence for survival on government loans and subsidies, and the protection they enjoy from competition from exports and from domestic producers. The recent reforms have addressed the problem by reducing the number of industries reserved for the public sector from 17 to 6, by instituting measures to improve the accountability of the enterprises and by announcing the intention of the government to divest up to 49 per cent of its equity in public enterprises. Are these measures adequate and why is the government keen on retaining 51 per cent of the equity for itself instead of going the whole hog on the road to privatisation? The simple answer to these questions has to be that India is a federation of states and the political realities are such that state governments would be loath to forego the power and patronage which state-owned enterprises provide. These political realities underlie the Fabian approach to the reform of public enterprises adopted by the policy makers. As the chief architect of the reforms, India's Finance Minister Manmohan Singh, observes:

> . . . we are in politics — we do not have a consensus in our government to go beyond the 49 per cent level. Certainly, if we were willing to offer an enterprise wholesale to private investors, probably we would get a better deal. But since we don't have a consensus in favour of that sort of thing, we have to live with what we have (*Financial Times*, 8 November, 1994).

A second issue relates to over-manning of industries and India's labour laws which do not allow for layoffs and shedding of redundant labour. The reforms provide for voluntary retirements, retraining of redundant workers and insurance schemes through the establishment of the National Renewal Fund. Admittedly, this may be too little and the measures may take time to yield results. But here again the words of wisdom of the Finance Minister, when he comments on the twin issues of divestment of government funds in public enterprises and labour over-manning, are to be heeded:

> If we reach an economic growth rate of 6 per cent, then I think we will reach conditions where jobs are being created and we can make changes. But we are not still there, so that is why we are deliberately going slow in this area (*Financial Times*, 8 November, 1994).

The third issue relates to education. It is a paradox that, in a land which boasts of rich endowments of scientific and technical personnel, the adult literacy rate is as low as 52 per cent. Perhaps the low level of literacy and education is to be attributed to education policies in the past which favoured higher education rather than primary education. More to the point, it may be both a consequence and cause of the low growth performance of India. In any case, the need to promote education of the labour force if India is to effectively compete in international markets cannot be exaggerated. The comment of one of the participants at the GATT review meeting, that India would be well advised to redirect the enormous subsidies it pays public enterprises towards primary education, is well taken.

6. CONCLUDING COMMENTS

Are the reforms credible? Will India persist with them and see the day when, as the Finance Minister hopes, the foreign trade system will have only moderate tariffs? There is much in the reforms, reviewed at length in the TPR, which suggests that they are credible. First is the breadth of the reforms which cover tariffs, exchange rates, de-licensing of domestic industries, foreign direct investment and public enterprises. Many of the reforms may not be deep enough, but the breadth of the reforms, unlike the piecemeal efforts in the past, suggests that policy makers are determined to see them through. Secondly, the comments of the Finance Minister, cited earlier, suggest that the policy makers are fully aware of the political realities and have made every effort to carry the politicians with them. Thirdly, the vastly altered international situation, in which India can no longer rely upon external sources of aid and assistance to bail her out of recurring crises, leaves India no option but to integrate its economy with the world economy through trade and private capital flows. Finally, there has been a change of guard in the ranks of policy makers and economists in India. The education, training and experience of the new guard are all attuned to the virtues of a liberal market-based economy as opposed to the blind ideological faith of the old guard in the inward-looking interventionist economic regime. This is evident from the candour with which the Indian Delegation and its leader responded to the debate on India's reforms at the GATT meeting. The two volumes on India's trade policy review provide not only a lucid account of India's economic performance and policies in recent years, but also an incisive analysis of the reforms.

REFERENCES

Bhagwati, J.N. (1993), *India in Transition: Freeing the Economy* (Oxford: Clarendon Press).

Bhagwati, J.N. and P. Desai (1970), *India: Planning for Industrialisation* (Oxford: Oxford University Press).

Bhagwati, J.N. and T.N. Srinivasan (1975), *Foreign Trade Regimes and Economic Development — India* (New York: National Bureau of Economic Research).

GATT (1993), Trade Policy Review — India (Geneva, GATT Secretariat).

Joshi, V. and I.M.D. Little (1994), *India: Macroeconomics and Political Economy, 1964–1991* (Washington, DC: The World Bank).

Lal, D. (1988), *The Hindu Equilibrium* (Oxford: Clarendon Press).

The GATT's Review of Australian Trade Policy

Kym Anderson

1. INTRODUCTION

WHEN the GATT's Trade Policy Review Mechanism (TPRM) was established in 1989 following the Mid-term Review of the Uruguay Round of multilateral trade negotiations, Australia volunteered to be among the first countries to come under review. The reasons were simple: Australia's trade policy was already more transparent than virtually any other country's,[1] and it had been liberalised substantially during the preceding 15 or so years and was continuing to do so. Its negotiating position in the Uruguay Round was likely therefore to be enhanced by allowing itself to be subjected to early review. That first report was published in 1990 (GATT, 1990), which meant its second report was due in 1994 since all but the largest traders are to be reviewed every four years. In fact the second review was released in January of that year (GATT, 1994).

This paper assesses that second report, focusing primarily on the first 200 pages written by the GATT Secretariat (the other 100 pages being written by the Australian Government). But it puts recent policy and trade developments in longer-term historical perspective than was appropriate in the review report itself, for the benefit of readers not familiar with the unusual features of Australia's trade pattern, policies and performance.

Section 2 summarises the main characteristics of Australia's trade that have made and continue to make it an outlier among OECD economies. It is an outlier both in the composition and in the direction of its trade, as well as in the timing of

KYM ANDERSON is from the Department of Economics and Centre for International Economic Studies, University of Adelaide.

[1] The major transparency institution is the Industry Commission, formerly the Industries Assistance Commission (IAC) and before that (pre-1973) the Tariff Board. Its success in prompting reform through exposing the extent and adverse effects of government intervention in the economy has prompted one commentator to suggest the need to internationalise the concept (Spriggs, 1991). In fact the IAC concept has been exported to several developing countries via the World Bank, and the GATT's Trade Policy Review Mechanism is itself a first step in that direction by GATT's contracting parties.

changes to its trade patterns. Section 3 then examines the country's recent trade-related policy changes and their effects on Australia's trade and growth performance. Those unilateral reforms have been a major break from past trends, in that they have gradually eliminated the (developing country-type of) bias in sectoral assistance policies that favoured Australian manufacturing relative to agriculture. The final section speculates on future prospects for continuing with rapid economic reform in Australia leading up to and beyond its centenary of Federation in 2001. It suggests that while trade policy reform has been an essential first step towards faster economic growth, much other policy reform remains to be implemented, especially in the labour market area.

2. THE UNUSUAL AUSTRALIAN ECONOMY[2]

Australia is an unusual industrial country in several respects. First, it is abundantly endowed with natural resources, having barely one twentieth of the global population density and more than ten times as much arable land and mineral reserves per capita as the rest of the world. Second, like New Zealand it is settled predominently by people from densely populated countries of the British Isles and Western Europe, has the trade advantage of English as its official language, and yet is more distant from the traditional centres of economic gravity on both sides of the North Atlantic than almost any other country. And third, it is comparatively close to the rapidly expanding centre of economic gravity in East Asia and is highly complementary to the densely populated industrialising economies of that region.

Being natural resource-rich and short of investable capital ensured that the antipodean colonies had close trade and investment links with imperial Britain in the nineteenth century, links that naturally carried over into the Australian Federation upon its formation in 1901. More than half Australia's foreign trade had been with Britain up to that time, and most of its foreign capital inflows had come from Britain. Exports were overwhelmingly farm products plus gold, which were exchanged mostly for manufactures. The growth of the United States as a major trader in the first half of this century led to some diversification of the direction of Australia's trade but to little change in its rural commodity concentration. It took the emergence of resource-poor but rapidly industrialising Japan and then the East Asian 'tigers' to bring some diversity to Australia's trade composition — if only in the form of a boom in exports of minerals and energy raw materials. The latter were helped along by the OPEC-induced oil price rises of the 1970s, so that by the early 1980s mining clearly dominated farming as the

[2] This section draws on Anderson (1995) and other chapters in Pomfret (1995).

TABLE 1
Composition of Australia's Exports of Goods and Services, 1950–51 to 1993–94
(per cent in current prices)

	Rural Products	*Fuels, Minerals and Metals*	*Other Merchandise*	*Services*	*Total*
1950–51	86	6	3	5	100
1960–61	66	8	13	13	100
1970–71	44	28	12	16	100
1980–81	39	34	11	16	100
1985–86	32	42	9	17	100
1989–90	26	41	14	19	100
1993–94	23	37	18	22	100

Sources: Australian Bureau of Agricultural and Resource Economics, *Commodity Statistical Bulletin* (1990), and *Australian Commodities* (December 1994, Canberra: Australian Government Publishing Service).

TABLE 2
Index of Net Export Specialisation, Australia, 1950–51 to 1993–94
(current value of exports minus imports/exports plus imports)

	Primary Products	*Manufactures*	*Services*
1950–51	0.67	−0.89	−0.45
1960–61	0.55	−0.70	−0.32
1970–71	0.73	−0.69	−0.23
1980–81	0.57	−0.72	−0.24
1993–94	0.66	−0.55	−0.04

Sources: See Table 1.

major export sector but Australia was still very much a net exporter of primary products and a net importer of other goods and services. However, by then it was trading much more intensely with East Asia than were other non-Asian countries, including New Zealand.

Then another trend break occurred. Since the mid-1980s, there has been a significant growth in the net exports of non-primary products from Australia. During the past decade the primary products share of exports has fallen from 74 to 60 per cent, the export share of other merchandise has doubled to 18 per cent, and the services share has risen from 17 to 22 per cent (Table 1). With little change in the sectoral composition of imports, that meant the net export specialisation indexes (exports minus imports as a ratio of exports plus imports) for manufactures and services have fallen even faster in recent times than in the earlier post-war years (Table 2). Indeed Australia is on the verge of becoming a

TABLE 3
Indicators of Increased Openness of Australia's Manufacturing Sector, 1968 to 1994

	Effective Rate of Government Assistance %	*Average Rate of Duty on Competing Imports* %	*Share of Production Exported* %	*Share of Imports in Domestic Sales* %	*Index of Intra-industry Trade*[a]
1968–69 to 1977–78	31	13	12	20	27
1978–79 to 1984–85	23	11	15	25	30
1986–87	19	10	17	30	32
1989–90	15	8	18	30	32
1991–92	13	7	21	31	37
1993–94	10	6[b]	na	na	38[b]

Notes:

[a] Defined as the trade-weighted average of the Grubel-Lloyd index for each 3-digit manufacturing industry, that index being the difference between exports plus imports and the modulus of exports minus imports, expressed as a percentage of exports plus imports. The index therefore takes on a value between 0 (no intra-industry trade) and 100 (when exports equal imports).

[b] 1992–93.

Source: Industry Commission (1995, Table A1).

net exporter of services, thanks to the growth of a wide range of services but especially tourism and education exports.

The increased internationalisation is especially striking in manufacturing, albeit from a low base. Prior to the 1980s Australia's exports of manufactures amounted to less than 10 per cent of manufacturing value added (compared with more than 100 per cent in the primary sectors), but that share had risen to 15 per cent by the end of the 1980s and to more than 20 per cent by 1992. As well, all the indicators in Table 3 show monotonic increases in internationalisation since the 1970s: effective assistance falling by two thirds, tariffs on competing imports more than halving, close to a doubling in the share of production exported, a 50 per cent increase in the share of imports in domestic sales, and 40 per cent increase in the index of intra-industry trade.

The associated dramatic jumps in the shares of Australia's trade, first with Japan and then with developing East Asian economies, is clear from Table 4: East Asia as a whole now accounts for nearly three fifths of Australia's exports and two fifths of its imports, compared with much less than one-fifth in the 1950s. A further five percentage points is now due to balanced trade with New Zealand.

Only part of those changing shares is due to the changing importance of different economies in world trade. To see that, it is useful to calculate intensity of trade indexes, defined as the share of Australia's exports (or imports) going to country or group X as a ratio of X's share of world imports (exports). Table 5

TABLE 4
Direction of Australia's Merchandise Trade, 1951 to 1993
(per cent)

	1951–55	*1968–72*	*1980–84*	*1990–93*
Exports				
United Kingdom	36	11	4	4
Other Europe	27	16	10	12
North America	10	16	13	11
New Zealand	4	5	5	5
Japan	8	26	27	26
Developing East Asia	6	12	20	31
Middle East	1	2	8	3
Other developing	8	12	13	8
Total	**100**	**100**	**100**	**100**
(of which APEC)	**28**	**49**	**65**	**74**
Imports				
United Kingdom	45	21	7	6
Other Europe	15	19	17	20
North America	15	27	25	25
New Zealand	1	2	3	5
Japan	2	13	21	18
Developing East Asia	7	7	14	20
Middle East	4	5	9	3
Other Developing	11	6	4	3
Total	**100**	**100**	**100**	**100**
(of which APEC)	**25**	**40**	**63**	**69**

Note: APEC comprises all the major trading economies of North America, East Asia and Australasia.
Source: Australian Bureau of Statistics, *Overseas Trade* (Canberra, various issues).

shows that in the early 1950s the shares of Australia's trade with the UK were four or five times greater than the UK's share of world trade whereas they are now barely equal to the UK's global trade share. That table also shows that the historically low intensity of Australia's trade with continental Europe has changed little, while its trade shares with East Asia are now two or three times greater than that region's shares of world trade (and with New Zealand they are twenty times greater, double the intensity of trans-Tasman trade that prevailed prior to the 1970s).[3] That is, the intensity of Australia's trade with its neighbours, after netting out their changing importance in world trade, has increased enormously during the post-war period, at the expense of the intensity of its traditional trade ties with the United Kingdom.

[3] While these data refer only to merchandise trade, the picture is similar with services trade. In 1992–93, for example, the indexes of intensity of Australia's services trade were around 0.5 with the European Union, 1.0 with North America, more than 2 with East Asia, and more than 15 with New Zealand (DFAT, 1995a).

TABLE 5
Intensity of Australia's Merchandise Trade, 1951 to 1993
(share of Australia's trade with country or group X as a ratio of X's share of world trade)

	1951–55	*1968–72*	*1980–84*	*1990–93*
Exports				
United Kingdom	3.8	2.0	0.7	0.8
Other Europe	0.7	0.3	0.3	0.3
North America	0.5	0.9	0.8	0.7
New Zealand	5.7	13.2	17.1	21.0
Japan	3.0	4.2	3.3	2.7
Other Northeast Asia	0.5	1.1	2.4	1.7
Southeast Asia	0.9	2.9	3.0	2.9
South Asia	1.5	1.6	1.9	2.2
Imports				
United Kingdom	5.2	3.5	1.3	1.0
Other Europe	0.4	0.4	0.4	0.4
North America	0.7	1.5	1.5	1.3
New Zealand	1.1	4.1	11.3	19.6
Japan	1.2	2.0	3.1	3.0
Other Northeast Asia	0.1	0.7	1.6	1.4
Southeast Asia	1.6	1.6	2.2	1.3
South Asia	1.9	1.3	1.1	1.1

Source: Calculated from data from the Australian Bureau of Statistics, *Overseas Trade* (Canberra, various issues), and United Nations, *Yearbook of Internatioinal Trade Statistics* (New York, various years).

Why was Australia so unusual (a) in having for so long its strongest trade ties with distant Britain rather than with its neighbours and then having that situation dissipate so quickly, and (b) in having its exports diversify away from farm products at such a late stage of the economy's development, first suddenly to mining products but then also to manufactures and services?[4] It cannot be explained by sudden changes in the relative distances of trading partners from Australia or in the country's relative abundance of natural resource per worker. Rather, policy changes abroad and then at home are the main explanators.

British Empire/Commonwealth tariff preferences and being part of the sterling currency area, together with antagonism towards Japan, are largely responsible for the trade bias towards Britain up to the 1950s. But then the thaw in relations with resource-poor Japan from the mid-1950s, and the adoption from the 1960s of outward-oriented industrialisation strategies in equally densely populated

[4] Another not-unrelated characteristic of Australia's trade has been the low propensity to engage in intra-industry trade. That propensity has almost doubled since the mid-1980s, but is still only three-quarters that of the average OECD country (GATT, 1994, p. 10). For details as to why Australia became so protectionist and why it reformed so belatedly, see for example Anderson and Garnaut (1987) and Garnaut (1994).

developing countries of East Asia, led to a rapidly growing demand for resource-intensive exports from Australia — mineral as well as agricultural. That prompted Australia to abandon its export prohibitions on such mining products as iron ore and to encourage, for the first time, substantial investments by multinational corporations in large-scale mining projects. Meanwhile, the United Kingdom was negotiating entry into the European Community, one consequence of which was the replacement of tariff preferences with much higher barriers to (particularly agricultural) imports from Australia. Those food import barriers continued to rise over the 1970s and 1980s, as did EC barriers to coal imports. Since those are two of Australia's major export items, it is hardly surprising that Australia's traders gradually turned their attention much more to East Asian markets.

The more recent changes in the commodity composition of Australia's trade — particularly the diversification of exports beyond primary products — are only partly due to the decline in the international terms of trade for primary producers since the heady days of the early 1980s. Much more important have been the economic reforms by the Australian Government during the past decade. It is those which are, appropriately, the subject of attention in the GATT Secretariat's review.

3. AUSTRALIA'S UNILATERAL ECONOMIC REFORMS

The extreme dominance of primary products in Australia's exports and non-primary products in its imports has prevailed since white settlement despite trade policies aimed at encouraging industrialisation. Tariff protection for the manufacturing sector carried over from the colony of Victoria into the Australian Federation in 1901, and was gradually raised over subsequent decades and supplemented with import quotas in the 1950s. Then Australia chose not to participate in the tariff reforms associated with the GATT's multilateral trade negotiations in the 1960s and early 1970s, out of frustration over the unpreparedness of other industrial countries to cut their agricultural protection (Arndt, 1965; and Snape, 1984). By 1970 Australia's manufacturing tariffs averaged 23 per cent, or more than twice those of most other OECD countries (Anderson and Garnaut, 1987, Table 2.1). As well, the economy had been shackled with numerous domestic regulations and policies that had substantially ossified economic activity and restricted internal (inter-state) trade.

One clear symptom of these policies being a problem was the steady erosion of Australia's rank on the ladder of national per capita incomes: having been perhaps the highest ranking in the latter nineteenth and early twentieth century, it dropped to third by 1950 (after the United States and Canada) and seventh by 1970 — and fell further to almost twentieth by the 1980s, including in terms of purchasing power parity (Anderson, 1995, pp. 45–46). Two other symptoms were the relatively slow growth (a) in Australia's total factor productivity, at half the OECD average since 1960 (GATT, 1994, Chart 1.1), and (b) in the internationalisation of the Australian economy, as measured by its share of real GDP traded which also had been growing at barely half the rate for other OECD countries during the post-war period (Anderson, 1995, Table 1.6).

The first tariff cuts came in 1973, with a 25 per cent across-the-board reduction. But that was aimed more at reducing the temporary supply constraints facing the new Labour Government than at reforming the economy. Indeed the Conservative Opposition continued to embrace protectionism, which helped it to win the election in 1975, after which it imposed increasingly protectionist import quotas on cars and on textiles, clothing and footwear.

By the early 1980s, however, there was widespread dissatisfaction with the country's economic performance and an expanding awareness of the economic costs of protectionism. That contributed to a change of government in 1983 which gave the new Labour Government a mandate to introduce an ambitious programme of economic reform, particularly in the manufacturing and service sectors (since the primary sectors were much more exposed to international competition). The currency was floated, financial markets and foreign direct investment were deregulated, public business enterprises began to be corporatised or privatised, and greater decentralisation of wage-setting began to be phased in. Standards, accreditation and government procurement procedures of the State Governments are being harmonised across states or made subject to mutual recognition; an exceptionally ambitious Closer Economic Relations Agreement with New Zealand was signed in 1983 and its implementation has been accelerated to speed the freeing up of trade in goods and services across the Tasman Sea (Lloyd, 1991); the remaining import quotas (on cars and textiles) have been removed, and import tariffs are being phased down together with producer subsides.[5]

The effects of these changes are clearly evident. At the macro level inflation has been brought down to among the lowest in the OECD (less than two per cent in the 1990s), GDP growth has been among the highest in the OECD recently (more than four per cent in 1993–94), and employment growth has been considerable (although the unemployment rate has fallen only slowly and in early 1995 was still almost nine per cent).

With respect to trade, the results are showing up as the country better exploits its comparative advantages not just in the strengthening of the country's trade with its neighbours and the diversifying of its export composition, but also in data

[5] An early set of analyses of the reforms is available in Forsyth (1992). The debates about the reforms have been vigorous, as they were under Thatcher in Britain. A sociologist's views are presented by Pusey (1992), and a collection of responses by economists is available in King and Lloyd (1993).

FIGURE 1
Share of GDP traded as goods and non-factor services, at constant prices, Australia, 1971 to 1991

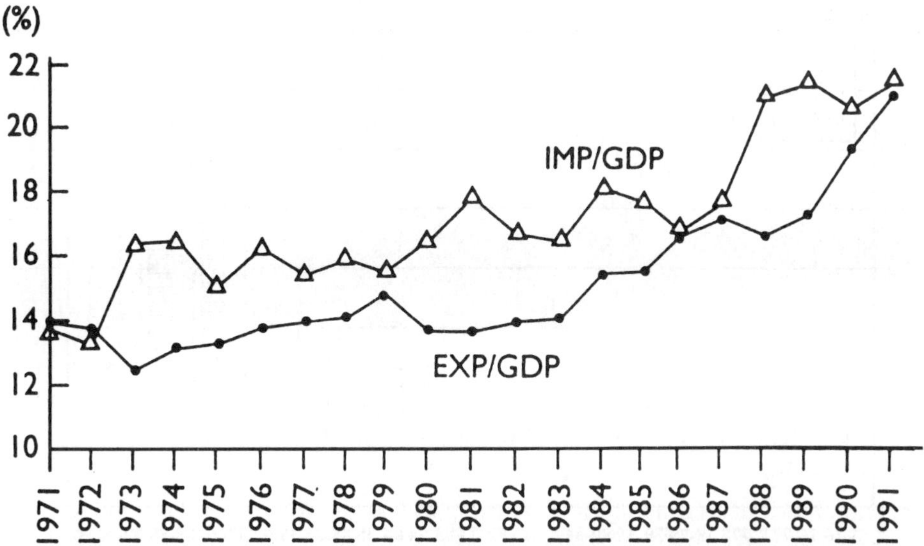

Source: World Bank (1993, pp. 96–7).

such as trade-to-GDP and foreign investment-to-GDP ratios. Figure 1 shows that between 1983 and 1991, the shares of GDP traded, rose from about 15 to 22 per cent at constant prices, during a period when that ratio for the rest of the OECD hardly grew at all. That represents a major reversal from a long run downward trend in that index of openness since the mid-nineteenth century which had set Australia apart from most other industrial countries whose economies had progressively become more trade-oriented (Anderson and Garnaut, 1987, Table 2.6). The freeing up of foreign direct investment, in an environment of major reform generally, simultaneously caused the trend level of both inward and outward investment flows to more than treble over the 1980s (Figure 2).

The reductions in trade barriers and subsidies are summarised neatly in the Industry Commission's estimates of assistance to tradables industries. There has been a gradual fall in the average rates of effective assistance to both the manufacturing and the agricultural sectors. By 1994, those rates were down to around ten per cent for both sectors (compared with nearly four times that in 1970 — Figure 3(a)). That is still well above the effective rate of assistance for mining (about −1 per cent), but the current plans for continuing the tariff and subsidy cuts are expected to halve the remaining difference by the turn of the century. The only assistance of significance still in place then will be for textiles, clothing and footwear and for motor vehicles and parts, but even those industries have been subjected to major tariff cuts since the mid-1980s and are scheduled for equally large additional cuts during the next five years (Figure 3(b)). By 1993

FIGURE 2
Inward and outward foreign direct investment, Australia, 1975 to 1992

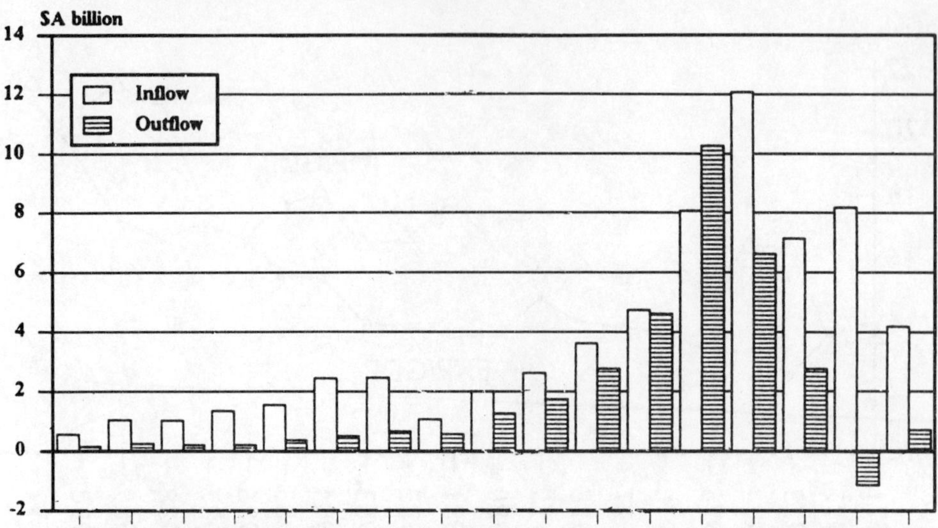

Source: GATT (1994, p. 33).

more than two-thirds of all imports actually entered duty-free and the unweighted average tariff was eight per cent. Most products are expected to have tariffs of five per cent or less from 1996, and the average is expected to be less than four per cent by the year 2000 (comparable with that for other OECD countries). At that time, tariffs on cars, footwear and textiles will be no more than 15 per cent and those on clothing no more than 25 per cent. As part of its Uruguay Round commitments, Australia has agreed to bind 94 per cent of its tariff items. This is about the same degree of binding as other OECD countries are committed to, but it contrasts with Australia's pre-Uruguay Round commitment to bind only 20 per cent of its tariffs. That previous low level of commitment was again a form of protest at the lack of progress on farm trade liberalisation in early GATT rounds.

Some export incentive schemes still remain, but they are of minor significance. In agriculture dairy farmers are levied to subsidise the export of manufactured milk products, the effect of which is to raise the domestic consumer price. A ceiling rate of 22 per cent of the export price is in place, but the actual level was closer to 15 per cent in the early to mid-1990s. It is scheduled to be phased down to no more than 10 per cent by the year 2000. Motor vehicle exporters are entitled to duty-free imports of cars and parts (an effective export subsidy) up to a proportion of the value added in the exported products. Textile, clothing and footwear exporters are also able to import certain products at reduced duties, again depending on the value added in their exports. Both rates of export assistance are to be halved by the year 2000. An Export Finance and Insurance Corporation, together with an aid-funded Development Import Finance Facility

FIGURE 3

Effective rates of assistance to Australia's manufacturing and agricultural sectors, 1968 to 2000

(a) Total Manufacturing and Agriculture

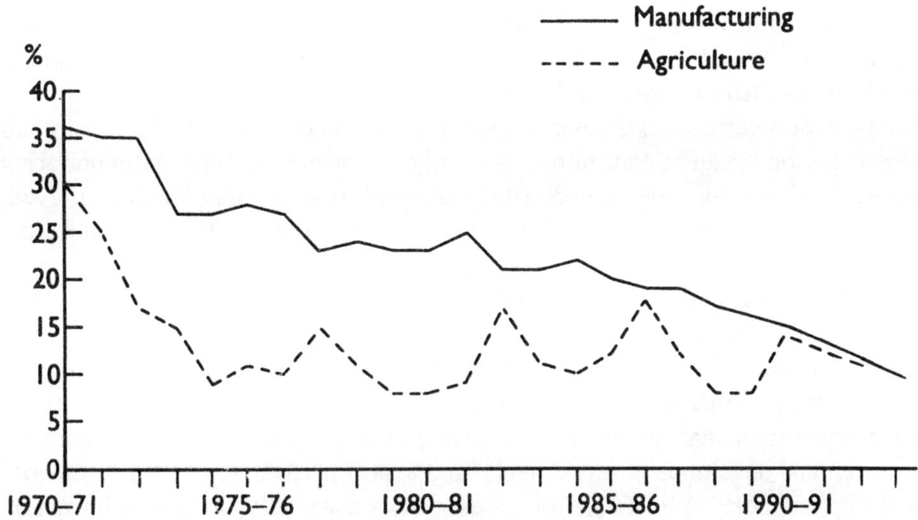

(b) Textiles, Clothing and Footwear (TCF), Motor Vehicles and Parts (MVP) and Other Manufacturing Industries

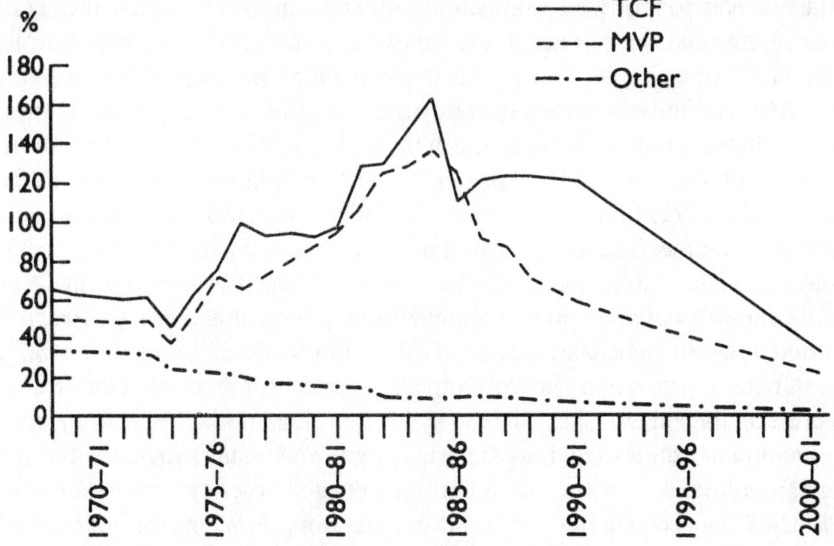

Source: Estimates by the Industry Commission (1994 and earlier editions).

to help developing countries purchase from Australia, also assists exports. All of these, other than car export facilitation, are tolerated by Australia's trading partners because they are within GATT and OECD guidelines. The car plan is tolerated, despite being a thinly disguised export subsidy, presumably because the firms abroad likely to be hurt by that subsidisation are, through their Australian subsidiaries, also the major beneficiaries in Australia (at the expense of the Australian taxpayer via lower customs revenue).

Few export controls exist. A coal export tax was abolished in 1992, and a small export tax on uranium concentrate is simply to cover environmental monitoring costs. Beef exports were 'voluntarily' restricted to the United States to prevent triggering duty increases, but that is disappearing with tariffication under the Uruguay Round. And most other restrictions are for environmental reasons under various international environmental agreements such as CITES, the Basel Convention, and the Montreal Protocol.

More-obtuse forms of assistance exist for a small number of industries, particularly pharmaceuticals and information technologies. They take the form of government/industry agreements on firm-specific targets such as local content, research and development investments, and export performance. Such 'strategic' industry support is difficult to assess and, especially in the information technology area, is changing continually because of the dynamics of the industries concerned.

A trade-related area that is receiving belated attention by Australia's reforming governments has to do with competition policy. In recent cases the Trade Practices Commission (TPC) has drawn an explicit link between competition and trade policies. For example, in the context of a planned takeover of New Zealand Steel by BHP (Australia's dominant steel producer), the TPC expressed concern about the reduced competition and recommended a tariff reduction. As a result, import tariffs on the relevant steel products were brought down from ten to five per cent in July 1992, four years earlier than scheduled under the general tariff reduction programme. The TPC's stated priorities, now that tariff reform is well underway for all tradables industries and an agreement has been reached with New Zealand to cooperate in the competition policy area, are to focus on competition laws in industries not exposed to international competition (e.g., because of natural protection via prohibitively high transport costs). The TPC has also expressed its concern that current legislation does not allow it to examine some government entities (such as electricity, gas and water providers and port authorities) and some non-corporate entities engaged solely in intra-state trade (such as legal and accounting services, and statutory rural marketing boards). However, the latter exceptions are among the many regulated activities that are starting to come under scrutiny following agreement between the Commonwealth and State Governments to address the recommendations of the milestone Hilmer Report (National Competition Policy Review, 1993).

4. FUTURE PROSPECTS FOR AUSTRALIA'S ECONOMIC REFORMS TOWARDS 2001

The decade-long new tariff reform programme announced in 1991, if maintained, will complete the conversion of Australia from one of the most protected industrial economies to one of the least protected in terms of external trade barriers: manufacturing tariffs will be no higher than for other OECD countries, and agricultural and mining protection and subsidies will continue to be far lower than elsewhere in the OECD. In the absense of 'voluntary' restraint arrangements, and assuming anti-dumping actions do not increase,[6] the insulating characteristic of Australia's trade policy will be a thing of the past by the time the country celebrates its centenery of federation in 2001. There is of course the possibility that policy reversals will occur, but the record of the past decade suggests that is unlikely, particularly now that the Conservative Opposition is in agreement with the Government on the need to keep the reform process going. The bipartisanship made it politically possible for the 1991 trade liberalisation package to be announced even though at the time the economy was quite weak; and, if anything, reform progress since then has been faster than in the original plan.

Why Australia (not unlike New Zealand) embarked on this reform when it did, and to the extent it has, is still being analysed, but an assessment by an economist directly involved in advising Prime Minister Hawke during the 1980s is available in Garnaut (1994). It is a complex story, but the changing climate of public opinion based on an improved understanding of the folly of protectionism, together with a leader coming to power who shared that view, were important contributing factors. It probably helped also that (as in New Zealand) it was a Labour Government doing the reforms, because the Labour Party owed less allegiance to business interest groups and was in a better position to placate the trade union movement than the Conservatives could ever have been.

Whether reform in other economic areas continues apace is less certain, not least because large groups of employees are affected when government business enterprises are threatened with competition, corporatisation, and in some cases privatisation. Nonetheless, the response by Commonwealth and State governments to the 1993 Hilmer Report on competition policy has been cautiously positive. If internal trade and competition are stimulated as a result, Australia's international competitiveness will be further enhanced which will make a reversal in trade policy reform even less likely.

[6] Australia's anti-dumping actions had been considerable in the 1980s and increased further towards the end of the decade, but recent changes in legislation have helped reduce their frequency and impact. In particular, the inclusion of a five-year sunset clause now restricts the longevity of any action, reducing the incentive for groups to lobby for such action. See GATT (1994, pp. 48–54).

Much remains to be done, however. The biggest bottleneck is labour market reform, with moves away from centralised wage-setting and towards enterprise bargaining progressing only slowly, thereby limiting the economy's capacity to reduce unemployment. One of the labour areas in need of greatest reform has to do with wharfs and shipping, an area that directly inhibits international trade in a significant way. Also far from optimal is the awkward mix of policies affecting telecommunications and Australia's access to the information superhighway. And attention needs to be focused as well on policies inhibiting household savings, so as to reduce the savings-investment gap and thereby lower Australia's excessive foreign debt.[7]

To conclude, a comment is warranted on Australia's commitment to the multilateral trading system. The GATT report correctly notes that Australia worked vigorously during the Uruguay Round to help bring the Round to a successful conclusion and thereby strengthen that rules-based, non-discriminatory trading system. Since that report was completed, however, there has been a discernible reduction in the Government's focus on the GATT/WTO relative to its interest in regional affairs (see for example, DFAT, 1995b). One reason may be disappointment at the extent of liberalisation in agricultural trade that was actually achieved in the Round (little more than a standstill it seems — see the various modelling results in Martin and Winters, 1995). Another reason may be that the current Prime Minister (Keating) sees more political mileage in focusing on initiatives within the East Asian and broader Asian-Pacific Economic Co-operation (APEC) region, particularly now that North America looks like extending NAFTA to embrace Chile and perhaps other Latin American countries. A more generous interpretation might be that this is simple posturing, along with Washington's, in an attempt to eventually re-focus West European attention away from further regional integration and towards multilateral trade issues before the end of the decade when a new round of WTO trade negotiations might begin. However, the Australian Government's apparent preparedness to now entertain the idea of a preferential trading area in the APEC region makes that interpretation less plausable than a year or so ago.

Overall, the GATT report provides a thorough and accurate assessment of the recent changes in Australia's trade-related policies up to the end of 1993. It is to be hoped that its next report, in 1998, is able to report (a) that the promised trade reforms continued to be carried out, (b) that substantial progress has been made on the remaining areas of microeconomic reform that at this stage still require attention, and (c) that Australia remains strongly committed to the multilateral trading system and against a preferential trading bloc in the Asia-Pacific region.

---

[7] Foreign debt as a percentage of GDP rose from around 10 per cent in 1980 to 30 per cent in the mid-1980s and to more than 50 per cent by 1992–93 (GATTm 1994, p. 43). Australia's domestic savings rate has been low by OECD standards, and had fallen to below one-sixth of GDP by the early 1990s.

REFERENCES

Anderson, K. (1995), 'Australia's Changing Trade Pattern and Growth Performance', Ch. 1 in R. Pomfret, (ed.), *Australia's Trade Policies*, (London, New York and Melbourne: Oxford University Press).

Anderson, K. and R. Garnaut (1987), *Australian Protectionism: Extent, Causes and Effects* (Boston, London and Sydney: Allen and Unwin).

Arndt, H.W. (1965), 'Australia — Developed, Developing or Midway?', *Economic Record*, **41**, 95, 318–40.

DFAT (1995a), *Trade in Services, Australia, 1993–94* (Canberra: Department of Foreign Affairs and Trade).

DFAT (1995b), *Winning Markets: The Next Steps* (Canberra: Department of Foreign Affairs and Trade (draft: 15 February)).

Forsyth, P. (ed.) (1992), *Microeconomic Reform in Australia* (Boston, London and Sydney: Allen and Unwin).

Garnaut, R. (1994), 'Australia', in J. Williamson (ed.), *The Political Economy of Policy Reform* (Washington, DC: Institute for International Economics), 51–72.

GATT (1990), *Trade Policy Review — Australia* (Geneva: GATT Secretariat).

GATT (1994), *Trade Policy Review — Australia* (Geneva: GATT Secretariat).

Industry Commission (1994), *Annual Report 1993–94* (Canberra: Australian Government Publishing Service).

Industry Commission (1995), *Australian Manufacturing Industry and International Trade Data 1968–69 to 1992–93* (Canberra: Australian Government Publishing Service).

King, S. and P.J. Lloyd (eds.) (1993), *Economic Rationalism: Dead End or Way Forward?* (Boston, London and Sydney: Allen and Unwin).

Lloyd, P.J. (1991), *The Future of CER: A Single Market for Australia and New Zealand* (Wellington: Institute of Policy Studies and Melbourne: Committee for Economic Development of Australia).

Martin, W. and L.A. Winters (eds.) (1995), *The Uruguay Round and the Developing Countries* (Washington, DC: The World Bank, forthcoming).

National Competition Policy Review [the Hilmer Report] (1993), *National Competition Policy* (Canberra: Australian Government Publishing Service).

Pomfret, R. (ed.) (1995), *Australia's Trade Policies* (London, New York and Melbourne: Oxford University Press).

Pusey, M. (1992), *Economic Rationalism in Canberra: A Nation-Building State Changes its Mind* (Cambridge, New York and Sydney: Cambridge University Press).

Snape, R.H. (1984), 'Australia's Relations with GATT', *Economic Record*, **60**, 168, (16–27 March).

Spriggs, J.D. (1991), 'Towards an International Transparency Institution: Australian Style', *The World Economy*, **14**, 2, 165–80.

World Bank (1993), *World Development Report 1993* (London and New York: Oxford University Press).

Trade Policy Review of the Republic of Turkey

Sübidey Togan

1. INTRODUCTION

THE recently published Trade Policy Review (TPR) of the Republic of Turkey which updates Krueger's (1974) comprehensive treatment of the Turkish foreign trade regime in the 1960s, investigates in detail the nature of Turkish trade liberalisation during the 1980s and 1990s, and provides a number of recommendations to policy makers. The study is based on two reports. The report by the GATT Secretariat is contained in Volume I, and the report by the Government of Turkey together with the statements by the discussants, members of the Council and the representative of Turkey in Volume II. The report by the GATT Secretariat begins with a discussion of the economic environment. After analysing rather comprehensively and exhaustively the trade policy regime in Chapter II and the exchange rate and foreign investment regime in Chapter III, the report studies the trade policies and practices by measure in a very thorough and useful chapter, namely Chapter IV. Finally, Chapter V considers the trade policies and practices by sector. The report by the Government of Turkey on the other hand consists of three chapters. The first chapter discusses the economic environment, the second chapter the trade policies and practices, and finally Chapter III the relations with EC, EFTA and other major trading partners. The ensuing discussion of the TPR is under the following headings: macroeconomic developments (Section 2), the achievements in the field of trade policy (Section 3) and problems faced by Turkey in the context of the formation of customs union with the European Union (Section 4). The paper concludes (Section 5) with a discussion of prospects and future issues.

2. THE TURKISH ECONOMY AND MACROECONOMIC DEVELOPMENTS

The economic developments in Turkey can be analysed by considering three sub-periods: the period before the 1980s, the 1980s, and the period after 1989.

SÜBIDEY TOGAN is from Bilkent University, Ankara, Turkey.

Until the 1980s Turkey followed an inward oriented development strategy. During the 1970s the increase in oil prices and the consequent world recession adversely affected the Turkish economy. Instead of adjusting to these external shocks Turkey attempted to preserve its growth momentum through rapid reserve decumulation and massive external borrowing. As a result of the oil price shock, the inefficiencies of the long standing inward-looking development strategy and inflationary financing of growing public sector deficits, the country faced crisis towards the end of the 1970s. Social and political tensions increased in the country. By the late 1970s, it was apparent that the strategy of economic growth based on import substitution and characterised by fixed exchange rates, regulation of imports through quotas, and high nominal and effective protection rates was no longer sustainable.

In January 1980, the government introduced a comprehensive policy package to correct the worsening economic situation. The immediate goals of the reforms were the reduction of inflation and of the balance of payments deficit. The policy makers further aimed at making the economy responsive to market forces in the long run, and in turn more dynamic and efficient. To this end, Turkey attempted to foster competition. It was recognised that the increased openness would be the most effective means to introduce greater competition in the economy. During the 1980s various economic reforms were introduced, and with significant consequences for the performance of exports, the balance of payments and real income. Exports increased from US$2.9 billion in 1980 to US$11.6 billion in 1989, the current account deficit decreased from US$3.4 billion in 1980 to a surplus of US$0.9 billion in 1989 and real income during 1981–1989 increased at the average rate of 4.8 per cent.

Furthermore inflation decreased from 116 per cent in 1980 to 39 per cent in 1987. Finally, one should note that the Turkish people started to realise that Turkey was capable of achieving international competitiveness. In March 1989 the Özal government lost the municipal elections. Thereafter the Özal government deviated from pursuing market oriented policies. It switched over to pursuing populist policies. During the 1980s the public sector borrowing requirements (PSBR) were kept under control. But after 1988 the PSBR/GNP ratio started to increase from its value of six per cent of GNP in 1988. The ratio became a double digit figure in 1990 and it continued to increase. In 1993 it reached 17 per cent. Behind this rapid growth of the ratio lie the fast growing deficits of the consolidated budget, the losses of state economic enterprises, the growing costs of social security organisations and the fiscal deficits of municipalities. During the years 1992–1993 there were no serious attempts either to increase the tax base and tax collection effectiveness or to improve the efficiency of public expenditures. As the growing PSBR was increasingly financed by Central Bank sources the money supply increased rapidly leading to increases in inflation.

A second important development in the Turkish economy was the growing trade and current account deficits. Since liberalisation of the capital account in 1989 the government opted for the policy of appreciating the real exchange rate after pursuing a real depreciation policy during the 1980s. The trade deficit increased from $2.7 billion in 1989 to $14 billion in 1993, while the current account deficit increased from a surplus of $0.9 billion in 1989 to $6.3 billion in 1993. The size of the external debt reached $67.4 billion by the end of 1993 of which $18.5 billion was short term. Simultaneously the domestic debt exploded. The share of long term borrowing of the Treasury for deficit financing has declined rapidly during the last few years. The projections for 1994 were that the PSBR/GNP ratio and the trade and current account deficits would further increase, leading to worsening macroeconomic imbalances. Because of the balance of payments crisis the government, in April 1994, decided to enter into negotiations with the International Monetary Fund and introduced a new stabilisation package. As a result of the stabilisation measures which were introduced, real GNP in 1984 decreased by 6.1 per cent and the current account deficit was completely eliminated and even moved into surplus in 1994. During 1994 however, inflation accelerated to about 125 per cent.

3. TRADE POLICY REFORM

Prior to the 1980s, all imports into Turkey were regulated by annual import programmes. Each programme was published in the *Official Gazette*. The import programme itemised commodities under the liberalisation list, the quota list, and a list enumerating the commodities to be imported under bilateral trade arrangements. Importation of goods not enumerated in any of the lists was prohibited. Of these the quota list and the liberalisation list were of major importance. The liberalised list contained commodities which were considered to be essential for the achievement of development plan objectives when domestic productive capacity was unavailable. They consisted mostly of capital goods and raw materials. The liberalisation list was further divided into a free import list (Liberalisation List I) and a restricted list (Liberalisation List II). Commodities on the free import list consisted of raw materials and spare parts. Commodities on the restricted list were mainly processed and semi-processed goods and raw materials. The quota list covered commodities of which there was some domestic production or which were considered not essential by plan objectives such as consumer goods. As soon as domestic production of an import competing product began, the import was transferred from the liberalised list to the quota list. When domestic production of a commodity was sufficient to meet the domestic demand, the item was removed from the quota list. Since commodities not specified on the import lists could not be imported, complete protection was then granted to local producers. This import regime remained in force until the 1980s.

In 1981, the quota list was partly phased out. In that year a large number of commodities were transferred from 'Liberalisation List II' to 'Liberalisation List I'. A major reform was introduced in January 1984, when all imports were classified into three lists: the 'prohibited list', 'imports subject to permission' and 'liberalised list'. Commodities that could not be imported under any circumstances such as arms and ammunitions were specified in the 'prohibited list'. 'Imports subject to permission' specified the items that could be imported with prior official permission, and the 'liberalised list' enumerated the commodities that could be freely imported.

In 1984 tariff rates were substantially reduced. But in order to reduce the import demand a new tax was introduced. The parliament in March 1984 approved the Housing Fund Law to finance the Government's low cost housing scheme for poor and middle income families. The fund has been financed mainly by specific or ad valorem surcharges levied on imports. In addition a number of other charges applied to imports: the municipality tax, transportation infrastructure tax, minerals surcharge, stamp duty, value added tax, housing fund tax, resource utilisation and support fund tax, and support and price stabilisation fund tax. As of 1992 stamp duty was levied at 10 per cent of the c.i.f. price of imports; municipal tax was charged at 15 per cent of the applicable customs duty on all imports; the transportation infrastructure tax was equal to four per cent of the tax-paid value of goods shipped by sea and three per cent for goods shipped by air or by road. A Support and Price Stabilisation Fund surcharge was levied at rates of three or ten per cent and the minerals surcharge stood at 2.5 per cent. Imports are also subject to value added tax. The base of the tax is the sum of the c.i.f. value, customs duty and all other surcharges.

At the beginning of the 1990s a second major reform was introduced. The import permit system was eliminated and all import formalities were eased and reduced to a minimum, including the abolition of the 'Import Guarantee Deposit Scheme'. Thus by the end of the 1980s all quantitative restrictions were abolished. Furthermore, under legislation adopted in late July 1992 all of the charges, in addition to customs duties, were abolished with effect from 1 January 1993, except the Mass Housing Fund Levy and the minerals surcharge. Further tariff concessions apply to raw materials, intermediate, and capital goods. Imports which were exempt from duty represented about 38 per cent of the total imports in 1992. In addition, holders of investment incentive certificates are eligible to import all investment machinery and equipment duty-free, and exporters are given the right to import intermediate inputs and other capital goods duty-free.

The balance of payments turnaround during the 1980s was achieved largely as a result of a dramatic improvement in exports. The increase in exports was achieved through a consistent export promotion policy, which relied on three primary instruments: exchange rate policy, credit policy, and fiscal incentives. During the 1980s the real exchange rate depreciated considerably. Furthermore, the government subsidised exports mainly through two channels: export credits and fiscal incentives. In the case of export credits the government has extended credit at preferential rates of interest to producers/exporters of selected products. During the first half of the 1980s, a substantial difference existed between the general lending rate and the rate of interest applied to export credits. That system however, was abrogated in 1985.

After 1987, preferential credits to exports were extended via the newly established Eximbank. The fiscal incentives (see Togan, 1994) have included the export tax rebates, cash grants financed by the 'Support and Price Stabilisation Fund', duty free imports of intermediates and raw materials, exemption from the production tax which was replaced later by exemption from the value added tax, foreign exchange allocations, exemption from the corporate income tax, rebate from the 'Resource Utilization Support Fund', exemption from various taxes related to alternative export transactions, and exemptions from freight rates.

- Export Tax Rebates: Reimbursement of indirect taxes for exporters was originally introduced in 1963. In April 1981, ten different lists of commodities were made eligible for rebates with the maximum rebate rate set at 20 per cent. In 1988 the maximum rate was set at 8 per cent and the system terminated at the end of the year.
- Foreign Exchange Allocations: The 'Export Promotion Decree' dated 25 January 1980, specified that exporters who hold Export Encouragement Certificates, granted by the Office of Incentives and Implementation at the State Planning Organisation, or letters of credit, could apply for foreign exchange. The exporter with a global sum of foreign exchange allocated had the right to duty free imports of intermediate and raw materials. The incentive value of the foreign exchange allocation was twofold. First, the exporter did not pay duties when importing the intermediates and raw materials; and second, at the beginning of the 1980s foreign exchange commanded a premium over its official rate.
- Payments from the Support and Price Stabilisation Fund: In December, 1986 a new system of cash incentives for exports was introduced. In general the premium provided through the Support and Price Stabilisation Fund was determined according to each ton of weight.
- Duty Free Imports of Intermediates: Exporters or manufacturer-exporters may import intermediates and raw materials to be incorporated in products that will be exported either directly by themselves or through subsidiary industries without paying customs duty and other related taxes.
- Exemption from Corporate Income Tax: In addition to the subsidy schemes

discussed above corporate income tax law has clauses on exemptions concerning exports. According to these clauses a portion of profits made on the export of industrial goods, fresh fruits and vegetables, marine products, as well as the revenues from freight to countries abroad and tourism revenues in foreign exchange, may be deducted from corporation income.

- Resource Utilisation Support Fund: Towards the end of 1984 the Government established at the Central Bank the Resource Utilisation Support Fund with a Decree dated 15 December 1984. The objective of the fund was to create additional resources for exports and investments in accordance with the objectives set out in the Annual Development Plans and Programmes. According to the regulations, all exports of commodities subject to the Price Stabilisation Support Fund would receive a two per cent subsidy, and all exports of commodities not subject to the Price Stabilisation Support Fund would receive a four per cent subsidy from the Resource Utilisation Support Fund. In April 1986 the two per cent rate was reduced to zero per cent, and the four per cent rate to two per cent. Export subsidies from the Resource Utilisation Support Fund were discontinued starting on 1 November 1986.
- Exemption from Freight Rates: According to the Communiqué dated April 1986 from the Money and Credit Board, a subsidy is to be paid for the transport of export products forwarded from Turkish ports to the ports of different groups of countries on a gross ton basis.
- Exemption from Various Taxes: All procedures related to exporting are exempt from taxes, duties and fees. The procedures include credits supplied by banks with the proviso that they be used for financing exports, fees charged by banks, insurance companies and public notaries related to the procedures they carry out concerning exports, taxes on bank and insurance company procedures and stamp duty.
- Fuel Oil and Electricity Subsidy: With a supplementary decree published on 11 May 1989, exporters could import the fuel-oil used in the production of goods to be exported without paying any customs duties and related taxes, and could buy the electricity used in the production of the goods to be exported with the Turkish Lira equivalent of US cent 1/Kwh.

Finally one should note that the use of restrictive export licensing schemes and export price controls was terminated in 1984 and export taxes were dismantled during the same period. Until the mid-1980s levies and surcharges were applied mainly to agricultural exports. Furthermore, voluntary export restraints apply in the textiles and clothing sector. In these cases exporters are allocated shares in the export quota for the EC, US and Canadian markets based on past performance. In 1985 Turkey joined the Subsidies Code, agreeing to eliminate export subsidies by 1989. In the meantime considerable progress has been made. Turkey has abolished the Resource Utilisation Support Premium Payments in 1986, Tax

Rebates in 1988, Support and Price Stabilisation Fund Payments in 1992, and the Corporate Tax Exemption in 1993. With the elimination of the difference between the market rate and the official rate of the exchange rate during the 1980s, the incentive value of the foreign exchange allocation schemes had already been reduced to zero during this decade. Furthermore, Turkey has eliminated all export taxes, and as a result of these changes has shifted from direct cash grants to a system of export credits and insurances.

Regarding the general trade policy orientation it should be noted that Turkey acceded to the GATT in 1951. It has accepted the MTN Agreements on Subsidies and Countervailing Measures and on Customs Valuation. It had observer status in other MTN Code Committees. Furthermore, Turkey has trade agreements with the European Union (EU), European Free Trade Association (EFTA) and Economic Co-operation Organisation (ECO). Turkey is a founding member of Black Sea Economic Co-operation (BSEC) and is a member of the Organisation of Islamic Conference (OIC). It is also a party to the GATT Protocol Relating to Trade Negotiations Amongst Developing Countries of 1971. The improvement of relations with the European Union is however considered to be the key objective of Turkey's trade policies.

4. TRADE RELATIONS WITH EUROPE

Turkey's application to the European Economic Community (EEC) was made on 31 July 1959. Following difficult and protracted negotiations, the application ultimately resulted in the signing in Ankara on 12 September 1963 of the Association Treaty. The Ankara Treaty came into force on 1 December 1964. The stated objective of the Agreement is to promote the continuous and balanced strengthening of trade and economic relations between the parties, while taking full account of the need to ensure accelerated development of the Turkish economy and the need to improve the level of employment and living conditions of the Turkish people. According to the Ankara Treaty, the association was to be implemented in three phases: a preparatory phase, a transition phase and a final phase. During the preparatory period, the EEC granted unilateral concessions to Turkey in the form of financial assistance and preferential tariffs on Turkey's traditional exports. In the meantime, Turkey didn't have to change its trade regime. On 16 May 1967, in Brussels, Turkey lodged its application for negotiations on entering the transition phase. The Additional Protocol to the Ankara Treaty was signed on 23 November 1970, and became effective on 1 January 1973.

The basic aim of the Additional Protocol was the eventual establishment of a customs union at the latest in 1995. During the first four years of the transitional period (1973–76), implementation of the Additional Protocol went ahead as planned. But at the beginning of 1973, the German government issued a ban on the recruitment of migrant workers from non-EC countries and the other member states soon followed suit. This was later supplemented by the introduction of visa requirements for Turks visiting EC countries. After 1976, Turkey-EC relations ran into problems. The process of implementing the Additional Protocol came to a virtual standstill. In January 1977, Turkey postponed the first step of its scheduled tariff alignment with the Common Customs Tariff. One year later it also postponed the third round of tariff reductions.

The government which came to power on 29 October 1979, launched a series of initiatives to revitalise the trade accord. But relations between the EC and Turkey were affected by the overthrow of the civilian government towards the end of 1980, and were not normalised until six years later. After the military take-over of 12 September 1980, the Community's aid programme to Turkey was frozen. With Turkey's possible exclusion from the Council of Europe, the relationship between Turkey and the Community became bitter. In 1984 a major reform was introduced in the Turkish import regime when the quota system was abolished. As a result Turkey has eliminated the use of quotas on all imports. Turkey – EC relations showed signs of normalisation only towards the end of 1986. On 14 April 1987, Turkey formally applied for EC membership. At the ad-hoc committee meeting in Brussels towards the end of 1988, Turkey promised to decrease the tariff rates on commodities in both the 12-year and the 22-year list by ten per cent each year during the period 1989 – 1992. Furthermore, Turkey promised to adopt the Common Customs Tariff of the Community over time. In particular, it was decided that Turkey should adjust its tariffs to the Common Customs Tariff of the Community by 20 per cent in 1989, by another 20 per cent on the 12-year list in 1991, and by an additional 20 per cent on the 22-year list in 1992. After the ad-hoc committee meeting, the tariff rates were in fact reduced by ten per cent at the beginning of both 1989 and 1990. Similarly, Turkey adjusted its tariffs to the Common Customs Tariff of the Community by 20 per cent in 1989.

On 5 February 1990, the EC member states concluded on the basis of the 'opinion' of the Commission on 18 December 1989, that it would be inappropriate for the Community which was itself undergoing major changes, while the whole of Europe was in a state of flux, to become involved in new accession negotiations. The completion in 1995 of the customs union, in accordance with the provisions of the Agreement, was considered by the Commission to be of prime importance for increased interdependence and integration between Turkey and the Community. At a meeting of the Association Council at ministerial level on 9 November, 1992, both sides agreed to restart the implementation of the provisions laid down in the Association Agreement. The Turkish government confirmed its readiness to finalise the establishment of a customs union with the EC by 1995 as foreseen in the agreement. The

Community agreed to the creation of an intensive political dialogue with Turkey at the highest level and showed its willingness to enhance economic and industrial co-operation. On 1 January, 1993, Turkey abolished all the non-tariff barriers to trade except the Mass Housing Fund duty and the EC Commission was informed that this would be phased out over the next five years at the latest. In March 1993 a common Steering Committee between EC and Turkey was set up in order to prepare for the completion of the customs union. Its work resulted in a list of topics to be discussed and solved in order to meet the 1995 deadline. The list was agreed at the November 1993 meeting of the Association Council. The list includes the free circulation of goods between the parties; implementation of the Community's common external tariff on goods from third parties; common trade policy; co-operation on the harmonisation of agricultural policy; mutual minimisation of restrictions on trade in services; harmonisation of commercial legislation as regards competition policy, state aids, anti-dumping legislation, intellectual and industrial property rights, and public procurement; and institutional provisions concerning decision-making and procedures of dispute settlement.

Table 1 provides estimates of nominal protection rates for the year 1994 as well as for the period after the formation of the customs union with the EU. From the table it follows that the economy wide nominal protection rate (NPR) in 1994 for trade with the EU amounts to 10.22 per cent and that the economy wide NPR in 1994 for trade with third countries amounts to 22.14 per cent. The frequency distribution of the NPR's reveals that among the 49 tradable goods industries considered, there were three (five) industries in 1994 which had a NPR higher than 50 per cent in trade with EU (third countries), and that there were 33 (28) industries which had a NPR of less than 20 per cent in trade with the EU and with third countries. Examination of the characteristics of the structure of protection in trade with the EU reveals that the highest NPRs in trade with the EU were in the sectors 'fruits and vegetables' (72.49 per cent), 'alcoholic beverages' (72.1 per cent) and 'nonalcoholic beverages' (56.92 per cent). In the case of trade with third countries we note that the highest NPRs were granted to the sectors 'processed tobacco' (99.91 per cent), 'alcoholic beverages' (94.28 per cent) and 'fruits and vegetables' (72.62 per cent).

With the formation of a customs union with the EU in 1995 Turkey has to reduce the nominal protection rates for all of the commodities belonging to the 12-year and 22-year lists to zero. As from 1995, Turkey does not intend to adjust its agricultural policy to the common agricultural policy. As a result nominal protection rates on agricultural commodities will remain unchanged. Table 1, column 3, shows the NPRs that will prevail after the completion of the customs union in 1995. From the table it follows that among the 49 tradable goods industries considered, there will be one industry which will have a NPR higher than 50 per cent in trade with the EU. There will be 44 (4) industries which will

TABLE 1
Nominal Protection Rates Before and After the Customs Union with the EU

1–0 Code	*Sector Name*	*NPR with EU in 1994*	*NPR with Third Countries in 1994*	*NPR with EU after Customs Union*
1	Agriculture	41.27	41.65	41.26
2	Animal husbandry	3.48	4.18	1.37
3	Forestry	0.01	0.10	0.01
4	Fishery	47.92	54.08	47.84
5	Coal mining	3.33	3.33	0.00
6	Crude petroleum	5.59	11.14	0.00
7	Iron ore mining	0.00	2.22	0.00
8	Other metalic ore mining	0.13	1.21	0.00
9	Non-metallic mining	9.09	11.02	0.00
10	Stone quarrying	1.95	2.18	0.00
11	Slaughtering and meat	10.21	10.21	10.21
12	Fruits and vegetables	72.49	72.62	68.01
13	Vegetable and animal oil	16.31	16.38	16.31
14	Grain mill products	41.33	41.33	41.02
15	Sugar refining	28.79	28.79	28.79
16	Other food processing	26.47	28.99	18.31
17	Alcoholic beverages	72.10	94.28	5.25
18	Non-alcoholic beverages	56.92	69.81	0.00
19	Processed tobacco	44.40	99.91	0.00
20	Ginning	0.00	2.22	0.00
21	Textiles	21.19	27.10	0.00
22	Clothing	14.75	20.65	0.00
23	Leather and fur production	7.85	12.57	0.00
24	Footwear	24.40	35.70	0.00
25	Wood products	15.25	18.97	0.00
26	Wood furniture	26.22	32.64	0.00
27	Paper and paper products	13.59	17.58	0.00
28	Printing and publishing	8.23	10.79	0.00
29	Fertilisers	8.22	16.38	0.00
30	Pharmaceutical production	3.33	8.99	0.00
31	Other chemical production	10.79	17.62	0.00
32	Petroleum refining	22.54	24.35	0.00
33	Petroleum and coal products	5.62	7.52	0.00
34	Rubber products	19.57	23.91	0.00
35	Plastic products	24.61	31.68	0.00
36	Glass and glass production	16.85	21.94	0.00
37	Cement	30.45	32.88	0.00
38	Non-metallic mineral	18.33	23.21	0.00
39	Iron and steel	8.00	10.70	0.00
40	Non-ferrous metals	4.52	8.43	0.00
41	Fabricated metal products	18.36	25.29	0.00
42	Non-electrical machinery	7.36	12.50	0.00
43	Agricultural machinery	6.98	12.18	0.00
44	Electrical machinery	9.69	16.64	0.00
45	Shipbuilding and repairing	6.13	12.89	0.00
46	Railroad equipment	0.00	4.61	0.00
47	Motor vehicles	27.33	33.10	0.00
48	Other transport equipment	0.01	1.76	0.00
49	Other manufacturing industries	2.92	8.19	0.00
	Mean[1]	10.22	22.14	1.34
	Standard Deviation	17.68	15.36	14.48

Note:
[1] Weighted by sectoral import values.

have a NPR of less than 20 per cent (between 20 and 40 per cent) in trade with the EU. After the formation of the customs union the average nominal protection rate will be reduced to 1.34 per cent in trade with the EU. Furthermore, we note that the highest NPR in trade with the EU will be granted to the sectors 'fruits and vegetables' (68.01 per cent), 'fishery' (47.84 per cent) and 'agriculture' (41.26 per cent).

In the case of trade with third parties, a distinction has to be introduced for trade with EFTA countries, the Mediterranean countries, the Central and Eastern European (CEE) countries, developing countries having GSP treatment, and the Lomé Convention countries. With each of these country groups the EU has concluded preferential agreements. Since Turkey, after the formation of the customs union, will have to apply the Community's common customs tariffs and accept all the preferential agreements which the EU has concluded over time, Turkey will be faced with a different set of tariff rates for different groups of countries. In the case of EFTA and the Central and Eastern European (CEE) countries the nominal tariff rates will be identical to those of the EU. Thus the NPR's given in column 3 of Table 1 will have to apply to about 53 per cent of imports. For these countries the average tariff rates will decrease from 10.22 to 1.34 per cent. Studies carried out on the tariff rates in the EU reveal that the average MFN tariff rates of the EU before the completion of the Uruguay Round were 4.2 per cent whereas the combined MFN-GSP rates were 2.5 per cent. Hence for these countries the tariff rates will decrease at different rates but in any case they will decrease substantially from the 22.14 per cent level.

Turkey considers the formation of the customs union with the EU as an intermediate step towards the achievement of full-membership of the European Union. The country recognises that increased competition to be achieved through the customs union will lead in the long run to improved resource allocation and thus to welfare gains. There will be static as well as dynamic gains for Turkey. Furthermore, the EU is likely to be the major source of technology and investment for Turkey in the coming decades. As a preferential trading arrangement, membership of the EU is seen as the first-best option. The membership would lock in political and economic reforms and provide the much needed credibility to political and economic reforms. On 6 March 1995, it was agreed at the Association Council meeting in Brussels that Turkey would join the European customs union starting on 1 January 1996. The Agreement will be effective after ratification by the European Parliament towards the end of 1995. According to the time table specified in the customs union agreement, Turkey will

(i) eliminate all customs duties, quantitative restrictions, all charges which have equivalent effect to customs duties, and all measures having equivalent effect to quantitative restrictions in trade with the EU, as of 1

January 1996,
(ii) adopt the Common Customs Tariff against third country imports by 1 January 1996,
(iii) adopt all of the preferential agreements which the EU has concluded with third countries by the year 2001,
(iv) incorporate within five years into its internal legal order the Community instruments relating to the removal of technical barriers to trade,
(v) implement the TRIPS Agreement until 1999, and
(vi) adopt the EU competition rules within two years (aid given for structural adjustment purposes will be considered compatible with the functioning of customs union for another five years).

As emphasised above, Turkey in 1994 has faced balance of payments crisis. It has introduced stabilisation measures and has signed a stand-by agreement with the International Monetary Fund. Currently the country is facing problems with increasing unemployment. Under these circumstances the adjustment of the Turkish economy to further competition from the EU and third countries will not be easy. Furthermore, a recent study conducted by the State Planning Organisation in Ankara reveals that the reduction in nominal protection rates after the formation of the customs union will result in a reduction of annual tax revenue amounting to about $2.3 billion. The country has to introduce new taxes if it does not want the reduction in tax revenue to result in higher PSBR/GNP ratios and hence in higher inflation rates. An alternative solution would be for the EU to finance the amount on an annual basis during the next few years.

Abstracting from this unlikely outcome, it should be emphasised that new taxes will have to be introduced at a time when adjustment in sectors where the country does not have comparative advantage will lead to further increases in unemployment. Social and political tensions in the country will increase. Furthermore, all these adjustments will have to take place when the government tries to privatise the public enterprises in an economy which has an insufficient social security net. As of 1995 Turkey is willing to bear all of the short run costs of establishing the customs union. It thus seems that the Turkish economy with the formation of the customs union will bear all of the costs of adjustment without getting the kind of assistance that Greece, Portugal and Spain received from the EU when they joined the Community. Furthermore, Turkey will have to fulfil most of the obligations of membership of the EU without being represented by its policy making bodies.

5 PROSPECTS AND FUTURE ISSUES

During the last decade when Turkey was engaged with problems of customs union, the eighth and most ambitious Round of multilateral trade negotiations carried out under the auspices of the General Agreement on Tariffs and Trade ended on 15 December 1993, with consensus. Besides the tariff reductions this Round dealt with complex issues like agriculture, textiles, trade in services, intellectual property rights and trade related investment measures. As a result 1995 has started with new hopes for international trade, with the new 'World Trade Organisation' established. The expected increase in global real income due to the Uruguay Round is estimated to range from $212 billion to $274 billion (in 1992 dollars), which is equivalent to about one per cent of world GDP in 1992. The largest beneficiaries will be the EU, the USA, the former USSR and Eastern Europe, third world manufactures and agricultural exports. On the other hand, Turkey expects to irrigate 1.6 million hectares of land alongside the Euphrates and Tigris rivers and their tributaries over the next decade with the completion of the Southeast Anatolian Project (GAP). This will result in substantially increased agricultural output in Turkey. Since the Uruguay Round is expected to lead to higher world agricultural prices as a result of reduced agricultural subsidies by the industrial countries, Turkey stands to gain from the liberalisation of agricultural trade. Similar considerations apply to trade in textiles and also in manufactures. Although Turkey will face increased competition from countries like China, India and Pakistan, Turkish industrialists are enthusiastic about the increased market access opportunities. Furthermore, Turkey as a result of improved rules on subsidies, anti-dumping actions, the framework for services, improvements in procedures for the settlement of disputes and higher standards of intellectual property is expected to gain. As competition increases within the country, resources will shift to more efficient sectors and as a result productivity and living standards will increase.

Turkey realises that the long run aim of increasing the GNP per capita over time can be achieved by having the customs union with the EU, but this is certainly not the only alternative. It is recognised that by opening the economy further to foreign trade and by taking the necessary measures to increase competition by following the rules of the Uruguay Round, Turkey will benefit from this increased competition. Policy makers being aware of these facts are willing to liberalise further the trade regime and implement effectively the measures regarding the intellectual, industrial and commercial property and export subsidies as specified by the Uruguay Round. On the formation of the customs union with the EU however, all of the main measures required by the Uruguay Round agreement will have to be implemented. In addition, Turkey will be required to introduce the EU rules relating to competition and also the provisions with respect to state aids.

Finally, the close relations between Turkey and the Republics of Central Asia and of Caucasus should be mentioned. Turkey is a key object of interest to the Republics, and a model of much attraction, economically as well as culturally. In the long run Turkey might find a natural market in the Republics which have attractive natural gas and hydrocarbon reserves. The Eurasian world around the Caspian Sea with as much as 50 bn barrels of reserves, second only to the Persian Gulf in terms of oil reserves, could become a stable source of oil for the West over the next decades. The region also has one third of the world's gas resources. As Western companies move towards the arrangement that will permit the development of Eurasian hydrocarbon reserves, the problem of how to get Eurasian oil and gas to the world markets remains to be solved. In this context it should be emphasised that the Baku-Ceyhan route to the Mediterranean via Turkey has emerged as one of the most viable routes. Thus Turkey is well positioned geographically and economically to act as an energy bridge between Western Europe and Eurasia.

REFERENCES

Krueger, A.O. (1974), *Foreign Trade Regimes and Economic Development: Turkey*. A Special Conference on Foreign Trade Regimes and Economic Development, Vol. 1 (NBER, new York).

Togan, S. (1994), *Foreign Trade Regime and Trade Liberalization in Turkey During the 1980s* (Avebury, Aldereshot).

GATT Trade Policy Review — South Africa: 1993

Merle Holden

1. INTRODUCTION

SOUTH Africa has finally emerged from the international isolation of the decades of the Apartheid era. In April 1994, the first democratic election was followed by the installation of a Government of National Unity under the leadership of Nelson Mandela. International sanctions have subsequently been lifted and South Africa is both free to trade and welcome to participate in international forums and organisations. However, while this political transformation continues, the accompanying economic transition is still to occur on a number of broad fronts. There is national recognition that emergence from the distorting and debilitating effects of apartheid and the resulting siege economy will entail a major reconstruction of the economy accompanied by substantial transition costs. The government has responded by advancing a strategy for a fundamental transformation that has been encapsulated in a White Paper on Reconstruction and Development. This blueprint for change was published in September 1994.

The 1993 GATT Trade Review for South Africa must be viewed against this background of profound political and economic change. How South Africa will be classified by the GATT has considerable bearing on these changes given the time frame allocated for the phasing in of proposed trade reforms. South Africa is currently classified as a 'developed' country and will be given three years for the elimination of certain trade interventions such as export subsidies. If the classification is changed to a 'country in transition', which many interested parties desire, these trade interventions can be phased out in eight years. If there is a weakness in the GATT Trade Review, it is the failure to address the thorny issue of the phasing in of trade reform in a country that will experience problems with transition while at the same time emerging from a prolonged recession and deeply engrained distortions in the economy.

MERLE HOLDEN is from the Department of Economics, University of Natal, South Africa.

This review summarises the main features of South Africa's trade policy regime and assesses its relevance to the present needs of the country. A brief overview of the economy is provided to facilitate an appreciation of its structure and performance in recent years. Against this background an attempt is made to assess the quality of the Trade Policy Review and establish the possibilities for future reform.

2. THE ECONOMY

South Africa has been classified as a middle income country that enjoys levels of per capita income of approximately US$2,800, or US$3,200 when expressed in terms of purchasing power parity. It is a country that is well endowed with many mineral resources. Notable among these is gold, which provides over 50 per cent of export earnings. Although the importance of the agricultural sector to the economy has diminished in terms of its contribution to Gross Domestic Product, agricultural exports remain an important mainstay of the balance of payments. Despite having followed a policy of import replacement, imports in the manufacturing sector in South Africa amount to 220 per cent of the manufactured goods exported (Industrial Development Corporation, 1990), while total imports are 16.2 per cent of GDP (Table 1).

In general, monetary and fiscal policies have been well managed. Although management of the exchange rate has been subject to criticism, the economy has been subjected to severe external shocks that have made the task difficult. Transport networks are well developed and electricity generation has not provided a constraint on growth. Nevertheless, economic growth has been disappointing since the early seventies, having declined from an average of five per cent per annum to zero per cent per annum from 1988 to 1993.

TABLE 1
Key Economic Features

Population	38.4
GDP	US$107.6bn
GDP per capita	US$2,803
Agriculture (% GDP)	5.0
Mining (% GDP)	11.0
Manufacturing (% GDP)	26.0
Merchandise exports (fob)	US$23.7bn
Merchandise imports (fob)	US$17.4bn
Merchandise exports (% GDP)	22.0
Merchandise imports (% GDP)	16.2
Current Account Surplus (% GDP)	5.0

The GATT Trade Review suggests both external and domestic reasons for this poor performance. External reasons range from the deleterious effects of drought on agricultural output, the declining price of gold and other minerals and the effects of both financial and goods sanctions during the eighties. The domestic reasons point to the pervasive effects of the anti-competitive stance followed by the apartheid regime in terms of the import replacement policies and the restrictions that were placed on the movement of black labour. The shortage of skilled, managerial and professional expertise that arose from the restrictions which were placed on black access to good education and jobs was also a major constraining factor on growth in South Africa throughout the post World War II period. The results of this labour market discrimination are reflected in high levels of income inequality. In 1991 the per capita income of whites was 12.3 times higher than African per capita incomes and 5.4 and 3.0 times higher than coloured and Asian per capita incomes, respectively. (See Whiteford and McGrath, 1994.)

In addition to intervening in the labour market, the State also sought to establish certain strategic industries to insulate the economy against international sanctions. The Review recognises the extreme form of import replacement that was followed in industries such as iron and steel, oil-from-coal and natural gas. It also conjectures that the cost of capital was kept low in order to finance such capital-intensive ventures. It has been through the establishment of such industries that the structure of industry is considered to be highly capital-intensive. In addition to negative real interest rates which kept the cost of capital low during the 1970s and early 1980s, tax incentives were used to stimulate capital formation. Furthermore, rising labour costs during the same period encouraged the observed trend towards greater capital intensity in industry. Research has shown that resource intensive industry and high levels of import protection have also contributed to high levels of concentration (Fourie and Smith, 1993), which have led to calls for unbundling and the implementation of tougher anti-trust legislation.

Despite such capital formation, growth in total factor productivity not only declined in the early seventies but became negative through to the early eighties (Fallon and Pereira de Silva, 1994). The Review is of the view that:

> Slow productivity growth and declining international competitiveness can be attributed both to the factor market distortions induced by South Africa's internal and external trade policies and to South Africa's international isolation, which has contributed to limiting both local and international competition and raising the price of imported technology (GATT Review, 1993, p. 11).

An interesting omission in the Review, however, is the extraordinarily limited role which is assigned to the real exchange rate in the development of the economy. It has been shown that movements in the nominal exchange rate have largely been driven by changes in the price of gold as well as by capital flows

(Gerson and Kahn, 1988). For example, the competitiveness of tradables was severely reduced by the real appreciations of the late seventies and early eighties. It is therefore not surprising that trade liberalisation efforts were suspended in 1983. The rand then depreciated in real terms in the middle eighties. This enhanced the competitiveness of exports in the face of international sanctions.

In recent years, the necessity to maintain current surpluses in the region of five per cent of GDP to finance the capital flight and foreign debt repayment has both driven the exchange rate and dampened growth. While considerations of competitiveness in the management of the exchange rate were overriding in the middle eighties, later in the decade the Reserve Bank sought to use the exchange rate to reduce the rate of inflation. This took place while the competitiveness of exports was maintained by the General Export Incentive Scheme.

3. TRADE POLICY OBJECTIVES

Trade policy in South Africa has largely been directed at substituting domestic production for imports. As early as 1956, the principle of infant industry protection was used by the Viljoen Commission to justify the use of protection in the drive towards industrialisation. This inward-looking trade regime was implemented by means of import tariffs and periodic quantitative restrictions. The severity of these import controls was determined by the state of the balance of payments.

In the 1970s, the process of dismantling import controls was commenced partly in response to pressure from trading partners. In addition, it was recognised that import substitution was no longer the engine of growth that it had been in the 1950s in the 'easier' consumer and intermediate goods industries (Scheepers, 1969). Both the Reynders Commission in 1973 and the Van Huyssteen Committee in 1980 stressed that trade policy should be orientated towards exports. These committees recognised that production of capital goods domestically would be uneconomic given the size of the domestic market. By 1980, exporters received uniform incentives through direct cash grants, tax concessions on export turnover, rail freight concessions, drawbacks and rebates of import duties on imported inputs, tax concessions based on the disadvantage of using tariff-laden inputs and tax concessions on profits derived from exports. These changes in trade policy are reflected in the relationship between exports and growth in South Africa. Between 1947 and 1970 it was growth in manufacturing output that promoted growth in exports, whereas between 1970 and 1987 it was exports that influenced growth in manufacturing (Holden, 1990). During this period, import substitution no longer promoted growth and exports were given more attention by policy makers.

The dismantling of import controls was temporarily halted in the early 1980s with the fall in the price of gold and the concomitant impact on the balance of payments. In 1983 the relaxation of controls was resumed and by 1985 a relatively small proportion, 28 per cent of the manufacturing tariff lines and 23 per cent of the value of imports, were still covered by import permits (Industrial Development Corporation, 1990). South Africa was also able to switch from a positive list of permitted imports, to a negative list of imported items which required approval. During this period import tariffs were raised to compensate for the loss of protection provided by the quantitative restrictions. In 1985 the foreign debt standstill resulted in the introduction of a ten per cent import surcharge. This was subsequently increased to 60 per cent in 1988 on certain luxury goods in an attempt to preserve the current account surplus. Since 1990 the import surcharge has been slowly lowered. In 1993 import controls only affected 15 per cent of all tariff lines (GATT Review, 1993).

In April 1990, the General Export Incentive Scheme (GEIS) was introduced to replace the earlier less transparent export incentives. This scheme incorporated selectivity, simplicity, and some protection against exchange rate fluctuations. Those industries which had a high value-added and high local content received a tax-free cash subsidy amounting to 19.5 per cent of export turnover. The scheme has cost approximately R1bn per annum in cash payments. However, as the GEIS contravenes the GATT and its financing has proved to be onerous, South Africa has announced its intention to phase out the scheme in 1995.

4. TRADE LAWS AND REGULATIONS

There are a large number of Acts of Parliament pertaining to trade policy. The most important of these are the Customs and Excise Act of 1964, the Import and Export Control Act of 1963 and the Board of Tariffs and Trade Act of 1992. The Customs and Excise Act provides the mechanism for levying tariffs and other import charges including import surcharges, anti-dumping and countervailing duties and refunds and rebates of duty. The Import and Export Control Act, on the other hand, provides the authority for quantitative border controls. The Minister of Finance can amend the schedules to the Act subject to ratification by Parliament. Appeals on customs valuation and tariff decisions are made to the Supreme Court. As the tariff schedules are unduly complex these appeals have proved to be very time-consuming for the Department of Customs and Excise. The Board on Tariffs and Trade Act was passed in order to alter the name of the Board of Trade and Industry and clearly define its functions. This Act also defines dumping and subsidisation of imports. Any countervailing action however is taken by the Minister of Trade and Industry which allows for trade policy to be integrated with industrial policy.

5. TRADE AGREEMENTS

a. Multilateral Agreements

Despite its previous pariah status in the international community, South Africa, was a founding member of the GATT. South Africa has accepted the MTN Tokyo Round Agreements on Customs Valuation and Import Licensing and has observer status in the MTN Agreements on Government Procurement, Anti-dumping, Subsidies and Countervailing Action. South Africa has not participated in the Multifibre Arrangement, but is involved in the International Dairy and Bovine Meat Arrangements. South Africa is also a member of the International Wheat Council, the International Cotton Advisory Committee and has acceded to the Convention on International Trade in Endangered Species as well as the Montreal Protocol.

At the time of the review, South Africa accorded most-favoured nation (mfn) treatment to all contracting parties except Egypt, India, and those countries that apply the GATT on a *de facto* basis (GATT Review, 1993, p. 47). Since the review, India and South Africa have accorded each other mfn treatment.

b. Regional Agreements

South Africa is a key member of the Southern African Customs Union (SACU), which contains Botswana, Lesotho and Swaziland and Namibia. This is the only customs union in Africa. As most of the external trade for these members enters through South Africa, the common external customs duties as well as excise duties are collected by South Africa. This common pool is then distributed according to a revenue-sharing formula which contains both a stabilisation factor and an allowance contribution for the effects of polarisation of industry towards South Africa.

The Review (p. 48) notes that South Africa contributes 90 per cent to the revenue pool and only retains 43 per cent, and comments on the importance of these payments to the smaller members of the union. The size of the revenue pool has grown as quantitative restrictions in South Africa were replaced by import tariffs with the implication that any contemplated move towards trade liberalisation on South Africa's part will have severe budgetary implications for these members (Lundahl and Petersson, 1991). Analysts of trade data for South Africa must be warned that because of SACU, exports and imports for South Africa are reported on a SACU basis.

c. Bilateral Agreements

South Africa has trade agreements with Zimbabwe and Malawi, and grants certain unilateral tariff concessions on imports from Mozambique. Until recently, Turkey enjoyed similar unilateral tariff concessions. Within the last year, trade agreements which exempted import surcharges were also concluded with Hungary, Romania, Poland and the Czech Republic.

Finally in 1994, GSP agreements will come on stream with the European Union and the United States. These will provide benefits to South African exporters amounting to an estimated R55bn and R10bn, respectively.

6. TRADE DISPUTES

The Review notes that no complaints have been brought against South Africa under the GATT dispute settlement procedures. Only one Article XXIII case was brought to the GATT by the South Africans in 1984. This case concerned the manner in which the provincial government of Ontario applied a retail sales tax to the sale of gold coins in order to protect the domestic production of gold coins. The Ontario government subsequently removed this differential tax treatment in 1986.

In 1988, South Africa notified the Uruguay Round Surveillance Body of the unilateral imposition of fixed quota requirements by Canada on imports of wool worsted fabrics and certain clothing. This resulted in a bilateral agreement setting quantitative restrictions which included an allowance for annual growth. South Africa also made a written submission as an interested third party regarding the quotas on dessert apples into the European Community. This resulted in the Council adopting the findings of the dispute settlement panel report in 1989. It is interesting that the Review makes no mention of how sanctions were treated by the GATT dispute mechanisms during the 1980s.

a. Type and Incidence of Trade and Industrial Policy Measures

By virtue of its large number of tariff rates, wide range of tariffs and high coefficient of variation, the system of protection in South Africa has been described as one of the most complex in the world by the World Bank (Fallon et al., 1993). Although the tariff is now the main instrument of protection in the manufacturing sector, it has nevertheless been described in the Review as lacking in transparency and characterised by great fluidity.

The tariff schedule comprises over 12,600 9-digit tariff lines under the Harmonised System, with the majority being applied on mfn terms. The GATT Tariff Study shows that in 1988 the average unweighted mfn tariff for all products was 22 per cent. This has to be compared with an average of 22.5 per cent on industrial products and 12.6 per cent on agricultural products. However, it must be borne in mind that formula duties, which are a characteristic of the South African system, distort these averages, while tariff equivalents for the import

TABLE 2
Nominal Rates of Protection, 1990 (%)

Category	*Tariff*	*Import Surcharge*	*Total*
Primary products	2.5	0.6	3.1
Processed primary products	12.0	2.5	14.5
Material-Intensive products	28.3	5.7	34.0
Manufactured products	26.9	13.4	40.3
Capital goods	9.8	10.4	20.2

Source: IMF (1992), Table 2.

controls on agricultural goods and textiles are not included. Nevertheless, these simple averages do not show the wide variation which exists between sectors. This ranges from 5.6 per cent on cut flowers and plants to 63.3 per cent on tobacco. Once tariffs have been cut in accordance with the Uruguay Round Agreement, the GATT Tariff Study estimates that the average tariff should fall to 13.9 per cent. The tariff schedule has also been shown to escalate from 2.5 per cent on primary products to 26.9 per cent on manufactured goods (Table 2).

Table 2 shows that in addition to the scheduled tariffs, the import surcharge increased the degree of escalation in the tariff. At the time of the Review this averaged six per cent and ranged up to 40 per cent on beverages, tobacco and clothing. Formula duties apply to approximately one-sixth of all tariff lines. This duty is calculated as a normal *ad valorem* plus the difference between a reference price and the fob price in the country of origin. The reference price is based on European or North American prices. The application of the formula has resulted in *ad valorem* equivalents being a multiple of the straight *ad valorem*.

The formula duty is applied when the export price is lower than the reference price. These duties have been justified on the grounds of protecting domestic firms against the effects of 'disruptive competition'. In many cases the *ad valorem* equivalent of the formula duties amounts to greater than 40 per cent. It is planned to phase out the formula duties when new anti-dumping legislation is introduced.

Less than 20 per cent of the tariffs are bound in terms of the GATT. However, with the South African offer in the Uruguay Round, the proportion bound will rise to just over 50 per cent. In addition, the average tariff on industrial goods will decline by a third, while the percentage of duty-free tariff lines will rise from less than 20 per cent to just over 25 per cent. South Africa's offer to the GATT therefore represents a significant improvement in trade liberalisation.

The Review correctly points to the *ad hoc* and selective manner in which tariff protection and rebates of tariffs have been granted in South Africa. The Board of Tariff and Trade has been known to adjust tariffs on a weekly basis which, when combined with the degree of complexity of the tariff machinery, lends itself to

TABLE 3
Estimates of Effective Protection: 1988 (%)

Subsector	*Protection on Inputs*	*Protection on Outputs*	*Effective Protection*
Food & Beverages	15.2	13.7	8.8
Textiles & Clothing	27.8	43.6	93.6
Wood & Wood Products	14.0	21.7	39.7
Paper & Paper Products	9.5	13.3	22.2
Chemicals	7.5	18.9	50.6
Non-Metallic Minerals	5.2	19.8	34.3
Basic Metals	4.7	11.2	23.2
Metal Products	17.1	18.2	20.3
Other Manufacturing	2.8	10.9	62.8
Total Manufacturing	12.6	17.8	30.2

Source: Ondersoek Na Die Tariefbeskermings Beleid. Ontleding van die Tariefstruktuur (Industrial Development Corporation, 1990).

confusion on the part of importers. It has also been coupled with evasion and corruption.

When considering applications for protection, the Board of Tariffs and Trade takes into account the degree of effective protection. The Board has stated that it will in general only support applications which lead to effective protection amounting to 30 per cent. Unfortunately, in the more recent studies of effective protection in South Africa, calculations of levels of effective protection have only taken into account the price-raising effects of tariffs. Tariff equivalents of the remaining quantitative restrictions on agricultural and textiles imports have not been included. Estimates of effective protection in 1988 for the manufacturing sector that were made on this basis by the Industrial Development Corporation are shown in Table 3.

These estimates of effective protection that take into account the tariff structure include the import surcharge but exclude the GEIS. Textiles and clothing, the most labour-intensive of the sectors, are paradoxically the most heavily protected, while food and beverages, which draw intermediate inputs from domestic agriculture and are protected by import controls, are the least protected sectors.

The percentage of tariff lines under import control by category varies quite substantially. Over 90 per cent of the tariff lines are affected in beverages, tobacco and rubber, 9 per cent of textiles and 59 per cent of clothing (GATT, Review). Although the Review states that the Industrial Development Corporation (1990) has estimated that these import controls add ten per cent to the nominal rate of protection, the research basis for such a conclusion is insubstantial without a comparison of international and domestic prices. Controls are in the process of being phased out, however, and, in agriculture, it is planned that they will be replaced by tariff equivalents.

Measures to address the anti-export bias inherent in the system of import substitution culminated with the introduction of the General Export Incentive Scheme (GEIS) in April 1990. The GEIS provides tax-free assistance to exporters based on export value, the degree of local content and extent of value-added. Primary products and motor vehicles are excluded from the GEIS. Other export promoting initiatives include duty-free inputs for export processing, low interest loans for investment in export capacity, attractive export credits and state reimbursement of outlays on export promotion. The accelerated depreciation allowances under Section 37e of the Income Tax Act, which encouraged the establishment of capital-intensive export capacity, was phased out in 1993. In 1992/93 over R2bn was disbursed in export subsidies with the GEIS accounting for just over R1bn. These amounts have to be measured against the total customs duty and import surcharges which amounted to R4.1bn for the same period.

The degree of anti-export bias inherent in the trade regime is not addressed in the Review, probably because in the past it has been difficult to obtain the necessary data, and the reviewing team did not see fit to make any estimates. Now that sanctions are no longer in force and international agencies such as the World Bank and the GATT are much in evidence in South Africa, pressure has been placed on government agencies to provide information. Research should now proceed in this area.

As a stop gap measure, incidence measures were estimated using a methodology developed by Greenaway and Milner (1987). This shows that for the period 1974 to 1987, when gold is included, protection of importables resulted in a substantial proportion of this protection (71 per cent) being shifted in the form of an implicit tax onto exportables. When gold is excluded, only 34 per cent of the protection was shifted onto manufacturing exportables (Holden, 1992). When the GEIS was introduced, a rough estimate that incorporated the GEIS and tariff protection only, was made for individual sectors. These estimates allowed for the tax-free status of the GEIS and the access to duty free inputs for exporters. It was found that with the GEIS, 27 industries would have found it attractive to produce for the foreign market, with 40 industries still preferring the domestic market (Holden, 1993). These estimates show that despite the GEIS, anti-export bias has not been fully addressed.

Research has been unable to establish the role of the GEIS in stimulating exports. In the past, South African exports have been shown to be very sensitive to the real exchange rate and the degree of excess capacity in the economy. Given that policy-makers in South Africa recognise that the GEIS directly contravenes the GATT (GATT Review, 1993, Vol. II), there is a real danger of stifling export-led growth if the GEIS is eliminated while protection is maintained. On the other hand, the GEIS has created the opportunity for corruption through firms importing goods, adding large mark-ups, claiming local content under the GEIS, over-invoicing exports and, finally, exporting goods of little value at high prices and then reimporting in a different form with low prices. The existence of such corruption coupled with the legality of the GEIS has led to cessation of its tax free status and a review by April 1995.

Industries which have received special treatment in South Africa and have been extensively commented on in the Review are motor vehicles, textiles and clothing. Manufacturers of textiles and clothing have been in conflict as to the form of intervention appropriate to their often conflicting interests. The protection granted to textiles and cotton growers has undermined the competitiveness of down-stream users, and duty-free imports of inputs for clothing exporters have been abused reducing the textile manufacturers' profits. As these sectors employ over 200,000 people, account for 15 per cent of total employment in manufacturing, and represent five per cent of manufacturing production, short-run employment losses will result from any trade liberalisation. This will have to be buffered with adjustment assistance.

The motor vehicle sector, is the third largest manufacturing sector employing 80,000 workers. It operates on a local content programme that is achieved by reducing imports or increasing exports. Firms are able to import components duty-free if they export. The scheme has not produced any significant savings in foreign exchange and has raised local content to 71 per cent at the cost of adding an estimated 12 per cent to the price of cars (GATT Review, 1993).

7. TRADE REFORM INITIATIVES

Trade liberalisation, as measured in the World Bank studies (Michaely et al., 1991), has proceeded in South Africa. Quantitative restrictions are being phased out and the exchange rate depreciated in real terms. Yet much remains to be done given the extreme selectivity in import protection and export promotion. The Review points to the lack of transparency and stability in the tariff structure and suggests greater uniformity in the tariff, a pre-announced schedule of tariff reductions, a phasing out of the import surcharge and a review of the system of duty rebates in order to provide a more stable and predictable trading environment for both South African and foreign firms.

The Department of Trade and Industry, at the behest of the Minister, is working with the Board of Tariffs and Trade and the Industrial Development Corporation to simplify the tariff system. The GATT offer included a cut in tariffs of approximately 30 per cent on 42 per cent of all tariff lines over a five-year period. Formula duties would be replaced with *ad valorem* duties with the overall intention to reduce tariffs to a maximum of 30 per cent on consumer goods and 15 per cent on other goods. The timing of such tariff cuts is critical as is also the necessity for adjustment allowances for affected firms and workers.

Improvements in the rebate and drawback procedures are being investigated. A quicker more automatic system of rebates is being considered and export processing zones are under discussion with the intention of establishing a free trade environment for exporters. Furthermore, financial assistance in the form of export insurance, export guarantees and export credit is being examined. These measures are recognised as being very necessary for the encouragement of exports once the GEIS is phased out.

In addition to the steps to reform trade which are in the process of being taken, significant progress has been made to reform industrialisation policy and privatise para-statals. While the Review points to the commercialisation of public enterprises, the Government of National Unity has recently announced the intention to privatise those public enterprises which do not play a 'developmental' role in the economy. Price control on a range of goods has been abolished and controls in the farm and food sectors are in the process of being deregulated with the phasing out of their marketing through Control Boards.

One of the last vestiges of the apartheid era, namely the decentralisation of industry policy, has been substantially modified. Wage, interest and relocation incentives are no longer offered and have been replaced with a profit incentive scheme for decentralised firms.

8. CONCLUSION

This review of trade policies in South Africa by the GATT is one of the most comprehensive reviews available and is proving to be an invaluable reference for policy makers, business, labour and academics. The Review establishes that although there had been favourable changes in trade policy in South Africa, international sanctions had slowed the pace of such reforms leaving the economy biased against exports whilst encouraging production for the domestic market. Nevertheless, there is a recognition in the Review that policy makers in South Africa intend to proceed with the liberalisation of markets. Many of the new initiatives which have come to fruition since the review bear testimony to this.

On a more personal note, it gave me as a researcher in South Africa, a great deal of pleasure tinged with some envy, to see data on trade, which in the apartheid and sanctions years were secret, now being freely available. As South Africa starts to enjoy greater transparency, the operation of government and business will be subject to much closer scrutiny and accountability, and the benefits and costs of policy changes clarified. In this era of change and transition it seems safe to predict that, as South Africa rejoins the international community, the benefits of an open economy will be magnified by a closer integration of markets and informational flows.

REFERENCES

Fallon, P., A. Aksoy, Y. Tsikata, P. Belli and L. Pereira da Silva (1993), 'South Africa: Economic Performance and Some Policy Implications', *World Bank Informal Discussion Papers on Aspects of the Economy of South Africa* (Washington DC).

Fallon, P. and L. Pereira da Silva (1994), 'South Africa Economic Performance and Policies', Discussion Paper No 7, *World Bank Informal Discussion Papers on Aspects of the Economy of South Africa* (Washington DC).

Fourie, F. and A. Smith (1993), 'Concentration, Tariff Protection and Industrial Performance in South Africa 1992–1988', unpublished manuscript.

GATT Trade Policy Review (1993), *The Republic of South Africa Vol 1 and Vol 2* (Geneva).

Gerson, J. and S.B. Kahn (1988), 'Factors Determining Real Exchange Rate Changes in South Africa', *The South African Journal of Economics*, **56**, 1.

Greenaway, D. and C.R. Milner (1987), 'True Protection Concepts and their Role in Evaluating Trade Policies in LDCs', *Journal of Development Studies*, **23**.

Holden, M. (1990), 'The Growth of Exports and Manufacturing in South Africa from 1947 to 1987', *Development Southern Africa*, **7**, 3.

Holden, M. (1992), 'The Structure and Incidence of Protection in South Africa', in P. Black and B. Dollery (eds.), *Leading Issues in South African Microeconomics* (Southern Book Publishers).

Holden, M. (1993), 'Trade Policy and Industrial Restructuring in South Africa', *Western Economic Association Conference* (Lake Tahoe, June).

Industrial Development Corporation (1990), *Modification of the Application of Protection Policy* (Sandton, June).

Lundahl, M. and L. Petersson (1991), *The Dependent Economy. Lesotho and the Southern African Customs Union* (Boulder CD: Westview Press).

Michaely, M., D. Papageorgiou and A. Chokski (1991), *Liberalising Foreign Trade: Lessons of Experience in the Developing World*, **7**, (Blackwell).

Scheepers, C. (1969), 'The Effect of Import Substitution on the Volume and Structure of South Africa's Imports 1926/27–1963/64', *Finance and Trade Review*.

Whiteford, A. and M. McGrath (1994), *Distribution of Income in South Africa* (Human Sciences Research Council, Pretoria).

White Paper on Reconstruction and Development (1994), *Government Strategy for Fundamental Transformation* (Cape Town).

A Review of Mexico's Trade Policy from 1982 to 1994

Timothy J. Kehoe

1. INTRODUCTION

FROM the early 1950s until the early 1980s Mexico, like many other developing nations, employed a growth strategy based on import substitution. Relying on protection from the world economy and government intervention in the domestic economy, this strategy encouraged investment in industry, suppressed agricultural prices (at least until the mid 1970s), and expanded government enterprises. Following its debt crisis in 1982, Mexico began to change course. Starting in 1985, under then President Miguel de la Madrid Hurtado, Mexico initiated a policy of openness (*apertura* in Spanish) to the rest of the world. In 1986 it acceded to the General Agreement on Tariffs and Trade (GATT), and in 1994, together with Canada and the United States, it formed the North American Free Trade Area.

Over the past decade Mexico has restructured its economy dramatically, cutting inflation sharply, privatising most government enterprises, deregulating domestic commerce, and eliminating barriers to foreign trade and investment. The successes of Mexican economic policy in recent years resulted in popularity for the ruling political party at home and respect and emulation abroad. Like a bucket of cold water over the head, however, the Mexican financial crisis of December 1994–February 1995 has caused most observers of — and participants in — the Mexican economy to stop and re-evaluate, not only the perceived successes of recent Mexican economic policy, but the policy itself.

During the 1988 Montreal midtern review of the Uruguay Round of the GATT, the contracting parties established, on a trial basis, a Trade Policy Review Mechanism. The trade policies of intermediate size nations like Mexico are reviewed every four years. This paper is a report on the Trade Policy Review (TPR) of Mexico, a review that was put together during 1992 and the beginning of 1993. The 1993 TPR did a good and balanced job of summarising and analysing Mexico's trade policy, in the context of its more general economic

---

TIMOTHY J. KEHOE is from the Department of Economics, University of Minnesota.

policy, during the period 1982–92. Events in Mexico in 1994 and early 1995 make even a critical assessment of the TPR a sterile undertaking for both the author and the informed reader. Consequently, this paper will do more than summarise and assess the review; it will also provide a critical history of the events leading up to the 1994–95 financial crisis and attempt to draw lessons from the experience gained during the crisis.

In one sense analysing the TPR — and with it Mexican trade policy — jointly with the 1994–95 financial crisis is easy, and in another sense it is hard. On the one hand, mistakes in policy are easy to identify after a crisis has occurred. Policy judgements involve calculated risks, and poor judgements are far easier to identify if there is a run of bad luck than if there is not. On the other hand, it is difficult to draw lessons from experience before the dust has settled and the debris cleared away.

The tentative conclusions of this paper — that presage a second TPR on Mexico in 1997— are that Mexico's trade and foreign investment policies from 1985 through 1993 were fundamentally sound. In 1994, however, faced with political instability, rising US interest rates, upcoming elections, and falling foreign investment, the administration of then President Carlos Salinas de Gortari made two decisions that later events proved unwise. First, it allowed the Mexican peso only a small devaluation (a nominal 12 per cent) against the US dollar, and in maintaining the value of the peso it lost much of Mexico's foreign reserves. Second, as the Salinas administration refinanced Mexico's government debt during 1994, it allowed the debt to become mostly short-term and dollar-indexed. The combination of these two policy decisions left Mexico open to a speculative attack, when investors realised that the *Banco de México* did not have enough reserves to continue supporting the peso, and, shortly afterwards and perhaps even worse, a bank-run situation, when bond holders realised that the *Banco de México* might not have enough reserves to meet the payments coming due on the dollar-indexed debt.

It is easy to identify these policy mistakes now. Yet they are related to longer term Mexican economic policies that, at least until 1994, seemed spectacularly successful: using the exchange rate as a nominal anchor in the anti-inflation programme by tying its value closely to that of the dollar and opening Mexico, not only to foreign direct investment, but to substantial portfolio investment. The financial crisis in Mexico calls both of these policies into serious question. The debate over the extent to which the combination of these two policies was to blame for the recent financial crisis is sure to continue for years both in Mexico and abroad. The verdict of this paper is mixed. Something like an exchange rate anchor was an effective policy instrument in 1987 when the economy was in danger of hyper-inflation and was relatively closed to foreign investment. As inflation fell and the economy opened itself to foreign investment, however, this policy became riskier in the face of volatile foreign investment.

One explanation of the crisis proposed by, among others, Dornbusch and Werner (1994) is, simply, that the Mexican peso was overvalued against the US dollar in 1994. The simple solution in terms of this simple explanation was a large devaluation. As Calvo (1994) has pointed out, however, this explanation of the problem and proposed solution to it are overly simplistic in that they ignore the effect that a devaluation would have on the credibility of Mexican policy makers and the impact that the loss of credibility following a devaluation would have on foreign investment. Subsequent events have painfully shown Calvo to be right.

It would have been difficult for the 1993 TPR to have foreseen the 1994–95 financial crisis. Hindsight allows us to see aspects of Mexican policy that could have been subject to more criticism, however. Principal among them is the way in which the Mexican government published data related to its international financial position — in particular, its foreign reserves and the composition of its debt — that is, with significant delay and, in the case of reserves, aggregated into monthly or quarterly, rather than daily, averages. The atmosphere of secrecy and rumour that surrounded the Mexican government's international financial position in 1994 contributed to the crisis.

2. A BRIEF ECONOMIC HISTORY 1970–1994

The import substitution strategy for development, once widely accepted by policy makers in developing countries and by a significant number of academic economists, has been so thoroughly rejected over the past ten years that it now seems absurd. It is important to remember, however, that at least in its early stages this strategy had some notable successes. Mexico was one of them. Between 1960 and 1981 Mexico experienced an average increase of real GDP of 7.0 per cent per year; even with the high rate of population growth in Mexico over that period, this translated into an average increase of GDP per capita of 4.0 per cent per year. (Unless explicitly stated otherwise, all real GDP figures are based on the purchasing-power-parity indices produced by Summers, Heston, Aten, and Nuxoll, 1995, and described by Summers and Heston, 1991).

During the *sexenios* (six year periods of presidential administrations) of Luis Echeverría Alvarez (1970–1976) and José López Portillo (1976–1982), however, the import substitution strategy began to unravel. As the 1993 TPR explains, partly in response to social and political tensions and partly because of a sense of increased prosperity resulting from the discovery of large oil reserves, the Echeverría and López Portillo administrations both followed policies of deficit spending and monetary expansion financed by public sector borrowing from international banks. The result of this policy was rising inflation, which together with a fixed nominal exchange rate led to substantial real exchange rate appreciation and growing current account deficits. At the end of each of the two administrations there was large devaluation: a devaluation of 60 per cent in late 1976, which was the first devaluation in Mexico since 1954, and a devaluation of 368 per cent in late 1982, which was followed by further devaluation over the next five years. In spite of massive economic imbalances during the Echeverría and López Portillo *sexenios*, the Mexican economy continued to grow, however, averaging a growth rate of real GDP of 6.2 per cent over 1970–82 (see Table 1).

In 1982, the Mexican import substitution strategy, and the Mexican economy with it, ran into a wall. Faced with a massive public debt owed to foreign banks, international interest rates that were rising sharply due to US monetary policy, and international oil prices that were falling due to the worldwide recession, Mexico found itself unable to meet its debt service obligations. In the final months of the López Portillo administration the government announced that it

TABLE 1
Major Mexican Economic Indicators 1970–1992

	Population[1]	*GDP*[2]	*GDP/Capita*[3]	*Exchange Rate*[4]	*Inflation*[5]
1970	50.3	200.4	3985	12.5	4.8
1971	52.0	218.9	4211	12.5	5.2
1972	53.7	236.4	4403	12.5	5.5
1973	55.4	255.5	4609	12.5	21.3
1974	57.2	273.4	4783	12.5	20.7
1975	58.9	290.1	4928	12.5	11.2
1976	60.6	301.2	4974	15.4	25.8
1977	62.2	305.0	4902	22.6	22.0
1978	63.8	332.5	5209	22.8	16.2
1979	65.4	367.9	5621	22.8	20.0
1980	67.0	405.7	6051	23.0	29.7
1981	68.6	443.6	6463	24.5	28.7
1982	70.2	417.2	5941	56.4	98.9
1983	71.8	387.7	5400	120.1	80.8
1984	73.3	405.0	5524	167.8	59.2
1985	74.8	420.3	5621	256.9	63.7
1986	76.2	402.4	5283	611.8	105.7
1987	77.6	408.0	5260	1378	159.2
1988	78.9	422.1	5347	2273	51.7
1989	80.3	447.0	5566	2461	19.7
1990	81.7	476.0	5825	2813	29.8
1991	83.3	501.1	6015	3018	18.8
1992	85.0	531.0	6250	3095	11.9

Notes:
[1] Millions.
[2] Purchasing-power-parity, Laspeyres index; billion 1985 US dollars.
[3] Purchasing-power-parity, Laspeyres index; 1985 US dollars.
[4] Yearly average; (old) pesos per dollar.
[5] Change in Consumer Price Index December to December.

Sources: Summers, Heston, Aten and Nuxoll (1995) and Banco de Mexico.

TABLE 2
Major Mexican Trade Indicators 1981–1994
(Billions of US Dollars)

	Gross Domestic Product	*Exports*	*Export Share Per cent Petroleum*	*Imports*	*External Debt*
1981	174.4	20.1	72.5	25.0	74.9
1982	170.5	21.2	77.6	15.0	86.7
1983	148.7	22.3	71.8	9.0	89.8
1984	175.6	24.2	68.6	12.2	96.4
1985	184.4	21.6	68.2	14.5	96.6
1986	129.5	16.2	39.0	12.4	101.0
1987	141.0	20.5	42.1	13.3	107.4
1988	172.9	20.5	32.7	20.3	100.9
1989	205.3	22.8	34.5	25.4	96.4
1990	241.8	26.8	37.6	31.3	98.2
1991	283.0	26.9	30.1	38.2	104.3
1992	327.6	27.5	30.2	48.2	116.6
1993	362.6	30.0	24.7	48.9	117.6
1994	355.8	34.6	21.4	58.9	130.2

Sources: GATT, *Trade Policy Review: Mexico 1993* and IMF, *International Financial Statistics*, various issues.

could not meet its obligations, the peso collapsed, the government nationalised banks, tight exchange controls were implemented, and the economy fell into deep recession. From 1981 to 1987 real GDP declined on average by 1.4 per cent per year and real GDP per capita declined by 3.4 per cent per year.

In late 1982 under newly elected President Miguel de la Madrid Hurtado, Mexico started on the long road to recovery. Because the Mexican government wanted to generate large trade surpluses quickly so that it could resume payments on its debt, restrictions on imports were initially tightened, and Mexico became even more closed: during 1982 and 1983 all Mexican imports required import licences, and imports fell from USD 25.0 billion in 1981 to USD 9.0 billion in 1983 (see Table 2).

The 1993 TPR employs the Organisation for Economic Cooperation and Development's (1992) division of the years 1982–91 into three distinct periods: a 1983–85 period of tight fiscal policy that saw modest reductions in inflation and the beginnings of resumption of growth; a 1985–87 period that saw a relapse into financial crisis, rapidly rising inflation, and falling output; and a 1987–period — which we will extend until the end of 1993 — that saw rapidly falling inflation and the resumption of economic growth. In addition, we will add a fourth period, 1994 and the first months of 1995, which constitute the events heading up to the recent financial crisis and the crisis itself.

During the 1983–85 period, with financial support from the International Monetary Fund, the de la Madrid administration implemented a series of policies designed to cut the public sector deficit and to turn the large trade deficit into a surplus. These policies included reductions in government expenditures, increases in taxes, increases in the prices of public services, elimination of many subsidies, and the closure of some public sector enterprises. Foreign trade and investment policies included the enforcement of licence requirements for all imports; the abolition of exchange controls, although a dual exchange rate was maintained; and, following a large nominal devaluation of the peso, the institution of a crawling peg against the dollar. Although this economic programme was successful in turning the trade deficit into a surplus and — more modestly — in lowering inflation and in raising GDP, it collapsed in late 1985: fiscal discipline began to falter, IMF funding ended, the earthquake in Mexico City caused disruption and imposed significant costs, and international oil prices started on a steep decline that was to continue into 1986 and 1987.

The 1985–87 period was one of falling output and accelerating inflation. It was during this period, however, that Mexico began some of the policy reforms crucial in the return to prosperity during the 1987–93 period. Specifically, the de la Madrid administration began the process of *apertura* — of opening Mexico to foreign trade and investment — and, starting in 1986, Mexico benefited first from the Baker Plan and later the Brady Plan for restructuring its debt.

The central feature of the 1987–93 recovery was a series of social pacts — generically referred to as the *Pacto* — negotiated by representatives of government, business and labour. The first version of the *Pacto*, the *Pacto de Solidáridad Económica*, was implemented in December 1987, during the de la Madrid *sexenio*. (The 1993 TPR mistakenly places this event during the Salinas *sexenio*, 1988–94). Subsequent versions of the *Pacto* have continued in force throughout the Salinas *sexenio* and, until 9 March, 1995, when the government announced an economic programme not officially backed by business and labour, during that of Ernesto Zedillo Ponce de Léon (1994–2000).

Under the *Pacto*, government, business, and labour leaders met unannounced, after financial markets closed for the day, and before markets opened the next day a new agreement was presented to the public. Policies enacted under the *Pacto* system included establishing the Solidarity Programme (*Programa Nacional de Solidaridad* or PRONASOL), a social welfare programme targeted at the poor; setting increases in the minimum wage, a wage level to which many labour contracts were then indexed; decreasing the value-added tax as improved law enforcement led to increased revenues from income taxes; controlling the increase in public sector prices, which became less important as the number of such prices was reduced by privatisation and the elimination of subsidies; and, under later versions, the issuance of guidelines for wage and price increases. Probably the most important elements of the *Pacto*, however, were those related to foreign trade policy: reductions in tariffs and commitments on the amount that the peso would be allowed to move against the dollar. Under some versions of the

Pacto the exchange rate was fixed, and under others a maximum daily devaluation was set.

The policies associated with the *Pacto* were successful in reducing inflation from an annual rate of 159.2 per cent in consumer prices in 1987 to 7.1 per cent in 1994. Furthermore, between 1987 and 1994, real GDP in pesos rose by 23.1 per cent, after having fallen by 8.0 per cent between 1981 and 1987, and real wages rose by 19.4 per cent, after having fallen by 30.0 per cent between 1981 and 1987.[1] Trade liberalisation and the nominal exchange rate anchor played major roles in establishing the credibility of the government's commitment to low inflation — credibility with its *Pacto* partners, with the Mexican public, and with foreign investors.

3. *LA APERTURA*

Between 1982 and 1994 Mexico went from being a relatively closed economy, even by developing countries' standards, to being one of the most open in the world. In 1982 tariffs were as high as 100 per cent, and there was substantial dispersion in tariff rates; licences were required for importing any good; and, as a general rule, foreigners were restricted to no more than 49 per cent ownership of Mexican enterprises. By 1994 the maximum tariff had been cut to 20 per cent, and the tariff code had been substantially simplified; import licences had been eliminated for 89 per cent of imports; and restrictions on foreign investment had been effectively eliminated for most industries and substantially reduced for many others.

As the 1993 TPR points out, in 1982–83 import licences, not tariffs, were Mexico's most significant trade barrier. Starting in late 1983, the de la Madrid administration began to replace quantitative restrictions with tariffs. The portion of tariff items subject to licence requirements fell from 100 per cent in 1983 to 65 per cent in 1984. The process accelerated in 1985, as this percentage fell to 10 per cent. By 1992 this percentage was 2 per cent. Even so, the portion of the value of imports subject to licence requirements fell more slowly: from 100 per cent in 1983 to 83 per cent in 1984, to 35 per cent in 1985, to 11 per cent in 1992. Import licences are still required for crude petroleum products, some basic agricultural and agro-industrial commodities, and for the automotive industry, although even here they are being phased out.

As import licences were replaced by tariffs as the principal tool of trade policy, average tariffs initially rose and then fell: the simple average of tariff lines went

[1] Data have been pieced together from various issues of IMF *International Financial Statistics* and the *Economist*; in terms of the purchasing-power-parity GDP data, real GDP rose by 30.1 per cent between 1987 and 1992 — the latest year for which such data are available — after falling by 8.1 per cent between 1981 and 1987.

from 23.2 per cent in 1983 to 23.3 per cent in 1984, to 25.4 per cent in 1985, to 13.1 per cent in 1992; the trade-weighted average tariff went from 8.0 per cent in 1983 to 8.5 per cent in 1984, to 13.3 per cent in 1984, to 11.1 per cent in 1992.

Equally significant with the changes in average tariff rates during the *apertura* was the simplification of the tariff schedule. The number of tariff rates was 16, with a maximum rate of 100 per cent, in 1982. The number of tariff rates fell to 13 in 1983, to 11 in 1986, and to 5 in 1987, where it currently remains. The maximum tariff fell to 45 per cent in 1986 and to 20 per cent in 1987. The dispersion of tariff rates (defined as the standard deviation of rates divided by the average rate) fell from 22.5 per cent in 1984 to 4.5 per cent in 1992 in terms of number of tariff items and from 11.9 per cent in 1984 to 6.7 per cent in 1992 in terms of trade-weighted tariff items. By 1992, for example, 48.9 per cent of Mexico's tariff items — accounting for 36.5 per cent of Mexico's imports — were subject to the 10 per cent tariff rate.

The impact of the unilateral reductions in Mexican trade barriers can be seen in the trade figures presented in Table 2. Notice the steady increase in exports starting in 1987 and the even more pronounced increase in imports from the low levels following the 1982 debt crisis.

The elimination of licence requirements and the simplification of the tariff schedule from 1983 to 1992 were major steps in making Mexican trade policy less protective and more transparent. These steps were accompanied by a number of other significant policies: Mexico acceded to the GATT in 1986, adopting the Harmonised Commodity Description and Coding System in 1987. In 1991 the 1985 Law on Procurement was modified to allow more foreign bidding on government procurement, although the law still recommends a preference for domestic suppliers. In connection with its accession to GATT, Mexico adopted a Foreign Trade Law in 1986 and the GATT Anti-Dumping Code in 1987, which allowed its Ministry of Trade and Industrial Promotion (*Secretaria de Comercio y Fomento Industrial* or SECOFI) to implement anti-dumping and countervailing duty provisions. While the Mexican government has made some use of these measures, especially against US, Brazilian and Chinese exporters, Mexican trade officials continually express distaste for them, and Mexican trade negotiators favour their elimination in GATT or greater restrictions on their use.

A significant change in Mexican policy that is only briefly discussed in the 1993 TPR is the 1992 agricultural reform. The 1917 Mexican Constitution had formalised the *ejido* system of community property rights in much of the agricultural sector. Under this system, which dates back to pre-Hispanic times in some areas, the *ejidatario* — the individual member of the *ejido* — had a right to work a specific plot of community land, but not to sell it, to use it as collateral in obtaining loans, or to rent it out. Furthermore, the maximum size of individual plots was tightly restricted. A substantial segment of the Mexican population are *ejidatarios*, mostly living in poverty, working small plots of rain-fed land in the

Southern and Central parts of Mexico, and cultivating maize. A change in the Mexican Constitution in 1992 allows the *ejidatario* the option of becoming the owner of the plot that he cultivates or of remaining part of the *ejido* system. Land can now be sold, used as collateral, or rented out. Restrictions on foreign investment in the agricultural sector are being gradually lifted. This agricultural reform, although not part of Mexican trade policy *per se*, is likely to have a major impact on Mexican trade patterns and on the Mexican economy in general, as many *ejidatarios* migrate off their lands, and crops are shifted away from maize.

Two other significant aspects of Mexican trade policy during the *apertura* were its negotiation of regional free trade agreements, especially NAFTA, and its reduction in barriers to capital flows. The changes in these two sets of policies and their impacts on the Mexican economy are discussed in the next two sections.

4. TRADE PATTERNS AND TRADE AGREEMENTS

During the *apertura* the size and composition of Mexico's foreign trade changed significantly, as Table 2 illustrates: exports grew, imports grew even more, and petroleum became less important an export as its relative price fell and manufacturing exports expanded. The reliance of Mexico on trade with the United States became even more pronounced over this period, going from 56 per cent of Mexico's trade in 1982 to 70 per cent in 1992.

Table 3 shows the composition of Mexico's trade in 1992. It is worth noting that the machinery and transportation category has replaced mineral fuels (petroleum) as Mexico's largest export. Looking at this process over the longer run, the 1993 TPR traces out the shift in the composition of exports from being largely agriculture and minerals and metals in the 1960s, to being largely fuels in the late 1970s and early 1980s, to being largely manufactures and fuels in the 1990s.

The TPR discusses a problem that plagued analysts of Mexico's trade patterns: what Mexican data said about imports and exports did not match what other countries' data said about these numbers. In 1990, for example, Mexican data say that Mexico exported USD 18.8 billion to the United States while US data say that the United States imported USD 30.8 billion from Mexico. The major problem was that Mexican data did not count into imports and exports the transactions made by *maquiladoras*. These are in-bond assembly factories, originally established by an agreement with the United States in 1965. Imports of unfinished goods enter Mexico duty-free, and the importer posts a bond that guarantees the export of the finished good. (If the good is not exported, the applicable duties on the unfinished goods are deducted from the bond.) Since 1965 the number of *maquiladoras* has expanded rapidly; *maquiladoras* have been built outside the US-Mexico border region; and the *maquiladora* programme has

TABLE 3
Mexico's Composition of Trade 1992
(Millions of US Dollars)

		Imports	*Exports*
0	Food and Live Animals	4,096	2,682
	04 Cereals	1,240	—
	05 Vegetables and Fruits	341	1,488
1	Beverages and Tobacco	315	331
2	Crude Materials	2,431	1,052
3	Mineral Fuels	1,675	8,114
	33 Petroleum and Products	1,210	7,932
4	Animal, Vegetable Oils	383	—
5	Chemicals	4,397	2,079
	51 Organic Chemicals	1,461	733
6	Basic Manufactures	6,655	3,105
	67 Iron and Steel	1,791	688
7	Machinery, Transportation Equipment	23,012	8,604
	71 Power Generating Equipment	1,098	1,577
	72 Specialised Machinery	2,627	166
	73 Metalworking Machinery	994	—
	74 General Industrial Machinery	3,257	502
	75 Office Machines	1,759	758
	76 Telecommunications	2,085	114
	77 Electric Machinery	2,578	877
	78 Road Vehicles	7,938	4,442
	79 Other Transportation Equipment	676	133
8	Miscellaneous Manufactured Goods	4,870	1,152
	87 Precision Instruments	1,045	102
9	Goods not Classified by Kind	43	58
Total		47,878	27,207

Source: UN, *1992 International Trade Statistics Yearbook*.

been expanded to include other countries (see US International Trade Commission 1990). Over 80 per cent of *maquiladoras* are still located in the US-Mexico border region, however, servicing the US market by assembling such goods as electronic products, textiles and apparel, furniture, and transportation equipment.

As the 1993 TPR points out, excluding *maquiladora* trade from Mexican trade statistics causes us to understate the importance of trade in manufactures. Using US trade data from 1990, for example, we could estimate that total Mexican exports, including those by *maquiladoras*, were 44 per cent higher than reported (USD 38.8 billion rather than USD 26.8 billion). Most of this difference is manufactured goods. Like the US-Canada Auto Pact of 1965, the *maquiladora* programme paved the way for the North American Free Trade Agreement (NAFTA). Fortunately, this problem with the data is rapidly disappearing for two reasons: first, starting in 1993, Mexico has begun publishing trade figures that include *maquiladora* trade, and second, as NAFTA is implemented, less and less trade will be done on an in-bond basis — instead it will be simply duty free.

In 1992 the United States accounted for 65.0 per cent of Mexican trade (see International Monetary Fund, 1994). If we include *maquiladora* trade, by following the TPR in inferring that it is the difference between Mexican trade data and US data, US trade with Mexico is as high as 74.4 per cent of Mexican trade (exports to the United States of USD 40,598 million out of 58,347 total imports and imports to the United States of 35,886 out of 44,396 total exports). Japan accounts for 5.2 per cent of Mexican trade, Germany 3.9 per cent and Spain for 2.7 per cent. No other country accounts for more than 2.5 per cent of Mexico's trade, and the rest of the Americas, led by Canada and Brazil, accounts for only 8.6 per cent.

On 1 January 1994, the NAFTA went into effect, linking the economy of Mexico with those of Canada and the United States. The 1993 TPR devotes significant attention to NAFTA, even though at the time the review was written the agreement had still not been approved by the US Congress. This attention was rightly placed because NAFTA can be viewed as a commitment by the Mexican government to the policies of the *apertura*. (Of course, NAFTA also represents significant commitments to free trade by the US and Canadian governments.) To be sure, NAFTA involved trade liberalisation on the part of Mexico that goes beyond that achieved during 1985–92: all tariffs among the three member countries are to be phased out over a fifteen year period. Remaining nontariff barriers, most significantly those in agriculture and transportation equipment, are being eliminated. Restrictions on foreign investment are being eased further; most significantly, US and Canadian providers of financial services in Mexico are to be accorded the same treatment as their Mexican counterparts. Dispute resolution mechanisms have been established, and, as part of side agreements negotiated after NAFTA itself, trinational commissions have been established to deal with issues involving labour rights and protection of the environment.

In general NAFTA does not raise barriers against nonmember countries, and the three member countries remain committed to further multilateral trade liberalisation within GATT. The 1993 TPR is not sufficiently critical of two significant moves towards protectionism embodied in NAFTA, however: First, the North American content provision that determines whether automobiles and light trucks qualify for duty free treatment has been raised to 62.5 per cent of net cost from the 50 per cent value-added provision in the US-Canada FTA. Second, Mexico, a major importer of sugar, has agreed to raise to US levels its external barriers to sugar imports from nonmember countries. Clearly, these provisions in

NAFTA were designed to make the agreement attractive — or less unattractive — to special interest groups in the United States.

As a member of the Latin American Integration Association, Mexico also gives preferential treatment to imports from a large number of Latin American countries. In addition, Mexico has signed FTAs with Chile (September 1991), Costa Rica (March 1994), Colombia and Venezuela (May 1994), and Bolivia (September 1994). These FTAs are not likely to have a significant impact in the near future on Mexican trade due to the small sizes of the other countries involved and the low current levels of trade with them. Nevertheless, these agreements are significant in that they demonstrate Mexico's commitment to extending free trade to the rest of Latin America.

5. EXCHANGE RATES AND FOREIGN INVESTMENT

Along with the liberalisation in trade policy that occurred during the *apertura*, Mexico significantly lowered its barriers to foreign investment. During the presidency of José de la Cruz Porfirio-Diaz Mori (1876–1910), the Mexican government encouraged foreign investment. During the Mexican Revolution, however, the government built restrictions on foreign investment into the 1917 Constitution. President Lázaro Cárdenas went as far as to nationalise all foreign owned oil companies in 1938. In 1973 Mexico combined the various restrictions on foreign investment that had accumulated since 1917 into a single Law to Promote Mexican Investment and to Regulate Foreign Investment. In general nonresident foreigners were restricted to 49 per cent ownership of Mexican companies, although companies that had been foreign-owned before 1973 were exempted.

Starting in 1984 Mexico began to lift restrictions on foreign ownership, not by changing this law, but by changing the administrative regulations and guidelines designed to enforce it. In 1989, the newly elected Salinas administration issued a comprehensive revision of these regulations. The Foreign Investments Commission (*Comisión Nacional para la Inversión Extranjera* or CNIE) had been empowered by the 1973 investment law to waive restrictions on foreign investment when it deemed the foreign participation to be in the public interest. Following the 1989 change in regulations CNIE granted automatic approval for investment projects in 'unrestricted industries' in cases that met guidelines designed to promote foreign trade and to create jobs outside of the major industrial areas of Mexico City, Guadelajara, and Monterrey. In cases where the industry fell outside of the unrestricted category or where the guidelines were not met, the foreign investor has to petition CNIE for approval of the project. The foreign investor was guaranteed a response within 45 days, otherwise approval was automatic. The 1993 TPR reports that since 1989 CNIE had approved 98.4 per cent of the investment projects proposed. In December 1993 a new Foreign

TABLE 4
Mexican Financial Flows 1981–1994
(Billions of US Dollars)

	Foreign Direct Investment	*Foreign Portfolio Investment*	*Current Acct Surplus*	*International Reserves*
1981	2.8	1.2	−16.1	4.1
1982	1.7	0.9	−6.3	0.8
1983	0.5	−0.7	5.4	3.9
1984	0.4	−0.8	4.2	7.3
1985	0.5	−1.0	1.1	4.9
1986	1.2	−0.8	−1.7	5.7
1987	1.8	−0.4	4.0	12.5
1988	2.0	0.1	−2.4	5.3
1989	2.6	0.3	−5.8	6.3
1990	2.5	−4.0	−7.5	9.9
1991	4.7	12.1	−14.9	17.7
1992	4.4	18.0	−24.8	18.6
1993	4.9	28.4	−23.4	24.6
1994	8.0	8.2	−28.9	5.8

Notes:
[1] End of year.
Source: IMF, *International Financial Statistics*, various issues.

Investment Law was enacted that did away with most of the restrictions in the 1973 law. There remain some sectors where foreign participation is prohibited or limited. These include the extraction of petroleum and natural gas, transportation services, and communication services.

The impact of the 1989 regulatory changes can be seen in the increase in foreign direct investment that has occurred since then (see Table 4). The sources of foreign direct investment in Mexico look like the list of Mexico's trade partners. Again, the United States dominates with 63.4 per cent of total foreign direct investment in 1991.

Perhaps more impressive, however, than the increase in foreign direct investment since 1989, has been the surge in foreign portfolio investment. In 1989 CNIE and the National Stocks Commission were authorised to approve trust funds through which foreigners could buy equities issued by Mexican firms without acquiring shareholder voting rights.

Foreign investors were attracted to the Mexican stock market by the large returns available. In 1991 share prices rose by 77.1 per cent in US dollar terms, by 49.4 per cent in 1992, and by 10.6 per cent in 1993. During the 1991–93 period Mexico was able to offset its substantial current account deficit with substantial inflows of foreign capital.

Over 1987–93, the Mexican peso appreciated substantially against the US dollar. Using consumer price indices from the two countries to calculate the real

TABLE 5
Real Appreciation of the Peso 1987–1994

	Peso/Dollar Exchange Rate[1]	*Mexican CPI*[2]	*US CPI*[3]	*Peso/Dollar Real Exchange Rate*[4]
1987	2.210	49	89	100
1988	2.281	73	93	72
1989	2.641	88	97	73
1990	2.945	119	103	64
1991	3.071	134	106	61
1992	3.115	149	109	57
1993	3.106	161	112	54
1994[5]	3.446	172	115	57

Notes:
[1] End of year; (new) pesos per dollar.
[2] End of year; 1990 average = 100.
[3] End of year; 1990 average = 100.
[4] Real exchange rate = Exchange rate × US CPI/Mexican CPI.
[5] 19 December 1994.

Source: IMF, *International Financial Statistics*, various issues.

exchange rate as in Table 5, we see that the value of the peso rose by 46 per cent compared to the dollar. The Mexican government over this period was letting the peso's value decline at a slower rate than the difference in inflation rates as part of its *Pacto* commitment to lowering inflation. Yet the *Banco de México* had no trouble maintaining the value of the peso. In fact, it had to intervene to keep the value of the peso down; as Table 4 shows, the *Banco de México* accumulated reserves every year from 1988 to 1993. Unfortunately, the situation changed in 1994.

6. THE 1994–95 CRISIS

On 20 December, the Mexican government announced that it would widen the band in which it let the peso move against the dollar. On currency markets the peso immediately fell to the floor of this band, 3.97 pesos/dollar as opposed to the level of 3.45 pesos/dollar. After two days at this level, the government announced that the *Banco de México* would no longer support the peso, and it fell even further.

The simple explanation of this collapse was that the peso had become overvalued during the period 1987–94, as shown in Table 5; the *Banco de México* spent most of its dollar reserves supporting the peso; and when it ran out of reserves the value of the peso plummeted. Although there is some validity to this story, it neglects two important facts. First, over the period 1987–93 the *Banco de México* was accumulating reserves, as shown in Table 4. Second, the peso depreciated in real terms against the dollar by 6.6 per cent from the end of 1993 until the onset of the crisis. If the peso was overvalued in 1994, it was even more overvalued in 1993, and yet there was no crisis in 1993.

What precipitated the crisis of December 1994–February 1995 was a combination of three factors. First, foreign portfolio investment fell sharply, as shown in Table 4, because of increased political uncertainty in Mexico and rising interest rates in the United States. Second, Mexican authorities did not react soon enough, in either tightening the money supply or letting the value of the peso fall in reaction to declining foreign investment, leading to a fall in reserves. Third, in an effort to decrease the debt service, Mexican authorities converted much of Mexico's public debt to short-term, dollar-indexed *tesobonos* from peso-denominated *cetes*.

1994 was a difficult year for Mexico politically: there was an uprising in Chiapas in January; the presidential candidate of the ruling Institutional Revolutionary Party (*Partido Revoluccionario Institutional* or PRI) Luis Donaldo Colosio, was assassinated in March; the Secretary General of the PRI, Jose Francisco Ruiz Massieu was assassinated in September; and there were threats of a new uprising in Chiapas in November.

Perhaps even more significantly, there were presential elections in August, with the new President, Zedillo, who had replaced Colosio as the PRI candidate, taking office in December. These elections were widely regarded as the most honest in Mexican history, and the victory by the PRI was considered as a mandate for the economic policies of the previous ten years.

Nevertheless, the change of government was, as it has been every six years in Mexico since 1928, a time of great uncertainty. At the end of each of the previous three *sexenios* there had been large devaluations. (The one at the end of the de la Madrid administration actually occurred in 1987 rather than 1988.) Mexicans and foreign investors feared another one.

While the Salinas administration might have considered devaluations during the summer of 1994, it is clear why it did not do so: reserves were at a high level by historical standards, a devaluation would have led to a loss of credibility for the government within Mexico and with foreign investors, it was hoped that the political shocks were transitory and that foreign investment would return, and there was a presidential election coming up. During the Fall of 1994, however, the situation became unsustainable.

7. WHAT HAPPENS NOW?

As its part of Clinton's 31 January package for Mexico, the IMF expanded its earlier line of credit for Mexico from USD 7.8 billion to USD 17.8 billion. In announcing this expansion of credit, the IMF Managing Director Michel Camdessus explained the move as a concrete illustration of the IMF's support for Mexico's unprecedented adjustment programme, the *apertura* of 1985–94 (*IMF Survey*, 6 February, 1995). Mexico has indeed come a long way since 1985, and prospects for its long-term recovery appear good.

Unfortunately, 1995 will be a difficult year for Mexico. The current economic programme includes an increase in the value added tax rate of 10 per cent to its 1983–91 rate of 15 per cent, a cut in government expenditures, and an increase in the minimum wage of 20 per cent, which will fall far short of the increase in prices. There are some good signs, however; the government remains committed to the policies of *apertura*. Zedillo himself currently enjoys a surprising amount of popularity, given the economic situation, for having appointed a member of the opposition National Action Party PAN as attorney general; reopening the investigations into the Colosio and Ruiz Massieu assassinations; insuring that the PRI gracefully acknowledged the victory of the PAN in gubernatorial and mayorial elections in Jalisco, home of Guadalajara, Mexico's second largest city; and showing his commitment to make Mexico a country where the law applies to everyone and where the political party in power receives no special treatment by the government. It is possible that the changes in Mexico's political system that will occur during the Zedillo *sexenio* will be as significant as the changes in the economic system that occurred during the de la Madrid and Salinas *sexenios*. It will be important for the 1997 TPR to focus some attention on these political changes. For the Zedillo administration to carry out political reforms, it needs to survive 1995 with a minimum of damage to the economy.

At the global level, we are still learning lessons from the Mexican crisis and its rapid spread to developing countries in Latin America and Southeast Asia and even to European countries like Italy, Spain, and Sweden. What seems to be needed is a new international monetary authority to serve as lender of last resort. To operate effectively, however, an international lender of last resort would need some regulatory power — imposing regulations before a crisis occurs, not only afterwards.

REFERENCES

Calvo, G. (1994), 'Comment on Dornbusch and Werner,' *Brookings Papers on Economic Activity*, 1, 298–303.

Dornbusch, R. and A. Werner (1994), 'Mexico: Stabilization, Reform, and No Growth,' *Brookings Papers on Economic Activity*, 1, 253–297.

General Agreement on Tariffs and Trade (GATT) (1993), *Trade Policy Review: Mexico 1993* (Geneva: GATT Publication Services, two volumes).

Organization for Economic Cooperation and Development (1992), *OECD Economic Surveys: Mexico* (Paris: OECD).

Summers, R. and A. Heston (1991), 'The Penn World Table (Mark 5): An Expanded Set of International Comparisons, 1950–1988,' *Quarterly Journal of Economics*, **106**, 327–368.
Summers, R., A. Heston, B. Aten, and D. Nuxoll (1995), 'Penn World Table (Mark 5.6),' (University of Pennsylvania, computer diskette).

An Economic Evaluation of the Uruguay Round Agreements

Robert E. Baldwin

1. INTRODUCTION

THREE criteria are relevant for assessing the economic welfare implications of the Uruguay Round agreements and for considering how the agreements can be improved in the future (see Office of US Trade Representative, 1993, for the text of the agreements). First, to what extent are the agreements likely to foster economic growth and raise living standards by bringing about a more efficient allocation of world resources? Second, recognising that nations use trade policies to promote certain non-economic objectives such as discouraging certain 'unfair' practices, e.g. dumping and easing economic adjustments to changes in comparative cost conditions, to what extent do the agreements achieve these goals without retarding growth or reducing economic efficiency? Finally, to what extent do the agreements strengthen the institutional mechanisms for achieving compliance with the trading rules embodied in the agreements and for settling disputes among trading partners?

On the basis of these three criteria, the Uruguay Round can be judged as very successful. This outcome is rather surprising in view of the bleak outlook for success that prevailed at the conclusion of the Brussels Ministerial Meeting in December, 1990. The Round was scheduled to be completed at that time, but it became evident that the major participants were far apart not just on the issue of agricultural liberalisation — the reason usually cited for the failure of the ministerial meeting — but on several other key issues. For example, the developed and developing countries were still far apart in the areas of protection for intellectual property rights and prohibiting certain trade-related investment measures. Furthermore, the developed countries had not as yet agreed to phase out so-called voluntary export restraints and some were still considering whether 'selectivity', i.e. non-most-favoured-nation treatment, should be permitted in safeguard actions. There were also important differences in the negotiating positions of the participants on such issues as anti-dumping policies, subsidies

ROBERT E. BALDWIN is from the University of Wisconsin-Madison.

and countervailing duties, and government procurement practices.[1]

Fortunately, between December 1990 and April 1994, when the agreements were signed in Marrakesh, the participants not only reached compromises on these and other issues, but, in doing so, managed to produce a set of agreements that promises significant progress towards achieving the goals incorporated in the three criteria set forth above. Among the agreements that will bring substantial benefits by accelerating economic growth and raising living standards are those dealing with the reduction of tariffs, the elimination of voluntary export restraints, the return of the textiles and agricultural sectors to the discipline of GATT rules, the strengthening of intellectual property rights, the extension of GATT rules to trade in services, the liberalisation of trade-related investment measures and the further opening of purchases by governments to international competition. Agreements that will operate to reduce the economic inefficiencies often associated with the use of trade policies to promote non-economic objectives are those covering safeguards, subsidies and countervailing duties, and anti-dumping measures. In addition, the new dispute settlement arrangements, the new trade policy review mechanism and, most important, the provisions replacing the GATT with a permanent international institution, the World Trade Organization (WTO), will make members more confident that all countries, large and small, will adhere to the trading rules embodied in the various agreements and that disputes among nations will be settled in a fair, expeditious manner.

The following sections of the paper describe the main features of various agreements and examine both how well they satisfy the three evaluation criteria and how they can be improved. The agreements are divided into three groups: (1) those dealing with issues not previously covered by the GATT, specifically, (a) trade in services, (b) trade-related aspects of intellectual property rights, and (c) trade-related aspects of investment measures; (2) those covering areas that had initially been covered by standard GATT rules but became excluded from GATT discipline for several reasons, namely, agriculture and textiles/apparel; and (3) those related to traditional GATT issues such as tariff liberalisation, subsidies, dumping, government procurement, technical barriers to trade, dispute settlement and institutional reform.

2. THE 'NEW' NEGOTIATING ISSUES

Technological and institutional developments are significantly changing the nature of commercial transactions among countries. The traditional view of these

[1] The differences in the negotiating positions of various countries are evident from the bracketed portions of the Draft Final Act prepared by the Director-General of the GATT for the Brussels meeting (GATT Secretariat (1990), Draft Final Act Embodying the Results of the Uruguay Round of Multilateral Trade Negotiations, MTN.TNC/W/35, November) and the comments on the various agreements in this document. The Briefing Book prepared for the US Delegation also summarises the differences in views of the participating countries on the various issues under negotiation.

transactions as consisting mainly of cross-border movements of homogeneous goods produced domestically by a nation's firms is increasingly inappropriate. Most modern manufactured goods produced by a firm are differentiated in important ways from the goods produced by other domestic or foreign firms in the same industry. Consequently, to compete successfully in foreign markets, it is no longer enough to deliver goods at a competitive price to foreign distributors who also handle identical goods produced by other firms. To sell successfully in foreign markets, a firm now often needs to establish its own sales, distribution, servicing and production facilities abroad. Foreign facilities are especially important for firms engaged in selling services to foreigners, a category of trade long ignored both under the traditional view of international trade and GATT rules. Furthermore, since the main basis of a firm's competitiveness often rests on a technological discovery, it must try to prevent foreign competitors from infringing on its intellectual property rights. Thus, the modern multinational firm must be concerned not just with border measures that impede its competitive ability, but with the many domestic regulations and market conditions in foreign countries that frequently seriously hamper its ability to sell in these countries.[2]

Foreign firms may, for example, be forbidden from establishing a commercial presence or be limited in the extent of their ownership. Even if establishment is permitted, the number of foreign firms allowed may be limited, or certain types of activities may be prohibited. Foreign firms may also be required to purchase a certain proportion of domestic input or employ a certain proportion of domestic personnel. Quantitative restrictions also frequently apply to imported services, e.g. motion pictures and air transportation.

A major accomplishment of the Uruguay Round has been to adopt new rules which take into account the fact that the distinction between border and internal regulations is becoming increasingly less meaningful for facilitating international transactions in goods and services. Three areas where new rules relevant to this point have been adopted are trade in services, trade-related aspects of intellectual property rights and trade-related aspects of investment measures.

a. Services

An important feature of the framework agreement negotiated for services is that it not only covers cross-border trade in services, but services supplied by foreign firms within a country to consumers in that country and services supplied by domestic firms to nationals of other countries who are visiting the country. The General Agreement on Trade in Services (GATS) commits WTO signatories

[2] See, for example, Sapir (1982) and Feketekuty (1988) for a description of various barriers to trade in services.

to a set of general principles that includes most-favoured-nation treatment (subject to specified exceptions), transparency with regard to any domestic laws or regulations affecting trade in services and progressive liberalisation in the services area.

The key part of the services agreement consists of schedules of commitments by GATT members in which they set forth specific terms and conditions on market access, conditions and qualifications on national treatment, and the time-frame for implementing such commitments. While most countries made commitments not to impose new restrictions against foreigners, there was a lack of significant liberalisation in such important sectors as financial services, air and sea transportation, and telecommunications. However, bilateral negotiations are continuing in some of these sectors. Thus, the most important accomplishment has been to bring the services sector under international trading rules and set the stage for later, significant liberalisation.

b. Intellectual Property Rights

In the modern global economy, economic growth is largely driven by technological progress. Moreover, to a significant extent, this technological progress is endogenous, depending on the level of research and development (R&D) expenditures by profit-oriented or government-owned firms and the level of funding for 'pure' research in academic and other non-profit institutions. Ensuring that optimal amounts of resources are devoted to both applied and basic research is a major economic problem for the international community.

Private firms engaged in R&D efforts face the problem that they may not be able to appropriate to themselves what consumers are willing to pay for the goods and services embodying the new knowledge they create. Other firms may be able to acquire the new knowledge freely because its nature can be discerned easily by examining the products themselves or observing the manner in which they are produced. Consequently, unless those who can acquire the new knowledge in this low-cost manner are enjoined from producing the products based on this knowledge and selling them at a cost that covers only their own costs of production, the firms creating the knowledge will not be able to recoup their R&D costs. This outcome will discourage future knowledge-creating activities on their part and thus slow the pace of economic development in the global economy.

There is another side of the knowledge-creation issue, however. Once created, knowledge has the characteristics of a public good. That is, the use of new knowledge by one party does not exclude its simultaneous use by other parties without additional resource costs. Therefore, it is socially efficient to disseminate existing knowledge as widely as possible.

Society must trade off the static economic gains from distributing an existing body of knowledge as widely as possible against the dynamic economic gains from the growth of knowledge stimulated by protecting those who create new knowledge. The patent and copyright systems, which prevent others from using new knowledge for a specific period of time without the permission of its creators, are the compromise that has been chosen in resolving this issue. Various conventions and agreements covering patents, copyrights and trademarks currently operate under the jurisdiction of the World Intellectual Property Organization (WIPO). However, the existing system has been criticised on at least four grounds: (1) a number of countries are not signatories to the existing agreements and thus not subject to their rules; (2) the rules themselves are not broad enough — for example, the Paris Convention on patents and trademarks permits exceptions from patent coverage for foods, drugs and chemicals; (3) the present system relies on the national treatment principle to provide protection, but the existence of weak standards of protection in many countries makes this arrangement inadequate; (4) there are no enforcement provisions in existing agreements, nor any dispute settlement mechanisms.

The Uruguay Round agreement on trade-related aspects of intellectual property rights made substantial progress in overcoming these drawbacks of the existing system. All GATT members are now required to provide copyright, trademark and patent protection for a specified number of years on the goods and services covered under the agreements to which most developed countries adhere, i.e. the Paris Convention, the Berne Convention, the Rome Convention and the Treaty on Intellectual Property in Respect of Integrated Circuits. The provisions of the agreement must be implemented within a year after the date of entry into force of the agreement, but developing countries and countries in transition from a centrally-planned to a market economy are given another four years. In addition, if a developing country is obliged to provide patent protection in an area not currently covered in its laws, e.g. pharmaceutical products, it may delay implementation of this protection for another five years. The least developed countries need not apply the agreement's provisions for ten years.

Specific enforcement procedures are also contained in the agreement. For example, countries are required to establish civil judicial procedures whereby individuals and firms can seek to enforce their intellectual property rights. Criminal procedures must also be put in place to deal with wilful trademark counterfeiting or copyright piracy on a commercial scale. A Council on Trade-Related Aspects of Intellectual Property Rights is established to monitor the compliance of countries with their obligations under the agreement, and if a country believes its rights under the agreement are being violated, it can utilise the standard dispute settlement procedures of the GATT.

The agreement represents an important step in encouraging additional R&D expenditures by private firms. The industrialised nations, where most R&D

activities take place, will clearly gain. While the developing countries will also gain in the long run as the increase in the level of technological knowledge leads to a greater supply of goods and services that raise their rates of income growth, and as these countries begin to develop new technologies themselves, some are likely to lose in the short run. Presumably, this is why developing countries have been given the five to ten year period within which to implement the various provisions.

c. *Trade-Related Investment Measures (TRIMS)*

An economically efficient global economy requires that direct investment among nations be as free from burdensome border and domestic controls as the movement of goods and services. Fortunately, more and more leaders of developing countries have come to realise that their economies can benefit from the considerable economic growth stimulus associated with liberal direct investment policies without becoming unduly dominated by foreign influences. However, there are still many countries that restrict foreign direct investment in various ways and also impose performance requirements on foreign firms operating in their territories.

Negotiations on trade-related investment measures were aimed at eliminating trading requirements imposed on foreign enterprises located within a country that do not also apply to domestically-owned firms. By specifying that the principle of national treatment must apply to foreign firms, such practices as requiring foreign enterprises to purchase a certain proportion of domestically produced goods or export a certain proportion of their output have become illegal under the TRIMS agreement. However, developing countries are given five years (least developed countries seven years) to eliminate such measures and can apply for an extension if they demonstrate particular difficulties in implementing the agreement.

While the TRIMS agreement represents an important step in eliminating discrimination against foreign investors, there is also a need for gradually reducing barriers that prevent investors in one country from establishing production facilities in other countries. A number of developing countries, who fear too much political influence by foreigners if direct investment is not controlled, strongly resisted efforts to deal with this issue in the Round. The costs of taking this position are very high in terms of preventing an acceleration of growth in these countries and thereby reducing the wide disparity in income levels between many developing and developed countries. However, the TRIMS agreement does contain a provision specifying that, in the course of reviewing the agreement within five years, the issue of including provisions on investment policy shall be considered.

3. AGRICULTURE AND TEXTILES/APPAREL

The Uruguay Round has been noteworthy not only for formulating international rules of 'good' behaviour in new areas such as trade in services and intellectual property rights, but in two traditional sectors that have long been excluded from the discipline imposed by GATT rules, namely, agriculture and textiles/apparel. The exclusion of agriculture from GATT rules goes back to 1955, when the United States obtained a GATT waiver permitting certain import practices that were illegal under the GATT but were mandated by US agricultural legislation. While the agricultural sector was never formally removed from GATT discipline, other countries have engaged in similar practices on the grounds that what was permitted for the United States should also be allowed for them.

The exclusion of textiles and clothing from GATT rules can be traced back to 1961, when the first of a series of multilateral agreements permitting bilateral quantitative restrictions went into effect. These agreements were supposed to be only temporary, but the current agreement, the Multifibre Arrangement (MFA), went into operation in 1974 and has been renewed several times since then.

a. Agriculture

In July 1987 the United States made the following proposal to the other Uruguay Round participants: (a) the complete phase-out over ten years of all agricultural subsidies which directly or indirectly affect trade; (b) the freezing and phase-out over ten years of the quantities of agricultural products exported with the aid of export subsidies; (c) the phase-out of all import barriers over ten years; and (d) the harmonisation of health and sanitary regulations, insofar as animal, plant and human health and safety are not affected. The European Community (EC) did not formally respond until December 1989 when, without mentioning a specific percentage figure, its negotiators proposed that support measures and protection be reduced. However, in July 1990, Community negotiators stated that the EC was willing to reduce farm support levels by 30 per cent over a ten-year period from their 1986 level. Because reductions had already taken place since that date, the proposal meant, in effect, that the EC would only be required to reduce support by about 15–20 per cent from 1990 levels.

The Community continued to offer to reduce support levels by only 30 per cent at the Brussels Ministerial Meeting in December 1990, where the negotiations supposedly were to be concluded. However, by this time the United States and the so-called Cairns Group, which was composed of most other agricultural exporting nations, had modified their position somewhat. They proposed reductions of not less than 75 per cent on a 1986 to 1988 average base period for commodity-specific support and a 30 per cent reduction over the same period for non-commodity-specific support.

At the Brussels meetings, neither the United States nor the EC was willing to make the significant compromises needed to bridge the wide gap between their two negotiating positions. Consequently, no agreement on agriculture was reached. Furthermore, since the United States insisted on an agreement in this sector as a condition for agreements in other issue areas in the negotiations, the meeting concluded without any agreements.

In November 1992, after nearly two years of difficult negotiations, US and EC negotiators agreed to support a Uruguay Round agricultural agreement requiring a 20 per cent reduction over a six-year period in the average level of farm supports from a 1986 – 1988 base. Since the United States had already reduced its supports relative to the base period, no further reductions were required for US commodities. Direct income payments linked to production-limiting programmes were also not subject to the reduction commitment. The negotiators also agreed to support a 21 per cent reduction in the volume of agricultural commodities that receive export subsidies and a 36 per cent reduction in the value of export subsidies. However, the French government balked at this arrangement on export subsidies and threatened to hold up the conclusion of the Round. But, after obtaining concessions from Community members in the form of additional compensation to French farmers who might be hurt by the agreement and from the United States in the form of a less rapid phase-out of export subsidies, the French withdrew their objections.

The market access features of the final agreement include replacing non-tariff border measures with tariffs and then reducing these by 36 per cent in the case of developed countries and 24 per cent in the case of developing countries. Another important feature is the establishment of minimum access commitments, equal initially to three per cent of the domestic consumption of a product and growing to five per cent over the implementation period. This provision will finally enable the United States to export rice to Japan and Korea. The implementation period for the various provisions in the agreement is six years for developed countries and ten years for developing countries.

While the pledged reductions are comparatively modest, the key point is that the agricultural sector is being brought under GATT discipline and will be subject to further cuts in support levels in future negotiations. However, since the commitment to integrate agriculture into the GATT was made at the outset of the negotiations, it is not evident that the difference between what was finally obtained and what the Community offered in 1990 was worth the long delay in the negotiations.

b. Textiles and Apparel

Other than agriculture, no commodity sector has been less subject to GATT rules than textiles and apparel. Beginning in the early 1960s, an international system of bilateral quantitative import restrictions developed for these products which has become increasingly comprehensive and restrictive. It has been estimated that the cost to consumers of the import protection for textile and apparel products in 1990 was $24 billion (Hufbauer and Elliott, 1994). This means that the average family paid about $360 more annually than would have been the case if there were no import protection for these sectors.[3] In launching the Uruguay Round, trade ministers took the bold step of declaring that the negotiations

> shall aim to formulate modalities that would permit the eventual integration of this sector into GATT on the basis of strengthened GATT rules and disciplines, thereby contributing to the objective of further liberalization of trade (GATT Press Release, 25 September 1986).

The final agreement in this sector represents an important step in carrying out these objectives.

The integration of textiles and clothing into the GATT system involves the elimination of bilateral quantitative restrictions and, thus, the end of the Multifibre Arrangement. Protection must take the form of tariffs. On 1 January 1995, each party must remove quotas on imports accounting for at least 16 per cent of its imports of textiles and clothing in 1990. At the beginning of phase 2 on 1 January 1988, quotas on an additional 17 per cent of 1990 imports must be eliminated, followed by another 18 per cent on 1 January 2002. All remaining quantitative restrictions must be removed by 1 January 2005.

For products remaining under quantitative import restrictions, at whatever stage, the agreement establishes a formula for increasing the growth rate of imports. During the 1995 to 1998 period, the annual growth rate must be not less than 16 per cent higher than the annual growth rate established for 1994 under the Multifibre Arrangement and, in the 1998 to 2003 period, this rate must be at least 25 per cent higher than the previous period. Between 2002 and 2004, the import growth rate must rise by 27 per cent compared to the previous period.

Safeguard actions in the form of country-by-country quantitative restrictions are permitted during the transition period. They can be imposed if increased imports cause, or threaten to cause, 'serious damage' to the domestic industry producing like or directly competitive products. These transitional safeguard measures can remain in place for up to three years but cannot be extended.

The postponement of the integration into the GATT system of a significant part of the textiles and apparel trade until the end of the transition period, and the relatively easy standards for invoking the safeguard provision, raise some concerns about whether the system of bilateral import quotas will actually come to an end, but there seems little doubt that significant progress in this direction will be made.

---

[3] The source for the number of families in 1990 (66 million) is the *Economic Report of the President* (1992).

4. TRADITIONAL GATT ISSUES

a. 'Unfair Trade'

One of the most significant developments in the international trading system in recent years has been the rapid increase in the number of cases of alleged 'unfair' trading practices brought by the two most important trading powers, the United States and the European Community. In recent years, US and EC negotiators have argued strongly that the competitive abilities of their producers have been seriously undermined by the dumping and subsidising activities of other countries and, therefore, that existing GATT rules need to be tightened to prevent these practices. In contrast, the trade representatives of most other countries have claimed that the current 'unfair' trade laws of the United States and the European Community, especially the anti-dumping laws of these countries, are being administered in a manner that unfairly discriminates against foreign producers. The anti-dumping and subsidies/countervailing duties agreements reached in the Uruguay Round address the concerns of both groups.

(i) Anti-dumping duties: A major complaint of US firms who have been successful in obtaining anti-dumping duties is that their effectiveness is often circumvented by the importation and assembly of the parts or components of the final products subject to the duties. The anti-dumping agreement does not explicitly mention anti-circumvention measures, but a ministerial declaration accompanying the agreement recognises the problem and the need to develop uniform anti-circumvention rules in the future. In the meantime, the United States can continue to apply such anti-circumvention measures as extending anti-dumping duty orders to parts or components.

A major complaint of foreign producers is that certain practices by the administrators of the US anti-dumping law have the effect of biasing upward the dumping margins that are found. These practices include (i) calculating anti-dumping margins by comparing the average foreign market value with each sale in the United States, (ii) throwing out negative dumping margins in calculating the dumping margin to apply to firms not investigated, and (iii) adding on eight per cent for profits and ten per cent for general expenses in cost-of-production calculations. Requiring foreign firms to submit extensive information about their selling practices on computer media is also widely considered to be unduly burdensome for small firms. The agreement deals with such concerns by spelling out in greater detail the procedures to be followed in determining dumping. For example, it calls for 'a fair comparison' between export price and normal value, and also specifies that, in determining the cost of production for a particular good, administrative costs and profits shall be based on actual data in the industry alleged to be dumping.

Another controversial matter considered in the agreement is forward pricing. An important feature of much modern, high-technology production is that there are large start-up costs in the form of research and development expenditures and outlays for plant and capital equipment, as well as strong learning-by-doing effects. Consequently, unit costs fall significantly as the cumulative volume of output increases. In addition, most manufactured products are differentiated from similar goods in diverse ways, and many have comparatively short product lives, since new and better products are being continuously developed through research and development activities.

As a consequence of these characteristics, firms take into consideration the volume of production over a product's life when setting the product's price. This forward pricing may mean that they set a price that does not cover average production costs during the early stages of a good's production life. Setting the price at the outset at a level sufficient to cover average costs could mean that a firm facing competition from other established producers would never sell a sufficient volume of output to cover its total costs. Therefore, most economists recommend that the rules on anti-dumping be changed so that the requirement of covering average costs refer to costs over a good's production life. US law permits the calculation of average costs 'over an extended period of time' in determining whether sales have taken place at less than average cost, but US anti-dumping administrators have interpreted this as being the last year or even the last six months. While the Uruguay Round anti-dumping agreement specifies an extended period of time as being normally one year but in no case less than six months, it does state that cost of production calculations shall take into consideration non-recurring costs, such as start-up costs, that benefit future as well as current production. In addition, if margins of dumping of less than two per cent are found, the dumping margin is to be considered *de minimis* and the case is to be terminated.

The procedures for determining material injury are also specified in greater detail. For example, the need to consider other possible causes of injury other than the dumped imports is stressed. However, in response to the wishes of the United States, the agreement does permit the investigating authorities to cumulate the injury effects due to dumped imports of a product from several countries. Other important features of the anti-dumping agreement are that anti-dumping measures shall expire in five years unless a determination is made that dumping would likely continue, and that dispute settlement panels can be established to determine if a country's administering authorities' establishment of the facts was proper and whether their evaluation of those facts was unbiased and objective.

While the agreement improves certain administrative features of the anti-dumping process, it is unlikely to bring about any significant changes in the way anti-dumping laws are being administered by such dominant trading powers as the United States or the European Union. In particular, it does little to deal with the criticism by many economists that anti-dumping laws are being used as an easy way to gain protection rather than to respond to practices that most would regard as being basically unfair (see Messerlin, 1989; Murray, 1991; Palmeter, 1991; Horlick, 1989; and Baldwin and Steagall, 1994). For this reason, it is the most disappointing of all the agreements. The failure to curtail the misuse of anti-dumping laws could prevent the international community from actually achieving the significant welfare gains that are implicit in most of the other Uruguay Round agreements.

(ii) Subsidies and countervailing measures: The Uruguay Round negotiators agreed to divide government subsidies into three categories: prohibited subsidies, actionable subsidies and non-actionable subsidies. An effort to introduce a similar classification was made in the Tokyo Round, but it was not successful. Economists have long recognised that the free market system does not always produce the most socially efficient allocation of resources and have pointed out that there is a theoretical case for the selective use of subsidies or taxes under certain circumstances.[4] For example, as pointed out in the discussion of intellectual property rights, research and development activities often produce beneficial spillovers that those undertaking the research are unable to capture. Thus, there will be a tendency to undertake less research than is socially desirable.

The agreement includes government subsidies for research activities in the list of non-actionable subsidies. However, recognising the problem of preventing politically influential sectors from misusing this provision, the agreement limits the proportion of research costs that can be subsidised to not more than 75 per cent of industrial research aimed at discovering new knowledge, or 50 per cent of pre-competitive development activity associated with translating industrial research into plans for new or improved products. Interestingly, in the early phases of the negotiations under the Reagan Administration, US negotiators opposed all forms of subsidies, but this position changed in the Bush Administration to one of supporting subsidies for research purposes. The Clinton Administration, which is more sympathetic to industrial policy involving active government participation than the previous two administrations, succeeded in raising the limits on industrial research from 50 per cent to 75 per cent and those on pre-competitive research from 25 per cent to 50 per cent.

Two other forms of subsidisation specified as non-actionable in the agreement are assistance to promote the adaptation of existing facilities to new environmental requirements and assistance to disadvantaged regions within a country. The case for making the latter type of subsidies non-actionable is

[4] For a survey of the various circumstances where government intervention is theoretically justified, see Bhagwati (1971).

questionable, since it is not based on international efficiency considerations and there are no time limits for the subsidies. In addition to these three specific forms of subsidisation, subsidies that are not specific, in the sense of being limited to a specific enterprise, group of enterprises or industry, are not actionable under the agreement.

Two types of subsidies are prohibited: subsidies contingent on export performance and subsidies contingent on the use of domestic goods over imported goods. Subsidies that cause injury to the domestic industry of another signatory, nullify or impair benefits accruing to other signatories under the GATT, or cause serious prejudice to the interests of another signatory, are actionable under the agreement in the sense of being subject to the consultation and dispute settlement procedures of the GATT, as well as being subject to countervailing duty actions.

An especially important provision of the agreement is that countervailing measures cannot be used against non-actionable subsidies. The current countervailing duty law of the United States and other countries permits countervailing duties to be imposed against any subsidy that materially injures or threatens to materially injure a domestic industry by reason of the subsidised imports. However, if a country believes the non-actionable subsidy of another country has resulted in serious adverse effects to a domestic industry, it can request the Committee on Subsidies and Countervailing Measures, which is established under the agreement, to investigate the matter. If the Committee agrees with the country's claim, it will recommend to the subsidising country that it modify its subsidy to eliminate these effects. If the recommendation is not followed, the Committee will authorise the country adversely affected to take appropriate countervailing measures.

The parts of the agreement dealing with countervailing measures, like the anti-dumping agreement, include provisions aimed at preventing the discriminatory administration of countervailing duty laws as well as the circumvention of countervailing duties by importation and assembly of parts or components of the final product subject to the extra duty. Countervailing duties must also be terminated within five years unless there is a determination that subsidisation is likely to continue.

Developing countries are afforded special and differential treatment under the agreement. Specifically, the least developed countries are exempt from the disciplines on prohibited export subsidies, while other developing countries are given eight years to comply with the prohibition of export subsidies. Countries in transition from a centrally-planned to a market economy do not have to phase-out prohibited subsidies for a period of seven years.

The agreement on subsidies and countervailing measures is a considerable improvement over the Tokyo Round agreement on this subject, which was vaguely and ambiguously worded. The new agreement tightens the administration of countervailing duty laws and explicitly recognises that some subsidies are clearly economically undesirable, others clearly desirable and many that must be examined on a case-by-case basis to determine their appropriateness on economic grounds.

b. Safeguards

Perhaps the most important feature of the safeguard agreement concerns a provision not included in the agreement. Despite considerable pressure from the EC to abandon the most-favoured-nation principle in safeguard cases, the agreement does not include a provision permitting the application of safeguard measures only against those countries from which imports have increased and caused serious injury to a domestic industry. The developing countries strongly opposed this selectivity principle and the United States, after seriously considering abandoning its traditional most-favoured-nation position, also finally opposed selectivity.

The agreement also specifies that GATT members must phase-out existing selective safeguard measures, such as voluntary export restraints, within four years.[5] Import quotas are permitted if administered in a non-discriminatory manner and if they do not reduce imports below the average of the last three representative years. However, an exception to non-discriminatory quantitative restrictions is permitted if it is demonstrated to the Committee on Safeguards that imports from some countries have increased disproportionately over the representative period.

Among other key parts of the proposed agreement are the requirements that safeguard measures last no more than eight years (four years at a time) and not be applied again for a period of time equal to that for which the measure had previously been applied (provided that this period is at least two years).[6] In addition, countries against whom safeguard measures are directed cannot demand compensation or undertake retaliatory action for the first three years that a safeguard measure is in effect.

Both of these provisions are aimed at encouraging industries to undertake appropriate adjustment actions in the face of serious import injury rather than attempting to obtain protection indefinitely. However, they do not deal directly with a fundamental flaw in the safeguard provisions of GATT. By standing ready to offset serious injury to domestic industries due to increased imports through the provision of import protection to these industries, governments' decisions to

---

[5] Each member can, however, retain one such measure through 1999.

[6] This provision was introduced into US law in 1988. Prior to the 1988 change, industries could petition for another eight years of protection two years after the expiration of the first eight-year period.

reduce levels of protection to promote economic efficiency and growth are not credible to the individuals employed in industries subject to such cuts (see Staiger and Tabellini, 1987 and 1991). Since they know that their governments will step in with assistance if they suffer harm from increased imports, these individuals will tend not to seek employment in other industries in response to the reduction in levels of protection. To avoid this outcome, trade measures should not be used for the purpose of helping import-injured industries. Instead, the legitimate goal of assisting injured workers should be carried out by providing income payments tied either to participation in retraining programmes and/or employment in other sectors. However, because such payments appear in governments' budgets, they are more difficult to implement politically than import duties or import quotas.

As in most of the agreements, developing countries are given special treatment. In the safeguard agreement they are permitted to grant import relief for up to ten years and can reintroduce protection in the same sector after waiting for a period of time equal to only one-half of the period that the measure had previously been applied. However, the Uruguay Round agreements do little to curtail the widespread use by developing countries of safeguards for balance-of-payments purposes, although members agree to give preference to price-based measures, e.g. import surcharges, for restricting imports for balance-of-payments reasons over quantitative measures.

The major accomplishment of the safeguard agreement was the banning of such measures as voluntary export restraints and orderly marketing agreements. In addition, the agreement has the merit of spelling out in more detail the procedures that must be followed in Article XIX determinations and in defining such key concepts as 'serious injury'. While the provisions concerning the frequency of petitions from a particular industry and compensation may help somewhat to bring about a more economically efficient adjustment process, the agreement does not deal adequately with the time-consistency issue.

c. Government Procurement

A new government procurement agreement was also reached in the Uruguay Round. However, unlike the other agreements discussed above, this is a plurilateral agreement in the sense that not all GATT members will be required to accept the agreement. The participants in the agreement are Austria, Canada, the European Community, Finland, Hong Kong, Israel, Japan, the Republic of Korea, Norway, Sweden, Switzerland and the United States. With the exception of Korea, this is the same list of countries who were participants in the government procurement agreement negotiated in the Tokyo Round. However, the scope of the agreement has been significantly expanded by including services, procurement at the subcentral governmental level, e.g. states and provinces, and procurement by public utilities. But, given the extent of the distortion to world trade caused by the preferences most governments give to domestic suppliers when making their non-military purchases of goods and services, much more negotiating work is needed in this field.

d. Technical Barriers to Trade (Standards)

The agreement covering technical barriers to trade extends and clarifies the agreement reached on this subject during the Tokyo Round. It stresses that technical regulations shall not be more trade-restrictive than necessary to fulfil a legitimate objective, taking account of the risks non-fulfilment would create. However, it recognises that each country has the right to establish and maintain standards and technical regulations that protect life and the environment, and can determine the appropriate level of protection for these purposes. All WTO members must adhere to the provisions of this agreement.

e. Dispute Settlement Procedures

Although GATT rules state that, unless otherwise specified, the majority voting rule determines the outcome of decisions where joint action is called for, there is, as Jackson (1989, p. 49) points out, 'a decided preference for "consensus" approaches' among GATT members. While this principle has been important in preventing the organisation from breaking up during times of difficult negotiations, it has also made the GATT ineffective in some circumstances. The dispute settlement process is an example of this ineffectiveness. Under the consensus approach that has been followed since the formation of the GATT, a defending party in a request for the establishment of a GATT panel has been able to block approval for the panel. Moreover, the losing party in a panel report (or any party) can block the adoption of the report and even block the winning party's request to retaliate if the losing party does not comply with a panel report that is adopted.

The Understanding on Rules and Procedures Governing the Settlement of Disputes reached in the Uruguay Round significantly changes the previous dispute settlement process. Most importantly, the principle of 'automaticity' has been introduced into the new agreement (Hudec, 1994). Now, formation of panels, adoption of their reports and, if a panel ruling is not complied with, retaliation are all automatic. This change in itself greatly strengthens the dispute settlement process.

There are several other ways in which the process has been strengthened. A unified system to settle disputes arising under the various agreements replaces the various different procedures for settling disputes under the Tokyo Round agreements. This system even applies to disputes arising over issues on which there are no specific legal obligations under the GATT. Time limits have also been established for carrying out the various steps in the settlement process. For example, panels appointed by the Dispute Settlement Body to render a decision of the merits of a complaint must normally report their findings within six months and in no event longer than nine months. Another important change is the creation of an Appellate Body to review panel decisions that are appealed. It will have seven members who are appointed for a four-year term. The decisions of this body must be made within 60–90 days.

It should be noted that panel rulings are *not* self-executing. If a country chooses not to change its laws or regulations to conform to a panel ruling, the penalty it will incur will be the possibility of retaliatory actions by its trading partners. However, such a country is likely to find it more difficult to persuade other countries of the merits of the cases it brings before the Dispute Settlement Body.

f. Market Access for Goods

Traditionally, the main focus of multilateral trade negotiations has been the reduction of tariffs. However, now that average duty levels of the major industrial countries are less than five per cent, the major efforts of negotiators have focused on the kinds of non-tariff issues discussed in this section. Nevertheless, import duties remain significant barriers to trade in some sectors and duty reduction was an essential goal of the Uruguay Round negotiations. On average, duty reductions of about 35 per cent on industrial products were achieved by the developed countries. Furthermore, the developed countries agreed to eliminate tariffs on construction, agricultural and medical equipment, steel, beer and distilled spirits, pharmaceutical products, paper, toys and furniture. Deep cuts on computer parts, semiconductors and semiconductor manufacturing equipment were also achieved. Most cuts will be phased in over five years, starting in January 1995, but reductions in some sensitive industries will be spread over ten years.

A particularly important feature of the agreement on tariffs is that tariffs will be bound on over 50 per cent of the imports of developing countries. This means that, unlike the past, these countries will not be able to change their tariff levels without providing compensation to their trading partners or risking retaliation from these countries. Although it is expected that these countries will set the bound levels higher than current tariff levels, this change represents an important step in locking-in the liberalisation that many developing nations have undertaken in recent years.

g. Agreement to Establish the World Trade Organization (WTO)

One of the biggest disappointments with the codes approach utilised in the Tokyo Round was that many countries did not sign some of the key agreements.

Thus, free-riding in the world trading system, which already was a serious problem due to the special treatment afforded to some members, became even more extensive. The effect was to increase the dissatisfaction of those members who assumed the full responsibilities of the GATT with the system and to induce some to seek alternative means of achieving their trade policy objectives.

In an effort to curtail free-riding and to bring together the existing and new international trading rules, the agreements and associated legal instruments covering goods, services, intellectual property rights, and the procedures for settling disputes and monitoring trade policies under a single institutional framework, the Final Act of the Uruguay Round establishes a new international organisation, the World Trade Organization (WTO). Members are required to accept all of its provisions, with the exception of the so-called Plurilateral Trade Agreements consisting of the agreement on government procurement, the agreement on civil aviation, the international dairy arrangement and the arrangement regarding bovine meat.[7]

The establishment of the WTO strengthens the institutional framework for administering the various rules pertaining to trade that have been proposed by some 120 trading nations. Because of the failure of the major trading powers to approve the International Trade Organisation (ITO) after World War II, while still accepting the ITO's provisions relating to trade in goods (GATT), a small Secretariat was established to help administer the agreement of trade in goods. Part of the weakening of the international trading system in recent years can be attributed to the inability of the small number of individuals involved in the Secretariat to monitor whether the rules were being followed and to exert pressure to secure compliance. The new organisation greatly improves the prospects that both the old trading rules and the new ones adopted in the Uruguay Round will be followed more closely.

5. FUTURE NEGOTIATIONS

As the preceding analysis indicates, the Uruguay Round agreements should significantly strengthen the multilateral trading system. However, further negotiations are needed to achieve the goals set at the outset of these negotiations. For example, additional negotiations are needed to achieve greater liberalisation and better international rules in such areas as trade in services, direct investment, agriculture, dumping and subsidisation, safeguards and government procurement policies. Furthermore, there is a need for new international trading rules in some

[7] Only the first of these four agreements has been discussed in this section. For details on this and other issues, see Jackson (1995).

areas not covered in the Uruguay Round. These include trade-related environmental matters and competition policy.

The growing importance of environmental issues is recognised by all and the Uruguay Round negotiators agreed that a work programme on trade and the environment should be developed within the WTO. Although there is less political pressure for developing international rules dealing with restrictive business practices, there is a growing recognition that the difficulty of penetrating domestic markets in some countries, for example, those in Japan, is due more to the collusive business practices of firms in these countries than to the policies of their governments. Unfortunately, even though business interests in other countries recognise the major cause of the market penetration problem in such countries, they fear that they too might be required to change some of their practices if rules dealing with competition policy are introduced into the WTO. In the meantime, consumers in the global economy appear to pay a very high price in terms of economic welfare for the absence of such rules.

On balance, the agreements represent a significant effort to strengthen the liberal foundations of the world trading system and to reverse the trend toward unilateralism and unequal treatment of trading partners that characterised the 1980s.

REFERENCES

Baldwin, R.E. and J.W. Steagall (1994), 'An Analysis of ITC Decisions in Anti-dumping, Countervailing Duty and Safeguard Cases', *Weltwirtschaftliches Archiv*, **130**, 2, 290–308.

Bhagwati, J.N. (1971), 'The Generalised Theory of Distortions and Welfare' in J.N. Bhagwati et al. (eds), *Trade, Balance of Payments and Growth*, (Amsterdam, North Holland).

Economic Report of the President (1993) (Washington, DC: United States Government Printing Office).

Feketekuty, G. (1988), *International Trade in Services: An Overview and Blueprint for Negotiations* (Cambridge, MA: Ballinger Publishing Co.).

Horlick, G.N. (1989), 'The United States Anti-dumping System', in J.H. Jackson and E.A. Vermulst (eds.), *Anti-dumping Law and Practice* (Ann Arbor: University of Michigan Press).

Hudec, R.E. (1994), 'Strengthening of Dispute Settlement Procedures', paper presented at a conference on Uruguay Round agreements from an Asia-Pacific perspective (sponsored by the Gaston Sigur Centre for East Asian Studies, George Washington University, 1–3 August 1994, Washington, DC).

Hufbauer, G.C. and K.A. Elliott (1994), *Measuring the Costs of Protection in the United States* (Washington, DC: Institute for International Economics).

Jackson, J.H. (1995), 'The World Trade Organization: Watershed Innovation or Cautious Small Step Forward?', *The World Economy Global Trade Review, 1995*, 11–31.

Messerlin, P.A. (1989), 'The EC Anti-dumping Regulations: A First Economic Appraisal, 1980–85', *Weltwirtschaftliches Archiv*, **125**, 3, 563–87.

Murray, T. (1991), 'The Administration of the Anti-dumping Law by the Department of Commerce', in R. Boltuck and R.E. Litan (eds.), *Down in the Dumps: Administration of the Unfair Trade Laws* (Washington, DC: The Brookings Institution).

Office of the US Trade Representative (1993), *Final Act Embodying the Results of the Uruguay Round of Multilateral Trade Negotiations (Version of 15 December 1993* (US Government Printing Office).

Palmeter, N.D. (1991), 'The Anti-dumping Law: A Legal and Administrative Non-tariff Barrier', in R. Boltuck and R.E. Litan (eds.), *Down in the Dumps: Administration of the Unfair Trade Laws* (Washington, DC: The Brookings Institution).

Sapir, A. (1982), 'Trade in Services: Policy Issues for the Eighties', *Columbia Journal of World Business*, 77–83.

Staiger, R.W. and G. Tabellini (1987), 'Discretionary Trade Policy and Excessive Protection', *American Economic Review*, **77** (December), 823–887.

Staiger, R.W. and G. Tabellini (1991), 'Rules Versus Discretion in Trade Policy: An Empirical Analysis', in R.E. Baldwin (ed.), *Empirical Studies of Commercial Policy* (Chicago: University of Chicago Press).

The Trade Policy Revolution in Developing Countries

Judith M. Dean

In a broad swing of the pendulum, developing countries have been shifting from severe and destructive protection to free trade fever.

R. Dornbusch (1992)

The 1980s have seen the beginnings of a change of heart among developing country policy makers with regard to trade policy. The import-substitution consensus of the previous decades, with its preference for high levels of tariff and non-tariff trade barriers, has all but evaporated.

D. Rodrik (1992)

1. INTRODUCTION

IN a recent discussion about the merits and limitations of trade liberalisation, there was little agreement between Dornbusch (1992) and Rodrik (1992), except on one issue. Increasing numbers of developing countries have unilaterally liberalised their trade regimes. During the 1980s liberalisation seemed to be contagious in the developing world. In Asia it spread from Taiwan and Korea to Southeast Asia and on to China. In Latin America, it spread from Chile to Mexico and beyond.

Two large-scale World Bank projects on trade policy reform have recently been published (Thomas, et al., 1991, and Papageorgiou, et al., 1991), evaluating reform episodes up through the mid-1980s. In addition, several smaller research projects on trade policy have been undertaken (Alam and Rajapatirana, 1993; Nogues and Gulati 1992; and World Bank, 1993), and the Bank's country operations maintain ongoing studies and reports on trade reform (e.g., World Bank, 1992). However, the recent and apparently broad move toward unilateral liberalisation across developing countries had not been documented in any comprehensive way. No compilation of data existed which showed changes in trade barriers across countries and over time,[1] nor were

JUDITH M. DEAN is from Johns Hopkins University, Washington DC. She wishes to thank James Riedel and an anonymous reviewer for very helpful comments.

[1] UNCTAD (1987) provides detailed data at the product level on both tariff and non-tariff barriers for a large number of countries. The data are usually for 1985/86, however. More recent UNCTAD work has updated the data for a few countries.

there any systematic comparisons of the type and magnitude of trade reform across countries or within regions.

'Trade Policy Reform in Developing Countries since 1985: a Review of the Evidence' by Dean, Desai, and Riedel (DDR) (1994) begins to fill this gap. It examines both the extent and the character of trade policy reform in 32 countries[2] in South Asia, Africa, Latin America, and East Asia, from the mid-1980s up to 1992/93. DDR (1994) discusses changes in tariffs, non-tariff barriers, foreign exchange markets, and export impediments and incentives. Data are presented on levels, range and dispersion of tariffs, and the coverage of quantitative restrictions (QRs) for the mid-1980s and the early 1990s.

The evidence presented in DDR (1994) shows that trade liberalisation has indeed occurred extensively, and sometimes dramatically, in South Asia, Latin America, and East Asia. Yet each region has shown a distinct difference in approach and in the degree of liberalisation actually achieved. The Latin American countries investigated stand out as moving sharply towards liberality in trade. In fact, they appear to be rapidly moving toward the level of liberalisation in the East Asian NICs. Only in Africa do we find little progress towards a liberalised trade regime. Here there have been several cases of reversal of previous liberalisation policy or of increases in import impediments.

This paper presents an overview of the trade policy revolution in developing countries, synthesising the evidence found in DDR. Section 2 outlines the approach adopted in DDR (1994) regarding definition and measurement of trade liberalisation. Section 3 presents evidence on the extent and character of trade policy reform. Section 4 discusses some patterns which emerge across regions.

2. DEFINING AND MEASURING TRADE LIBERALISATION[3]

The conflict between various definitions of trade liberalisation makes it difficult to assess the extent to which it has occurred (Greenaway, 1993; and Edwards, 1989). In general, liberalisation has been equated with becoming more 'outward oriented.' This may refer, however, to a move toward neutrality, liberality, or openness (Pritchett, 1991). A move toward neutrality involves equalising incentives, on average, between the export and import-competing sectors. A more liberal regime is one where the level of intervention has been

[2] Bangladesh, India, Pakistan, Sri Lanka; Cameroon, Cote d'Ivoire, Ghana, Kenya, Madagascar, Malawi, Mali, Nigeria, Senegal, South Africa, Tanzania, Uganda, Zaire; Argentina, Brazil, Chile, Colombia, Costa Rica, Mexico, Peru, Venezuela; China, Indonesia, Korea, Malaysia, Philippines, Thailand, Vietnam. These countries together account for about 60 (80) per cent of the population of the (low-income) developing world.

[3] DDR (1994) also considers the issues of design of liberalisation. This is particularly important as most liberalisation is piecemeal, giving rise to issues of the second-best. In addition, questions of credibility and feasibility arise.

reduced. Finally, an increase in openness is equated with an increase in the importance of trade in the economy (e.g., as a per cent of GDP). Clearly, a more neutral regime does not necessarily mean a more liberal one. In addition, even in a world without distortions, a small country will usually be more open (as defined above) than a large country.

The DDR study adopts an approach similar to Edwards (1989) in evaluating the character and extent of trade reform. This approach defines liberalisation as a continuum. A policy action which reduces the scarcity premium attached to controls (Krueger, 1989) would be considered 'mild liberalisation.' A move to neutrality (Bhagwati, 1988) would be a more intensive liberalisation. Finally, a reduction in levels of intervention (increased liberality) would constitute a more drastic form of liberalisation.

Measuring the extent of trade liberalisation is severely impeded by the lack of an aggregate measure which possesses a minimal set of desirable properties.[4] Of the numerous attempts to develop such a measure,[5] those which are most comprehensive are not objective, and those which are objective are not necessarily sensitive to policy changes.[6] The index used in Papageorgiou, et al. (1991), for example, is constructed separately for each country, by weighting and aggregating many individual indicators. As the authors note, subjective assessments were used in the choice of components and weights, making cross-country comparisons impossible. An alternative measure, Leamer's (1988) index, uses residuals from a regression of net exports on factor endowments to capture the effect of the difference between an individual country's trade restrictions and the average trade restrictions of the sample. As Leamer points out, the residuals clearly could represent non-linearities and/or unmeasured resources, as well as trade barriers, making it difficult to link changes in the residuals to changes in restrictiveness of the trade regime.

DDR (1994), therefore, examines four individual categories of indicators for evidence of liberalisation — import tariffs, QRs on imports, export impediments and incentives, and the degree of exchange rate misalignment — recognising that changes in one indicator are not easily weighed against changes in the others. Several other limitations are also stressed. Average nominal tariffs will be biased upwards, since quite often the highest rates apply to only a few goods. Import-weighted averages will have a downward bias, since the most restrictive barriers receive the smallest weights. Weighting tariffs by the amount of domestic

---

[4] Objectivity would allow for cross-country comparisons. Comprehensiveness is critical to account for interaction among policy changes. In addition, an index should measure changes in both the magnitude and coverage of barriers. Finally, a direct link between changes in trade restrictions and the index would avoid treating trade liberalisation as a residual.

[5] See Harrison (1991) and Pritchett (1991) for a review of a large number of these measures.

[6] A new measure being developed to better meet these criteria is the trade restrictiveness index (Anderson and Neary, 1994).

production they 'protect' may be superior, since heavily protected sectors receive higher weights.

Some barriers may be redundant. Very high tariffs may imply 'water in the tariff' or may apply to very few goods. Large reductions in such barriers will be necessary before any impact on imports occurs. Alternatively, a good may be restrained by both quotas and tariffs. If the quota is binding, reductions in tariffs will have little impact on trade flows. This same problem arises if the binding constraints on trade are due to foreign exchange restrictions rather than trade barriers.

Finally, several aspects of trade distortions cannot be easily quantified. For example, many goods are restricted by licensing procedures, but not bound by any specified quota. The procedures themselves act as a non-tariff barrier.[7] Although it is possible to measure the coverage of a licensing system, or of specific QRs (incidence), it seems virtually impossible to assess the degree to which they distort relative prices (severity). This is also true of many export incentives, such as removal of marketing boards, increases in exporters' foreign exchange retention rates, and access to bonded warehouses.[8]

3. THE EXTENT AND CHARACTER OF TRADE REFORM

South Asia

Between 1985 and 1990, with the exception of Sri Lanka, the pattern of reform in South Asia was one of moving toward a more neutral trading regime, with much less progress towards liberality. Sri Lanka had been essentially free of QRs prior to 1985, and during this period focused on both reducing tariff levels and removing disincentives to exporters. In India, Bangladesh and Pakistan, some selective reductions in QRs took place, as well as rationalisation of the tariff structure and some small reduction in tariffs. Despite these changes, both tariffs and QRs remained significant impediments to trade in these three countries.

Since 1991, however, trade reform has been accelerated dramatically in India and Bangladesh. Significant cuts have been made in import impediments, and radical reforms have occurred in the foreign exchange market. Although import barriers remain high relative to other regions, recent budgets project a continuation of these moves toward liberality.

---

[7] Countries often maintain negative and/or restricted lists, or positive lists. The former specify goods which are banned, are restricted by quotas, or can only be imported with a licence. The latter stipulate which goods may be imported (after obtaining a licence). Goods not on the positive list are in effect banned. Licensing procedures vary widely and are not very transparent. Official exemptions, discretionary administration, and smuggling increase the difficulty of assessing changes in restrictiveness using only data on official barriers.

[8] Comprehensive data on official export taxes and subsidies were also unavailable.

TABLE 1
South Asia

	Average Nominal Tariff[a]		*QR Coverage*[b]	
	Pre-reform[c]	*Current*[d]	*Pre-reform*[c]	*Current*[d]
Bangladesh (1989, 1993)	94	50	40	10
India (1990, 1993)	128	71	93	<50
Pakistan (1987, 1990)	69	65	63[e]	33[e]
Sri Lanka (1985, 1992)	31	25	a few	0

	Average Black Market Premium[f]	
	Pre-reform[g]	*Post-reform*[h]
Bangladesh (1991)[i]	113	113
India (1991)	12	24
Pakistan (1987)	20	8
Sri Lanka (1987)	15	19

Notes:
[a] Unweighted, rounded to the nearest integer.
[b] The percentage of tariff line subject to quotas, bans or licensing requirements, rounded to the nearest integer. Data for India and Pakistan are production weighted.
[c] Prior to the most recent trade reform. First date in parentheses.
[d] Second date in parentheses.
[e] 'Pre-reform' is 1980; 'current' is 1986.
[f] The premium is calculated as [(black market rate-official rate)/official rate]*100, and rounded to nearest integer. Data are from *IMF International Financial Statistics*, and *World Currency Yearbook*.
[g] Pre-reform averages are calculated from 1980 up to and including the reform year.
[h] Post-reform averages are calculated from the first year after reform up to and including 1992.
[i] Year of reform in parentheses.

Table 1 reports changes in average nominal tariffs, QR coverage and black market premia for South Asia. All four countries reduced tariff rates during the period, lowering the regional average from 80 to 53 per cent. However, the average nominal rate remained at 50 per cent or higher for three of the four. Only Sri Lanka, already very open to trade, succeeded in reducing average nominal rates to 25 per cent.

Rationalisation of the tariff structure also took place. Prior to reform, maximum tariffs exceeded 100 per cent. All four countries reduced the range of tariffs and number of tariff rates. Maximum rates fell dramatically, although they remain at 50 per cent or higher. In at least three of the four the dispersion of rates also fell considerably. Despite these changes, all countries still exhibit significant tariff escalation.

With the exception of Sri Lanka, the South Asian countries in the sample had extensive and elaborate QR systems prior to the most recent reforms. These were likely to be more significant in restraining trade than the relatively high tariffs which prevailed. Sri Lanka reduced the relatively small number of items still subject to licensing requirements. The other three countries (especially Bangladesh) made large reductions in the coverage of QRs. However, in the two most restrictive regimes — India and Pakistan — QRs still cover about one-half and one-third of domestic production, respectively.

Prior to reform, the systems of QRs consisted of negative and restricted lists. India appears to have had the most complex system, with 26 such lists. In all cases reform meant reducing the number of lists to a maximum of two (one negative and one restricted), and reducing the number of goods on the lists. Notably, all three countries have removed virtually all intermediate and capital goods imports from these lists, raising the likelihood of increased effective protection. This is particularly likely in India, where all consumer goods imports are still effectively banned.

In India and Bangladesh, remarkable reforms have occurred in the foreign exchange market. Both countries had maintained severe restrictions on foreign exchange, which are reflected, in Bangladesh, in an average black market premium of 113 per cent.[9] Both maintained dual exchange markets with multiple exchange rates during this reform period. However, in both countries the number of items eligible for foreign exchange was increased over time. Between 1992 and 1993, the dual market was used to facilitate transition to a unified market with a floating rate.[10] All four countries also achieved a real exchange rate depreciation in the first year after reform began, with three seeing continual real depreciation through 1992.

Three of the four South Asian countries maintained significant export taxes prior to reform. All four countries made efforts to increase incentives to exporters. These commonly took the form of establishing or expanding duty drawback systems, implementing tax holidays for exporters, simplifying direct subsidy schemes, and/or paying tax rebates. In most cases, direct controls on imported intermediate goods for use in export production were reduced. On net, these efforts may have helped to neutralise the effect of remaining import barriers in Bangladesh and Sri Lanka. In India and Pakistan, they may have done more to simply offset simultaneous export taxes or controls.

Africa

By 1985 the binding constraint on trade in the non-CFA African countries in the sample was the extensive use of quantitative import restrictions and foreign exchange controls. In virtually all of these countries, QRs covered all product

---

[9] India's low premium may partly reflect a low inflation rate in the latter part of the 1980s.
[10] Note that the Indian and Bangladesh reforms accelerated dramatically in 1992. Not surprisingly, the impact of this is not reflected in Table 1, where 'post-reform' includes only 1992.

lines (Table 2). Restraints were either imposed directly on imports (quotas, bans, or prior licensing arrangements), or indirectly through elaborate foreign exchange rationing schemes. The latter restrictions seemed particularly important, judging from the real exchange rate appreciation experienced by many of these countries, and the large and rising black market premia prior to reform. Nigeria, Tanzania, Uganda and Ghana stand out with average black market premia ranging from 210 to 985 per cent, prior to their recent reform efforts. Ghana, Nigeria, and Zaire also maintained multiple exchange rate systems during this period.

Almost all non-CFA African countries in this sample attempted to reform the foreign exchange market first.[11] Most of these countries achieved significant real depreciation as a result of reform, and reduced the complexity of their licensing systems (or eliminated them). As shown in Table 2, the five countries with the most distorted regimes succeeded in reducing the black market premium substantially. Seven of the nine countries achieved sustained and continual real depreciation by the end of the period. However, as Nash (1993) has noted, none of these African countries has achieved full convertibility of currency, and some still maintain heavily managed foreign exchange systems.

Unlike the other regions examined in this study, several African countries (Ghana, Nigeria, and Uganda) established a secondary auction market to gradually free access to foreign exchange, and eventually reach a unified market-determined exchange rate. Madagascar, Uganda, and Tanzania began liberalising foreign exchange through the establishment of Open General Licensing Schemes (OGLs), and allowing the use of own funds.[12] Although these two methods ostensibly reduced the restrictiveness of the systems, they also tended to generate multiple exchange rates, leaving the net impact on incentives for exporters unclear. Another common practice was to simply raise the retention rate allowed exporters (especially exporters of non-traditional goods), which meant increased foreign exchange supplied to the parallel market.

Virtually all countries undertook (or planned to undertake) reductions in QRs. Sometimes these reforms were simultaneous with exchange market reforms, as the method of foreign exchange allocation was through import licensing systems. Table 2 shows evidence of these rather dramatic reductions. Of the eleven countries for whom data are available, eight reduced coverage and five virtually

---

[11] The CFA countries faced significant real appreciation during the first half of the decade due to declining terms of trade, and the appreciation of the French franc relative to the US dollar. Failed attempts on the part of some countries to implement a mock devaluation, coupled with lack of progress on other trade reforms, contributed to the 1994 devaluation of the CFA franc.

[12] OGLs involve a specified amount of foreign exchange which is made available to fund imports of certain products automatically (without a licence). 'Own funds' are foreign exchange from the importer's own sources. Legalisation of their use usually means that no licence is required for goods imported with such funds.

TABLE 2
Africa

	Average Nominal Tariff[a]		*QR Coverage*[b]	
	Pre-reform[c]	*Current*[d]	*Pre-reform*[c]	*Current*[d]
Cameroon (PR, CR)[e]	59[f]	59[f]	hundreds[g]	hundreds[g]
Côte d'Ivoire (1985, 1989)	26	33	38[f]	38[f]
Ghana (1983, 1991)	30	17	all[e,g]	2[e,g]
Kenya (1987, 1991)	40	34	71	0
Malawi (1986, 1991)	26	na	all[g]	few[g]
Madagascar (1988, 1990)	46	36	100[h]	0
Mali (1990, -)	25	na	58[e,g]	0[e,g]
Nigeria (1984, 1990)	35	33	all[g]	17[g,i]
Senegal (1986, 1991)	98[j]	90[j]	na	15[g,e]
South Africa (1984, 1993)	na	29	55[f]	23[f,k]
Tanzania (1986, 1992)	30	33	all[e,g]	100[e,g]
Uganda (1986, -)	30	n.a.	n.a.	5[e,g]
Zaire (1984, 1990)	24	25	100	100

	Average Black Market Premium[l]	
	Pre-reform[m]	*Post-reform*[n]
Ghana (1986)[p]	985	17
Kenya (1988)	16	9
Madagascar (1987)	37	13
Malawi (1988)	51	12
Nigeria (1986)	210	27
South Africa (1989)	0	3
Tanzania (1984)	242	119[q]
Uganda (1987)	303	79
Zaire (1986)	71	9

Notes:

[a] Unweighted, rounded to the nearest integer.
[b] Per cent of tariff lines covered by QRs and licensing procedures, unweighted, rounded to the nearest integer.
[c] Prior to most recent trade reform. First date in parentheses.
[d] Second date in parentheses.
[e] PR: pre-reform; CR: current regime. Exact dates are unavailable.
[f] Data are import-weighted.
[g] Number of goods or categories.
[h] 'Pre-reform' is 1986.
[i] 'Current' is 1988.
[j] Includes surcharges.
[k] 'Pre-reform' is 1984; 'current' is 1990.
[l] The premium is calculated as [(black market rate — official rate)/official rate]*100, rounded to nearest integer. Data are from *IMF International Financial Statistics*, and *World Currency Yearbook*.
[m] Pre-reform averages are calculated from 1980 up to and including the reform year.
[n] Post-reform averages are calculated from the first year after reform up to and including 1992.
[p] Year of reform in parentheses.
[q] This premium virtually disappeared by 1993.

eliminated QRs. Of the six which maintained 100 per cent coverage of QRs prior to reform, four made significant cuts.

In contrast, there has been essentially no action on tariff barriers. Of the thirteen countries examined, all but two reduced the range of tariffs, and at least four reduced the number of formal tariff rates. However, average nominal tariffs (unweighted) have remained fairly high. The current average for the region is about 37 per cent — the same as the pre-reform average level. Although Ghana, Kenya, and Madagascar made significant tariff cuts, Cameroon, Cote d'Ivoire and Zaire show virtually no signs of liberalisation with respect to tariffs or QRs. In the latter two, tariff levels actually rose.

Reversal of reform in Africa has been frequent. In seven of the countries examined, restrictions which were removed were reinstated, or some existing barriers were strengthened to offset reductions in others.[13] In some cases the motive for reversal appears to be pressure from import-competing industries as they begin to experience competition from abroad. In others, resurgence of foreign exchange shortages has slowed the liberalisation of tariffs, or reversed the foreign exchange market reform itself.

Certainly, the reduction of overvaluation in many African countries constitutes a reduction in the degree of anti-export bias. However, explicit restraints on exports were also reduced. Almost all countries lowered export taxes during this recent reform. Two eliminated export monopolies of major crops, and five allowed producer prices of coffee to rise (via reductions in taxes). Five countries also reduced the extent and severity of export licensing systems. At the same time, all but three have implemented some form of direct incentive scheme, particularly for non-traditional exports. Six countries have increased exporters' access to imported inputs, through reductions in tariffs, rebates, or increased access to foreign exchange. A few explicitly raised foreign exchange retention rates, or implemented tax incentives/subsidy schemes. Only a few have formal duty drawback schemes or export processing zones. In most of these cases, however, these schemes have not been very effective due to complex procedures, time lags, and eligibility requirements.

Latin America

The eight Latin American countries surveyed here can be grouped into early and late reformers. Chile, Mexico, Colombia, and Costa Rica began significant trade reforms between 1984 and 1986. Peru, Argentina, Brazil, and Venezuela, in contrast, did not begin major reforms until 1988/89 at the earliest. The late

[13] Nigeria, though it eliminated most quotas and licensing, increased dramatically the number of import bans. Ghana, which was the only country to make great strides in cutting formal tariffs, reversed this with the implementation of large special taxes on imports. Cote d'Ivoire raised tariffs significantly, after having reduced QRs.

TABLE 3
Latin America

	Average Nominal Tariff[a]		*QR Coverage*[b]	
	Pre-reform[c]	*Current*[d]	*Pre-reform*[c]	*Current*[d]
Argentina (1988, 1992)	29	12	88	a few
Brazil (1987, 1992)	51	21	39	minimal
Chile (1984, 1991)	35	11	minimal	0
Colombia (1984/5, 1992)	61	12	99	1
Costa Rica (1985, 1992)	53[e]	15[e]	na	0
Mexico (1985, 1990)[f]	24	13	92	20
Peru (1989, 1992)	66[e]	17	100[g]	0
Venezuela (1989, 1991)	37	19	40	10

	Average Black Market Premium[h]	
	Pre-reform[i]	*Post-reform*[j]
Argentina (1989)[k]	40	21
Brazil (1987/88)	44	52
Chile (1985)	16	16
Colombia (1985)	9	13
Costa Rica (1986)	215	17
Mexico (1985)	15	10
Peru (1989)	82	12
Venezuela (1989)	103	5

Notes:
[a] Unweighted, rounded to the nearest integer.
[b] Per cent of tariff lines covered by QRs and licensing procedures. Unweighted, rounded to the nearest integer.
[c] Prior to the most recent trade reform. First date in parentheses.
[d] Second date in parentheses.
[e] Includes surcharges.
[f] Production weighted data.
[g] 'Pre-reform' is 1988.
[h] The premium is calculated as [(black market rate — official rate)/official rate]*100, and rounded to nearest integer. Data are from *IMF International Financial Statistics*, and *World Currency Yearbook*.
[i] Pre-reform averages are calculated from 1980 up to and including the reform year.
[j] Post-reform averages are calculated from the first year after reform up to and including 1992.
[k] Year of reform in parentheses.

reformers are characterised by extensive foreign exchange controls. Argentina, Peru, and Venezuela maintained multiple exchange rate systems, with Peru having six different rates by 1988. As shown in Table 3, all four had QRs covering at least 40 per cent of product lines. Prior to the late 1980s, NTBs had been extended and average tariff rates increased. Venezuela and Peru maintained 41 and 56 different tariff rates, respectively. Just prior to reform in Brazil, Argentina, and Peru, inflation had escalated to 682, 3,080, and 3,398 per cent, respectively.

Of the early reformers, Chile had pursued extensive reforms prior to the 1980s, and had already eliminated QRs. By the mid-1980s, it had a relatively low uniform tariff (Table 3). Mexico and Colombia, on the other hand, had virtually all trade covered by QRs by 1985, and Costa Rica maintained very high tariffs as part of the regional arrangement (CACM). Only Mexico had a dual exchange rate system, although all but Chile had extensive foreign exchange restrictions.

All eight of these countries made dramatic and significant reforms between 1985 and 1993. Liberalisation took place simultaneously, in terms of import impediments, export impediments, and the foreign exchange market. Quite unlike other regions, Latin American countries made significant reductions in tariff barriers, concomitant with radical removal of QRs. Export taxes and restrictions were reduced, while indirect support for exports was expanded. These reforms appear to have moved beyond efforts at neutrality to increased liberality.

Three of the late reforming countries (Argentina, Peru, and Venezuela), as well as Colombia, stand out as having implemented extensive reforms extremely rapidly. In Brazil some new trade taxes have been implemented, and the process seems to have halted, due to the inability to reduce soaring inflation. For the remainder of the sample, however, no reversals have taken place. Liberalisation, as measured by all four indicators, appears to be continuing.

All eight countries reduced tariffs, lowering the regional average from 44 per cent to about 15 per cent. No country has an average rate above 25 per cent, and Chile and Mexico stand out with average rates at 10 and 11 per cent, respectively. Of the seven countries other than Chile,[14] at least five reduced the number of tariff rates sharply, and all seven reduced the range of tariffs. For the four early reformers, the maximum tariff is now less than 25 per cent. Most countries removed (or reduced to low levels) duties on non-competing inputs and capital goods imports. However, reductions in rates for more processed goods have been smaller, preserving tariff escalation.

Radical removal of QRs has taken place in the seven countries which retained such controls in the mid-1980s. Prior to reform, six countries had QRs covering 40 per cent or more of product lines, with three countries requiring prior licensing for virtually all products. Five out of seven countries have essentially eliminated all QRs on imports, while the remaining two reduced coverage to 25 per cent or less of their pre-reform levels. This shift from reliance on quantitative restraints to tariffs took the form of progressive reductions in the number of items subject to licensing (or other QRs) in Brazil, Argentina and Mexico. In the other four there was a radical simplification or removal of the entire licensing system. Colombia stands out in its efforts to convert QRs to tariffs using a quota auction

---

[14] Chile had already moved to a uniform tariff.

initially. However, it, too, eventually simply abolished the QR system, given the limited success of the auction.

All eight countries reduced the extent of intervention in the foreign exchange market. The four countries which had maintained multiple exchange rates prior to reform unified the market and abolished most foreign exchange controls.[15] In addition, five of the eight countries reduced inflation significantly during the reform process, with Argentina and Peru achieving radical reductions from an initial hyper-inflationary state. As seen in Table 3, all countries except Brazil and Columbia succeeded in reducing the size of the average black market premium. Both Venezuela and Peru (late reformers) made a radical shift from highly distorted regimes to relatively low levels of distortion.

Export taxes were either reduced or eliminated in the five countries where they were significant. Of the five countries maintaining export licensing requirements, three reduced the number of goods subject to licensing, and simplified the procedures; the other two countries eliminated all such requirements. At the same time, of the six countries maintaining explicit export subsidies, only Argentina, Peru, and Venezuela managed to reduce them. Six of the eight Latin countries examined either maintained, introduced, or expanded indirect subsidy schemes.[16]

East Asia

Trade policy in East Asia from 1985 to 1992 became decidedly more liberal. However, the character and pace of trade liberalisation differed from country to country, reflecting the differences across the East Asian countries in level of development, in progress made in trade reform prior to 1985, and in macroeconomic circumstances during the 1985–1992 period. In spite of these differences, a common pattern in the sequencing of trade reforms does emerge from the East Asian experiences. The first phase of trade policy reform in all the countries was one of removing the obstacles to exporting, which typically involved unifying and devaluing the exchange rate and removing quantitative restrictions on imports of intermediate and capital goods. In addition, during this phase direct inducements to exporting were generally provided in the form of duty drawback schemes and preferential export financing. The second phase, during which remaining quantitative restrictions were largely eliminated and tariffs began to be gradually reduced, generally commenced only after balances of payments were strengthened.

---

[15] Currencies are now allowed to float in Venezuela, Peru, and Argentina. Brazil, however, still maintains significant exchange controls.

[16] Among these were: duty drawback schemes, tax exemptions and/or rebates on income from exports, and tariff exemptions on imported inputs used for production of exportables.

TABLE 4
East Asia

	Average Nominal Tariff[a]		*QR Coverage*[b]	
	Pre-reform[c]	*Current*[d]	*Pre-reform*[c]	*Current*[d]
China (1986, 1992)	38	43	na	70[e]
Indonesia (1985, 1990)	27	22	32	10
Korea (1984, 1992)	24	10	23	<5
Malaysia (-, 1993)	na	14	<5[f]	<5[f]
Philippines (1985, 1992)	28	24	100[g]	<5
Thailand (1986, 1990)	13[e]	11[e]	<5	<5
Vietnam (-, 1991)	na	11	na	100

	Average Black Market Premium[h]	
	Pre-reform[i]	*Post-reform*[j]
China (1984)[k]	20	88
Indonesia (1986)	8	9
Korea (1987)	4	3
Malaysia (1991)	1	0
Philippines (1986)	11	5
Thailand (1989)	−1	1
Vietnam (1987)	359	108[l]

Notes:
[a] Unweighted, rounded to the nearest integer.
[b] Per cent of tariff lines covered by QRs and licensing requirements. Rounded to the nearest integer.
[c] Prior to the most recent trade reform. First date in parentheses.
[d] Second date in parentheses.
[e] Data are import weighted.
[f] 'Pre-reform' is 1985; 'current' is 1992.
[g] 'Pre-reform' is 1983.
[h] The premium is calculated as [(black market rate — official rate)/official rate]*100, and rounded to the nearest integer. Data are from *IMF International Financial Statistics* and *World Currenty Yearbook*.
[i] Pre-reform averages are calculated from 1980 up to and including the reform year.
[j] Post-reform are calculated from the first year after reform up to and including 1992.
[k] Year of reform in parentheses.
[l] By 1992 this premium had been largely eliminated.

In Taiwan and Korea, the second phase began in the latter half of the 1970s; in Malaysia it began about 1980 and in Indonesia and Thailand in the second half of the 1980s. In the Philippines, attempts to advance into the second phase of trade liberalisation in the early 1980s were derailed by macroeconomic instability and severe debt problems. China and Vietnam have yet to begin the second phase trade policy reform, but they have made significant progress reforming trade policy so as to promote export expansion.

The progress in East Asia in eliminating quantitative import restrictions is shown in Table 4. It is difficult to characterise the extent of quantitative restrictions in China and Vietnam under their complicated systems of import licensing. For example, in Vietnam, quantitative restrictions per se have been largely eliminated, yet goods cannot be imported without first obtaining licences and permits, which in practice operate much like quantitative restrictions. Elsewhere in East Asia, quantitative restrictions have been largely eliminated. Korea, Malaysia and Thailand had already eliminated them before 1985, while Indonesia and the Philippines achieved the elimination during the 1985–1992 period.

While substantial progress was made in East Asia in eliminating quantitative restrictions, much less was achieved by way of lowering tariffs. Table 4 indicates that Korea was the only East Asian country in our sample to reduce tariffs substantially[17] cutting its average tariff by more than half between 1984 to 1992. In China, the average tariff rose over the period under study, while in the Philippines, Indonesia, Malaysia and Thailand it declined modestly, albeit in the latter two countries from an already relatively low base. In the case of Vietnam, one cannot talk of a tariff reduction, since prior to 1985 Vietnam had no use for tariffs in its state trading system. When it did establish a tariff system it did so with a relatively low average tariff (11 per cent).

The black market exchange rate premium is not, as we know, a fool-proof indicator of trade liberalisation. Changes in the black market premium in the East Asia countries are, nonetheless, consistent with what we know about changes in protectionism, especially in the form of quantitative restrictions, during the period. As Table 4 suggests, the countries which have made the most progress in eliminating quantitative restrictions generally have the lowest black market premia.

Trade reforms since 1985 were initiated with substantial real devaluations in only four of the countries (China, Philippines, Indonesia and Vietnam). Of these, only China and Indonesia succeeded in maintaining a real depreciation by the end of the period. In Korea and Malaysia, the reform programme was accompanied by real appreciation. The departure of the latter two countries from the normal pattern, we suspect, is due to the fact that their trade liberalisation in the period from 1985 to 1992 was from a relatively low base of protectionism and was spurred by very strong balance-of-payments positions which were attracting unwelcome attention of their trade partners (principally the United States).

4. EMERGING PATTERNS IN TRADE REFORM ACROSS REGIONS

The recent reductions in trade barriers across the developing world are dramatic. Unlike earlier periods, this liberalisation has been unidirectional and

[17] Taiwan also made significant cuts during this time; Hong Kong and Singapore have virtually no tariff barriers.

continual in most countries outside Africa. Reform has been significant in scope and magnitude, even in countries which had long maintained high levels of protection and extensive restrictions on foreign exchange. Perhaps the most remarkable change is found in Latin America, where trade restrictions appear to have fallen to the low levels of East Asian NICs. However, liberalisation is also beginning to accelerate in South Asia — especially in India and Bangladesh. East Asian countries vary in their speed of reform, but show continued movement towards neutrality and liberality. Only in Africa do we find little progress towards a liberalised trade regime. Here there have been cases of reversal of policy, no liberalisation, or increased import impediments during this period.

The small number of countries within each region casts doubt on the statistical significance of any relationships found in the data. However, at least six interesting similarities emerge from an evaluation of these extensive reforms across regions. First, there appears to be a positive correlation between the height of average nominal tariffs pre-reform and the magnitude of tariff reductions during the period. Countries which maintained the highest tariffs pre-reform made the largest *percentage* reductions in tariffs. This correlation is positive for all but East Asia, and significant at the 10 and 15 per cent levels for Latin America and Africa, respectively. Although this may support the view that there has been a radical departure from protectionism, it may simply reflect reductions in very high redundant tariff rates. In many countries the highest rates applied to very few goods, or were accompanied by numerous official exemptions. Though elimination of these rates would have a large impact on the average unweighted nominal tariff for the country, it would not signal significant liberalisation of imports.

Second, there is some evidence that tariff reductions may indeed have been held up due to dependence on import tariffs (and other import surcharges) for tax revenues — 'revenue dependence.' In South Asia and Africa, countries show a relatively high level of revenue dependence. Within all four regions, there is a positive correlation between revenue dependence of a country (mid-1980s) and its level of tariffs prior to these recent reforms. For Africa and Latin America, this correlation is significant at the 2 per cent and ~8 per cent levels. Countries which relied more on imports for tax revenues maintained higher levels of tariffs in the mid-1980s than did their counterparts with lower levels of dependence. Within South Asia, East Asia, and Africa, this positive correlation between revenue dependence and tariff levels continues in the early 1990s (though it is significant at the ~8 per cent level only in Africa).

Latin America is the interesting exception. Though a significant positive correlation exists between revenue dependence and tariff levels prior to the recent reforms, there is no such correlation in the early 1990s. This suggests that Latin countries' tariff reforms were not limited by 'revenue dependence.' It would be useful to investigate whether or not domestic tax reform policies in Latin America facilitated a move away from dependence upon trade taxes.

Third, in all four regions, countries with the largest black market premia did succeed in achieving the largest real depreciations. In addition, a positive correlation emerged between the magnitude of real depreciation in the initial years of reform, and the ability of a country to sustain a real depreciation through 1992. For countries with severely overvalued currencies, this suggests the importance of achieving a significant depreciation at the outset, if such a depreciation is to be maintained.

Fourth, virtually all countries have made significant progress in reducing QRs. A large proportion of the countries in Latin America, East Asia, and Africa essentially eliminated explicit QRs and complex licensing systems which previously had restrained nearly all imported goods. In most countries, reductions took the form of shifting from a positive to a negative list, and then reducing the number of items subject to this list. It is unclear whether the level of protection on these goods rose or fell when QRs were replaced by tariffs. However, certainly incentives for rent-seeking were reduced and transparency increased. Since QRs were the binding constraint on trade in many countries, these reductions do represent a significant move towards liberalisation.

Fifth, rationalisation of tariffs has taken place in many countries. The number of rates, as well as their dispersion, have been reduced, and many tariff exemptions have been eliminated. These reforms have contributed to more uniformity in the tariff structure. At the same time, elimination of duties or QRs on imported capital and intermediate goods has tended to increase effective rates of protection on imported final goods (especially competing consumer goods).

Sixth, in all regions, liberalisation has included some removal of direct disincentives for exporters. At the same time, new incentives have been created — usually in the form of a duty drawback scheme or a tax rebate scheme. These schemes are often designed or operated inefficiently, however, leading to low levels of participation by exporters, and unknown effects on incentives.

There seems little doubt that a small revolution in trade reform has taken place across the developing world. Many interesting questions remain, however. Have tariff reductions, and removal of QRs, actually had a liberalising effect on trade? How have domestic reforms (e.g., tax reform) impeded or facilitated these trade reforms? Have incentives to exporters actually reduced distortions? Finally, what has contributed to the success of Latin America at trade reform? Answers to these questions may help to finally change the African experience.

REFERENCES

Alam, A. and S. Rajapatirana (1993), 'Trade Policy Reform in Latin America and the Caribbean in the 1980s,' *World Bank Policy Research Working Paper*, No. 1104 (February).

Anderson, J. and J.P. Neary (1994), 'Measuring the Restrictiveness of Trade Policy,' *World Bank Economic Review*, **8**, 2, 151–169.

Bhagwati, J. (1988), 'Export Promoting Trade Strategies: Issues and Evidence,' *The World Bank Research Observer*, 3, 27–58.

Dean, J., S. Desai, and J. Riedel (1994), 'Trade Policy Reform in Developing Countries Since 1985: A Review of the Evidence,' *World Bank Discussion Paper* No. 267.

Dornbusch, R. (1992), 'The Case for Trade Liberalization in Developing Countries,' *The Journal of Economic Perspectives*, **6**, 1, 69–86.

Edwards, S. (1989), 'Openness, Outward Orientation, Trade Liberalization and Economic Performance in Developing Countries,' (The World Bank).

Greenaway, D. (1993), 'Liberalizing Foreign Trade Through Rose-Tinted Glasses,' *The Economic Journal*, **103**, 208–222.

Harrison, A. (1991), 'Openness and Growth: A Time Series, Cross Country Analysis for Developing Countries,' *World Bank Background Paper*, WDR 1991.

Krueger, A. (1986), 'General Issues in Economic Liberalization' in A. Choksi and D. Papageorgiou (eds.), *Economic Liberalization in Developing Countries* (Oxford: Basil Blackwell).

Leamer, E. (1988), 'Measures of Openness,' in R. Baldwin (ed.), *Trade Policy Issues and Empirical Analysis*, a National Bureau of Economic Research Conference Report (The University of Chicago Press).

Nash, J. (1993), *Implementation of Trade Reform in Sub-Saharan Africa: How Much Heat and How Much Light?* Policy Research Working Paper 1218 (World Bank, Trade Policy Division).

Nogues, J. and S. Gulati (1992), 'Economic Policies and Performance Under Alternative Trade Regimes: Latin America During the 80s,' *World Bank Latin America and Caribbean Technical Department Regional Studies Program* (Report No. 16).

Papageorgiou, D., M. Michaely and A. Choksi (1991), *Liberalizing Foreign Trade*, Vol. 7: Lessons of Experience in the Developing World.

Pritchett, L. (1991), 'Measuring Outward Orientation in Developing Countries. Can It Be Done?' *World Bank Policy Research Working Paper* No. 566.

Rodrik, D. (1992), 'The Limits of Trade Policy Reform in Developing Countries,' *The Journal of Economic Perspectives*, **6**, 1, 87–105.

Thomas, V. and J. Nash and Associates (1991), *Best Practices in Trade Policy Reform* (Oxford: Oxford University Press).

UNCTAD (1987), *Handbook of Trade Control Measures of Developing Countries: Supplement*.

World Bank (1992), *Trade Policy Reforms under Adjustment Programs* (World Bank Operations Evaluation Department).

—— (1993), *Adjustment in Africa: Reform, Results, and the Road Ahead*, A World Bank Policy Research Report (Washington DC).